Neoliberalism and Educatio

C000256682

Neoliberalism and Education: Rearticulating social justice and inclusion offers a critical reflection on the establishment of neoliberalism as the new global orthodoxy in the field of education, and considers what this means for social justice and inclusion. It brings together writers from a number of countries, who explore notions of inclusion and social justice in educational settings ranging from elementary schools to higher education. Contributors examine policy, practice, and pedagogical considerations covering different dimensions of (in)equality, including disability, race, gender, and class. They raise questions about what social justice and inclusion mean in educational systems that are dominated by competition, benchmarking, and target-driven accountability, and about the new forms of imperialism and colonisation that both drive, and are a product of, market-driven reforms. While exposing the entrenchment, under current neoliberal systems of educational provision, of longstanding patterns of (racialised, classed, and gendered) privilege and disadvantage, the contributions presented in this book also consider the possibilities for hope and resistance, drawing attention to established and successful attempts at democratic education or community organisation across a number of countries. This book was originally published as a special issue of the *British Journal of Sociology of Education.*

Kalwant Bhopal is Professor of Education and Social Justice at the University of Southampton, UK. She has published widely on educational inequalities, focusing on marginalised and excluded groups. She is the author of *The Experiences of Black and Minority Ethnic Academics: A comparative study of the unequal academy* (Routledge, 2015). She is currently conducting research exploring successful support strategies for BME senior leaders in higher education.

Farzana Shain is Professor of Sociology of Education at Keele University, UK. Her research and writing focuses on educational inequalities and social justice, and on young people's understandings of the politics of oil. She is the author of *The New Folk Devils: Muslim Boys and Education* (Trentham, 2011), and *The Schooling and Identity of Asian Girls* (Trentham, 2003), which both explore the social and political identifications of young people in a schooling context in England, against the backcloth of the global 'war of terror'. She has also written widely about the politics of educational change in the further education sector in England.

Neoliberalism and Education

Rearticulating social justice and inclusion

Edited by
Kalwant Bhopal and Farzana Shain

Routledge
Taylor & Francis Group

LONDON AND NEW YORK

First published 2016 by Routledge

2 Park Square, Milton Park, Abingdon, Oxfordshire OX14 4RN
711 Third Avenue, New York, NY 10017

Routledge is an imprint of the Taylor & Francis Group, an informa business

First issued in paperback 2017

British Library Cataloguing in Publication Data
A catalogue record for this book is available from the British Library

ISBN 13: 978-1-138-18253-0 (hbk)
ISBN 13: 978-1-138-30628-8 (pbk)

Typeset in Times New Roman
by RefineCatch Limited, Bungay, Suffolk

Publisher's Note
The publisher accepts responsibility for any inconsistencies that may have
arisen during the conversion of this book from journal articles to book chapters,
namely the possible inclusion of journal terminology.

Disclaimer
Every effort has been made to contact copyright holders for their permission to
reprint material in this book. The publishers would be grateful to hear from any
copyright holder who is not here acknowledged and will undertake to rectify
any errors or omissions in future editions of this book.

Contents

CONTENTS

Citation Information

The chapters in this book were originally published in the *British Journal of Sociology of Education*, volume 35, issue 5 (September 2014). When citing this material, please use the original page numbering for each article, as follows:

Introduction
Educational inclusion: towards a social justice agenda?
Kalwant Bhopal and Farzana Shain
British Journal of Sociology of Education, volume 35, issue 5 (September 2014)
pp. 645–649

Chapter 1
Interrupting the interruption: neoliberalism and the challenges of an antiracist school
Assaf Meshulam and Michael W. Apple
British Journal of Sociology of Education, volume 35, issue 5 (September 2014)
pp. 650–669

Chapter 2
Fighting for the 'right to the city': examining spatial injustice in Chicago public school closings
Carl A. Grant, Anna Flock Arcello, Annika M. Konrad and Mary C. Swenson
British Journal of Sociology of Education, volume 35, issue 5 (September 2014)
pp. 670–687

Chapter 3
Just imaginary: delimiting social inclusion in higher education
Trevor Gale and Steven Hodge
British Journal of Sociology of Education, volume 35, issue 5 (September 2014)
pp. 688–709

Chapter 4
Re-articulating social justice as equity in schooling policy: the effects of testing and data infrastructures
Bob Lingard, Sam Sellar and Glenn C. Savage
British Journal of Sociology of Education, volume 35, issue 5 (September 2014)
pp. 710–730

Chapter 5

Beyond the education silo? Tackling adolescent secondary education in rural India
Orla Kelly and Jacqueline Bhabha
British Journal of Sociology of Education, volume 35, issue 5 (September 2014)
pp. 731–752

Chapter 6

Pakistani and Bangladeshi young men: re-racialization, class and masculinity within the neo-liberal school
Mairtin Mac an Ghaill and Chris Haywood
British Journal of Sociology of Education, volume 35, issue 5 (September 2014)
pp. 753–776

Chapter 7

Disability and inclusive education in times of austerity
Wayne Veck
British Journal of Sociology of Education, volume 35, issue 5 (September 2014)
pp. 777–799

Chapter 8

Transforming marginalised adult learners' views of themselves: Access to Higher Education courses in England
Hugh Busher, Nalita James, Anna Piela and Anna-Marie Palmer
British Journal of Sociology of Education, volume 35, issue 5 (September 2014)
pp. 800–817

Chapter 9

Home education, school, Travellers and educational inclusion
Hugh Busher, Nalita James, Anna Piela and Anna-Marie Palmer
British Journal of Sociology of Education, volume 35, issue 5 (September 2014)
pp. 818–835

For any permission-related enquiries please visit:
http://www.tandfonline.com/page/help/permissions

Notes on Contributors

Michael W. Apple is Professor of Curriculum and Instruction and Educational Policy Studies in the Department of Educational Policy Studies at the University of Wisconsin-Madison, WI, USA. His research centres on the limits and possibilities of critical educational policy and practice in a time of conservative restoration. His most recent books include *Education and Power* (Routledge, 2012), *Global Crises, Social Justice, and Education* (Routledge, 2010), and *The Routledge International Handbook of the Sociology of Education* (with Ball and Gandin, Routledge, 2010).

Anna Floch Arcello is a Graduate Student in the Department of English at the University of Wisconsin-Madison, WI, USA, specialising in the area of composition and rhetoric. Her interests include emotion and vulnerability in education and writing contexts, composition pedagogy, and exploring the role of gender, identity, and race in meaning.

Jacqueline Bhabha is Professor of the Practice of Health and Human Rights in the John F. Kennedy School of Government at Harvard University, Cambridge, MA, USA. She was previously a practicing human rights lawyer in London, UK, and at the European Court of Human Rights. She is the editor of *Children Without A State* (2011), author of *Moving Children: Young Migrants and the Challenge of Rights* (2014), and the editor of *Coming of Age: Reframing the Approach to Adolescent Rights* (2014).

Kalwant Bhopal is Professor of Education and Social Justice at the University of Southampton, UK. She has published widely on educational inequalities, focusing on marginalised and excluded groups. She is the author of *The Experiences of Black and Minority Ethnic Academics: A comparative study of the unequal academy* (Routledge, 2015). She is currently conducting research exploring successful support strategies for BME senior leaders in higher education.

Hugh Busher is Senior Lecturer in Education at the University of Leicester, UK. He researches critical perspectives on people, power and culture in education-based communities, including representations of students' and teachers' voices, and hybrid learning communities using ethical visual and online methods. His most recent book is *Online Interviews: Epistemological, Methodological and Ethical Considerations in Qualitative Research* (with Nalita James, 2009).

Kate D'Arcy is Acting Principal Lecturer in Applied Social Sciences at the University of Bedfordshire, Luton, UK. Her working practice has been situated on the margins of education, supporting a variety of vulnerable and often disengaged young people in a variety of educational settings. She is the author of *Travellers and Home Education: Safe Spaces and Inequality* (2014).

Trevor Gale is based in the School of Education at the University of Glasgow, UK. He is the author of *Rough Justice: young people in the shadows* (2005).

Carl A. Grant is Professor of Education in the Department of Curriculum and Instruction at the University of Wisconsin-Madison, WI, USA. He has written many books on multicultural education and teacher education, including *Bringing Teaching to Life* (1982), *After the School Bell Rings* (with Sleeter, 1986), *Making Choices for Multicultural Education* (with Sleeter, 1988), *Preparing for Reflective Teaching* (1984), *Community Participation in Education* (1979), *Research and Multicultural Education* (1992), and *In Praise of Diversity* (1977).

Chris Haywood is Senior Lecturer in the School of Arts and Cultures at Newcastle University, UK. His main interests focus is on the men and masculinities, and he is currently working on exploring how men negotiate different dating practices in the areas of speed dating, online dating, and mobile romance. He is the editor of *Education and Masculinities: Social, Cultural and Global Transformations* (with Mairtin Mac an Ghaill, Routledge, 2013).

Steven Hodge is a Lecturer in Adult and Vocational Education at Griffith University, Brisbane, Australia. His research expertise is in competency-based training, vocational education and training, adult education, curriculum studies, and the philosophy of education.

Nalita James is a Senior Lecturer in the Vaughan Centre for LifeLong Learning at the University of Leicester, UK. Her research interests lie in the sociology of education and include: higher education; transitions from school to university and from education to work; changing patterns of education, work and identity; lifelong learning; and education policy. She is also interested in the impact of creativity on adults' learning. She is the author of *Online Interviews: Epistemological, Methodological and Ethical Considerations in Qualitative Research* (with Hugh Busher, 2009).

Orla Kelly is a Research Associate in the FXB Center for Health and Human Rights at Harvard University, Cambridge, MA, USA.

Annika M. Konrad is a Graduate Student in the Department of English at the University of Wisconsin-Madison, WI, USA, specialising in the area of composition and rhetoric. Her interests include composition pedagogy, narrative, disability rhetoric, community writing, and the administration of writing programs.

Bob Lingard is a Professorial Research Fellow in the School of Education at the University of Queensland, Brisbane, Australia. His work was collected in *Politics, Policies and Pedagogies in Education: The selected works of Bob Lingard* (Routledge, 2014).

Mairtin Mac an Ghaill is Professor of Multi-Professional Education at Newman University, Birmingham, UK. He has expertise in the areas of educational and social inequalities, ethnicity, racism and cultural belonging, the sociology of masculinity, and the Irish diaspora in Britain. He is the editor of *Education and Masculinities: Social, Cultural and Global Transformations* (with Chris Haywood, Routledge, 2013).

Assaf Meshulam is Senior Teacher in the Department of Education at Ben-Gurion University of the Negev, Beer Sheva, Israel. He has contributed articles to *Teachers College Record* and the *British Journal of Sociology of Education*. His research interests include bilingual education, neoliberalism, studies of educational policy, and alternative and non-formal education.

Anna-Marie Palmer was a Graduate Research Assistant at the University of Leicester, UK, working on the British Academy- and Aim Higher-funded project entitled 'Opening Doors to Higher Education? Access Students' Learning Transitions'.

Anna Piela is a Research Assistant working on a British Academy- and Aim Higher-funded project entitled 'Opening Doors to Higher Education? Access Students' Learning Transitions', based in the School of Education at the University of Leicester, UK. She holds a Ph.D. in Women's Studies from the University of York, UK.

Glenn C. Savage is a Researcher and Lecturer in Education Policy in the Graduate School of Education at the University of Melbourne, Australia. His research focuses on education policy and governance at national and global levels, with a specific interest in policies relating to curriculum, equity, marketisation and teaching standards.

Sam Sellar is a Professorial Research Fellow in the School of Education at the University of Queensland, Brisbane, Australia. He is the editor of *Globalizing Educational Accountabilities* (with Rezai-Rashti and Martino, Routledge, 2015). He is currently working on three ARC projects investigating national and global education policy, new accountabilities in schooling, and the aspirations of young people in high-poverty regions.

Farzana Shain is Professor of Sociology of Education at Keele University, UK. Her research and writing focuses on educational inequalities and social justice, and on young people's understandings of the politics of oil. She is the author of *The New Folk Devils: Muslim Boys and Education* (Trentham, 2011), and *The Schooling and Identity of Asian Girls* (Trentham, 2003), which both explore the social and political identifications of young people in a schooling context in England, against the backcloth of the global 'war of terror'. She has also written widely about the politics of educational change in the further education sector in England.

Mary C. Swenson is based in the Department of English at the University of Wisconsin-Madison, WI, USA.

Wayne Veck is Senior Lecturer in Education Studies at Winchester University, UK. His main areas of expertise are inclusive education, disability studies, values in education and research, and the philosophy of education.

INTRODUCTION

Educational inclusion: towards a social justice agenda?

Kalwant Bhopal and Farzana Shain

Social justice and inclusion are complex and contested terms that feature prominently in current global and national education policy rhetoric. The latest Global Monitoring Report (UNESCO 2014), for example, assesses progress against the Education for All (EFA) goals[1] that were established in 2000 with the aim of securing universal access for all children to basic education by 2015. The EFA framework, along with the United Nations Millennium Development Goals,[2] is underpinned by a particular view of social justice as 'distributional justice' (Gewirtz 1998) and an assumption that the provision of standardised systems of teaching, learning and assessment to support 'the weakest learners' will bring about 'equality for all' (UNESCO 2014, i). However, as Connell (2012) has argued, social justice in education is not just about equality in the distribution of, or access to, an educational service, which is important, but 'social justice concerns the nature of the service itself, and its consequences for society through time' (2012, 681).

What Connell means is that the shape and direction of education is never neutral but is influenced and structured by dominant agendas and interests that shift over time to reinforce and reproduce particular forms of privilege and inequality. In the last two decades, educational sociologists have mapped the various ways in which 'Western-centric' (Amin 2010) neoliberal policies have come to be both embedded and resisted within educational sectors – albeit unevenly across different locales and with different effects. As Ozga (2011, 307) notes, market mechanisms are displacing the State, services are being outsourced to hybrid public–private organisations, and there is an increasing devolution of responsibility for self-management, choice-making and the management of risk to individuals and families and away from State institutions. As transnational actors such as the World Bank, the International Monetary Fund and the Organisation for Economic and Cooperative Development (OECD) increasingly (since the 1990s) set the agenda for regional and national education policies, questions emerge about the social justice implications of this direction of travel and the means by which it is being rolled out. Neoliberal policies are being promoted through the EFA framework and the policies of the World Bank as the ideal and only way of bringing economic prosperity to the poor and for driving up 'standards' in the context of western economic decline.

Even before the onset of the Global Financial Crisis in 2008, it was clear that neoliberal policies had not delivered the promised economic growth and that income inequalities had increased (Jessop 2002; Peck and Tickell 2002; Harvey 2005; Amin 2010). However, the austerity measures that have imposed large public spending cuts in countries such as Portugal, Spain, Ireland and Greece have further sharpened longstanding inequalities by hitting directly on the State's ability to deliver on equity. In England, for example, policy measures introduced since 2010, in the name of austerity, include the abolition of the Educational Maintenance Allowance – a grant of around £30.00 per week that was aimed at helping poorer 16–17 year olds to stay in education. This development has occurred alongside a tripling of higher education fees from £3000 to £9000 per annum creating new barriers in terms of access to higher education. Those most affected include poor, working-class and minority ethnic young people with consequences for their chances of social mobility and future success in the labour market (Sutton Trust 2013).

Against this background, this special issue of *British Journal of Sociology of Education* explores notions of inclusion and social justice in educational settings ranging from elementary schools to higher education. The nine contributions inevitably discuss only a selection of social justice and inclusion issues, and all but one focus on education in the 'neoliberal heartlands' (Peck and Tickell 2002) of Western Europe, North America and Australia where market-oriented policies have been pursued relentlessly since the 1980s. Collectively, the papers explore policy, practice and pedagogical considerations covering different dimensions of (in)equality including disability, race, gender and class. They raise questions about what social justice and inclusion mean in educational systems that are dominated by competition, benchmarking and target-driven accountability and how new forms of imperialism and colonisation both drive and are a product of market-driven reforms. The papers also point to the resources that teachers, pupils and parents (might) draw on to counter the negative impacts of market-oriented policies. Finally, a range of 'policy buzzwords' (Cornwall and Brock 2005) including 'participation', 'empowerment' and 'involvement' appear across several of the contributions. These terms, which speak ostensibly to social justice and inclusion agendas, are also critically considered in terms of what they mean in practice. We turn now to a brief description of each paper in the issue.

Meshulam and Apple highlight the challenges involved in enacting social justice even in a school that has a history of fighting for it. They draw on the case study of a US public elementary bilingual and multicultural school. Despite being a pioneer of an 'inclusive' anti-racist curriculum, they find that under an onslaught of neoliberal policies, the school has had to make concessions that serve paradoxically to reinforce the cultural domination, marginalisation and exclusion of its African American students. Grant,

Floch Arcello, Konrad and Swenson, likewise, explore the mechanisms that serve to reproduce the unequal and racialised opportunity structure in the United States. Their discussion of the closure in 2013 of 50 out of the 54 Chicago public schools is framed by a 'critical spatial perspective' in which the closure of 'underperforming' schools is seen as counterproductive to the 'rights to the city'. Like Meshulam and Apple, Grant et al. find African American students to be at the sharp end of the neoliberal restructuring policies. The authors conclude by calling for increased democratic participation from students, parents and community leaders who are involved in urban school systems on a national and international basis to resist these new forms of gentrification and colonisation.

Turning the emphasis to higher education, Gale and Hodge draw on Australia as a case study for exploring the 'policy effects' (Ball 1993) of current social inclusion policies within OECD nations. They argue that a new 'imaginary' has emerged in the 'Asian Century', about higher education's role in interrupting the declining advantage of OECD nations in the 'rapidly changing profile of the global economy'. This new imaginary supports an expansionist agenda that shows evidence of widening access to education; however, it fails to translate into a second-order effect of challenging existing relations of domination and patterns of privilege. Staying with Australia and the OECD's role in the global governance of education, Lingard, Sellar and Savage consider the ways in which social justice is being rearticulated as 'equity' in education. Examining mechanisms of national and global testing, such as the National Assessment Programme – Literacy and Numeracy and the Programme for International Student Assessment, they conclude that standardised systems of measurement and comparison 'have become central in contemporary education policy regimes and that this has weakened the influence of conceptual-discursive accounts of what constitutes social justice schooling'.

Taking up the EFA agenda and turning to issues of access and inclusion in secondary education in rural India, Kelly and Bhabha explore the gendered power dynamics that restrict poorer girls from benefiting from widened access to secondary education. Drawing on Connell's gender and power framework, the authors' question whether the Indian government's focus on extending education programmes to rural communities can deliver equal opportunities for girls. They assert that, without challenging existing material inequalities, and the dominant cultural values and patriarchal frameworks that underpin family and education systems, the possibilities for a redistribution of opportunity are not only extremely limited but potential exists for further marginalisation based on gender, class and caste. Mac an Ghaill and Haywood explore what inclusion/exclusion means to a group of young British Pakistani and Bangladeshi men in English Schools who experience education against the backdrop of the US-inspired global 'war on terror'. Focusing their analysis on reconstructions of masculinity, class and the emergence of a schooling regime that operates through neoliberal policies, they note 'the increasing ambivalence surrounding race/ethnicity and the growing visibility of a neo-conservative nationalism that impels an absolute cultural (moral) difference, means that categories of same and other are moving into sharper distinction'.

With a focus on the United Kingdom, Veck critically considers austerity policies and approaches to understanding the education of disabled people in relation to the decline of community and the longing for its existence. Drawing on the work of Arendt and Bauman, he argues that, '… in a society where individuals are increasing indifferent to one another, addressing disability means defending community and its possibilities for generating and sustaining caring, responsive and inclusive relationships'. Keeping the focus on community, but moving to a discussion of adult learners, Busher, James, Piela and Palmer focus on learner identities in 'access to higher education' courses that are delivered in the further education sector in England. The students in their research study were marginalised by formal learning processes but were able to enhance their social and cultural capital by being active participants in their learning. They achieved this by working with teachers to form collaborative learning cultures through communities of practice.

Finally, drawing on a critical race theory, D'Arcy focuses on the policy of elective home education for Traveller families in England. Her argument is that this apparently inclusive policy facilitates the exclusion of Traveller children. She challenges the dominant discourse that frames elective home education as a 'free choice' deriving from Travellers' mobility. Instead, D'Arcy finds that the take-up of elective home education is often linked to the experience of racism and discrimination so that families who are deeply committed to their child's education are forced to make the choice to home school their children.

The papers presented in this issue enable us to reflect on the establishment of neoliberalism as the new global orthodoxy in the field of education and to begin to analyse what this means for social justice and inclusion. The papers raise possibilities for hope and resistance, drawing attention to established and successful attempts at democratic education or community organisation. However, they also expose ongoing tensions between recognition and redistribution as principles for social justice and the entrenchment, under current neoliberal systems of educational provision, of longstanding patterns of (racialised, classed and gendered) privilege and disadvantage that need to be highlighted and addressed.

Notes

1. These goals are to: expand early childhood care and education; provide free and compulsory primary education for all; promote learning and life skills for

young people and adults; increase adult literacy by 50%; achieve gender parity in education by 2005, and gender equality by 2015; and improve the quality of education. Although UNESCO's statistics show that the number of children out of school fell by almost one-half between 1999 and 2011, 57 million children were still out of school by 2011. In sub-Saharan Africa, 22% of the region's primary school-age population was still not in school by 2011, and by all accounts the targets are unlikely to be met by 2015.

2. See http://www.un.org/millenniumgoals/.

References

Amin, S. 2010. *Ending the Crisis of Capitalism or Ending Capitalism?* Oxford: Pambazuka Press.

Ball, S. J. 1993. "Education Markets, Choice and Social Class: The Market as a Class Strategy in the UK and the USA." *British Journal of Sociology of Education* 14 (1): 3–19.

Connell, R. 2012. "Just Education." *Journal of Education Policy* 27 (5): 681–683.

Cornwall, A., and C. Brock. 2005. "What do Buzzwords do for Development Policy? A Critical Look at 'Participation' 'Empowerment' and 'Poverty Reduction'." *Third World Quarterly* 26 (7): 1043–1060.

Gewirtz, S. 1998. "Conceptualizing Social Justice in Education: Mapping the Territory." *Journal of Education Policy* 13 (4): 469–484.

Harvey, D. 2005. *A Brief History of Neoliberalism.* Oxford: Oxford University Press.

Jessop, B. 2002. "Liberalism, Neoliberalism, and Urban Governance: A State-theoretical Perspective." *Antipode* 34 (3): 452–472.

Ozga, J. 2011. "Governing Narratives: 'Local' Meanings and Globalising Education Policy." *Education Inquiry* 2 (2): 305–318.

Peck, J., and A. Tickell. 2002. "Neoliberalizing Space." *Antipode* 34 (3): 380–404.

Sutton Trust. 2013. *Advancing Access and Admissions.* London: Sutton Trust.

UNESCO. 2014. *Teaching and Learning: Achieving Quality for All.* Education for All Global Monitoring Report, UNESCO.

Kalwant Bhopal
University of Southampton, UK

Farzana Shain
Keele University, Keele, UK

Interrupting the interruption: neoliberalism and the challenges of an antiracist school

Assaf Meshulam[a] and Michael W. Apple[b,c]

[a]*Department of Education, Ben-Gurion University of the Negev, Beer Sheva, Israel;* [b]*Department of Curriculum and Instruction, University of Wisconsin, Madison, WI, USA;* [c]*Department of Educational Policy Studies, University of Wisconsin, Madison, WI, USA*

The article examines a US public elementary bilingual, multicultural school that attempts to interrupt the reproduction of existing relations of dominance and subordination across a variety of differences. The school's experiences illuminate the complex reality of schools as a site of struggle and compromise between at times contradictory interests, agents, and ideologies and the powerful forces in the (racial) state and civil society that make educating for social equality and justice difficult to accomplish. The article considers the concessions the school has made, and how and why, even in this most antiracist of schools, issues of race and racism persist.

Introduction

The bottom-up struggles of creating and defending an education for a democratic and more socially just society are especially difficult today. There is an intensified neoliberal assault on public education. Any socially committed educational endeavor in the public system faces ongoing budget and resource cutbacks and constraints, inbuilt biases within the state, and the increasing commodification of education and its accompanying alterations in commonsense (Apple 2006). Yet in the face of all of these pressures, some counter-hegemonic institutions survive. They do so through a combination of partial victories, what may seem to be necessary compromises, and, at times, partial losses. But they do last.

In this article, we examine a public elementary school in the United States that is well known for its attempt at building and then defending a socially transformative education that seeks to challenge existing relations of dominance and subordination across a variety of differences. Opening its doors in 1988, this school is particularly distinguished by two flagship programs: its dual bilingualism (English and Spanish) program, and its grounding in critical multiculturalism. The latter in particular is organized around an overtly antiracist set of goals. Yet even with such goals, the school lives in the real world. Its experiences can tell us a good deal about a number of the challenges facing critical education today. It can illuminate how schools act as a site of constant struggle and compromise between different, at times contradictory, interests, agents, and ideologies. And, at the same time, it can demonstrate some of the powerful forces in the (racial) state and civil society that make educating for social equality and justice difficult to accomplish, even in a school that is deeply committed to interrupting the reproduction of the unequal structure of class and race relations within the school itself.

As we shall document, even with the school's strong commitment to and struggle for inclusion – racial, cultural, political, social – in both its pedagogy and curriculum, racializing forms arise. Despite the predominance in numbers of African-American students at the school from the outset, African-American identity as a distinct community has been subsumed, while African-Americans have been marginalized in school governance and staff representation. This process has been intertwined with the erosion of the school's antiracist program due to the neoliberal and neoconservative challenges to such curricula in public education. This combination has led to a complex reality in which the partial victories involving innovative curricula that promote and support the transformation of unequal power relations are accompanied by partial losses in which cultural, racial, and class inequalities are reproduced.

The article begins by presenting the historical and socio-political contexts to the establishment of the school and the background to its bilingual, multicultural, antiracist agenda. We examine the features of the school that have made it a pioneer on the educational landscape in the United States, in particular its antiracist multiculturalism program and the collaborative curriculum development process it hinges on. We then consider the challenges to implementing the school's antiracist vision due to neoliberal demands and pressures to which the school is subject. We examine the complex factors and dynamics in the concessions the school has made, and consider how and why, even in this most antiracist of schools, issues of race and racism persist.

Methods

The findings presented in this article are from a larger study on multicultural, bilingual schools educating for democracy and social justice in different national, political, and cultural contexts (Meshulam 2011). The school was selected based on its reputation as an example of 'thick' democratic education pursuing social justice and equality. The names of the school and participants are withheld to protect their anonymity.

Ethnographic methods were used to collect data during two months of intense research in the school in 2009. Twenty semi-structured, open-ended individual interviews with the school's principal, teachers, a multi-racial group of parents, and founding members, past and present, were conducted. The research also included in-class and out-of-class observations (classroom activities, teacher meetings, school council meetings, recess activity, field trips, and various extracurricular activities) and document analysis, in particular a number of books composed by school staff and community activists summarizing the first four years of the school's operation. All interviews were audio-recorded and transcribed, and all collected data were triangulated and organized to attain a thick description of the central themes of the study. The interviews focused broadly on questions about: the socio-political and historical contexts of the school's establishment; its structure and governance; its vision and goals, particularly regarding bilingualism, multiculturalism, and antiracism; its pedagogy and curriculum; and the kind of critically democratic identity the school seeks to cultivate. Added to the interviews and observations was a detailed examination of documents related to the history of the school and the social context of the city in which it sits.

The socio-historical contexts of antiracist schooling

Any substantive understanding of the socio-historical contexts on which we focus here must rest on two interrelated realities about the racial structuring of the United States. First, powerful forms of segregation persist in US society in general; and in particular in public schools, which are more segregated than ever (Orfield 2009). Second, race itself and racializing policies and practices, inside and outside education, are primary factors accounting for this segregation in education: 'Issues of race and racism permeate US culture – through law, language, politics, economics, symbols, art, public policy – and the prevalence of race is not merely in those spaces seen as racially defined spaces' (Ladson-Billings 2004, 5). Decades after the US Supreme Court's significant *Brown vs. Board of Education* decision in 1954, in which official segregation was ruled unconstitutional, the public school system continues to be a space in which unequal race relations are sometimes challenged but, by and large, also reproduced and reinforced.

How this works out, however, is always conjunctural. As Stuart Hall (1996) reminds us, race and racialization – and how the state operates as a *racial* state – are not always the same, nor do they operate in the same ways in every context (see also Mills 1997). The contexts of this particular city and school clarify why Hall's point is important and requires that we spend time critically examining their racial history.

The city in which the school is located, as well as its public education system, provides a fine example of the complex socio-historical conditions in which schools of this type function. An industrial Midwest port city, it has traditionally drawn immigrants from across the world as well as within the United States, who have brought with them cultural and social diversity. By 2008/09, the year in which the school was researched, the city's population was 40% White, 38% Black, 15% Hispanic, 3% Asian, and about 1% Native American (US Census Bureau 2008).

Yet, despite a strong tradition of social progressiveness and activism, the city also has been notorious for its deep-rooted segregation and racial inequality. This gives credence to Mills' (1997) argument that social democracy is based on a *racial contract*, a contract that can be weakened and even withdrawn when the 'Other' enters into the geographical and political space. Thus, racism, discrimination, and inequity prevail to this day, suffered most acutely by African-Americans, but also by the city's Latino/Latina population (Miner 2013).

Two prominent socio-political movements in the city served jointly as the breeding ground and setting for the school and its antiracist, multicultural, bilingual agenda: the battle, since the 1960s, of civil rights activists against segregation in housing and education; and the Spanish-speaking community's demand and struggle for bilingualism in public education. Despite the 1968 enactment of a federal open housing law and the passage of a local ordinance essentially making segregated housing illegal, residential segregation in the city continued. Real-estate agents, city zoning laws, and lending institutions prevented African-Americans from moving into White neighborhoods, while suburbanization led to the abandonment of the inner city to African-Americans and other minoritized people.

An intensification of neighborhood segregation was the result, which inevitably produced and exacerbated segregation in the city's schools. Because the city was so segregated geographically, its schools did not integrate following *Brown*. Only in 1976 did a federal court rule that the city's schools were illegally segregated and order their immediate integration, and only in 1979 did the public school-board follow this up with a five-year desegregation plan. Yet, when the school first opened in 1988, the city was ranked amongst the top five most racially segregated cities in the United States (Year One 1989). This led to even further mobilizations, especially within the African-American community (Miner 2013).

Parallel to the efforts to desegregate neighborhoods and schools, a wide mobilization around the need for bilingual education in the city's schools emerged within the Latino/Latina community. In 1968 the Bilingual Education Act was passed, allocating federal funding to 'encourage local school districts to try approaches incorporating native-language instruction' (History of Bilingual Education 1998, 1). This legislation and the city's failure to implement it served as the impetus for protests and walk-outs by Mexican and Puerto-Rican parents and students, who demanded the establishment of Spanish–English bilingualism programs in the city's schools.

In addition, a movement emerged to build new high schools in minority communities, with a coalition forming between African-Americans, Mexican-Americans, and White working-class groups towards this cause. Such joint mobilizations are unusual in many parts of the United States, where inter-ethnic solidarity is often made more difficult by dominant groups' ideological work using racializing discourses to enhance differences.

At the city and state levels as well as within the affected communities, the promotion of antisegregationism, bilingualism, and critical visions of multiculturalism gained political momentum. Yet in spite of its growing strength, this activism did not have a meaningful impact on segregation in the city's public school system or on educational equality in the schools. The system remained unequal, segregated, and seemingly indifferent to the needs and rights of the minoritized populations it served.

In the 1986/87 school year, one year before the school opened, the Grade Point Average for Black high-school students was 1.46 and for Hispanic students 1.67 out of a possible 4.0. The completion rate for entering ninth-graders in the city stood at 46% for Blacks and 49% for Hispanics, as opposed to 62% for Whites (Year One 1989). Against this backdrop of sweeping social and political activism alongside ongoing inequalities and racism in public education, a strong dual (Spanish–English) bilingual, multicultural school was envisioned: 'We started to dream about a school that would provide the highest quality education for our children, Black, White, and Hispanic,' explained a community parent and representative (Year One 1989, 68).

Building a collaborative, community school

The school opened its doors in September 1988 as a public pre-K–5 elementary school (ages 4–10) in a working-class neighborhood populated by the communities most impacted by the city-wide discrimination and inequality. Its continued racial and cultural diversity and integration, despite a 'parade of change' in its demographics over the decades (Tolan 2003), have always been unique in the city. The 2000 census data portray the neighborhood as 'one of the city's – and state's – most integrated' neighborhoods, 'one of just four in the state with the most equal proportions of black, white, and Hispanic residents' (Tolan 2003, VIII). This has been critical to both the success in mobilizing the community to fight for the school's establishment and the school's ability to serve and promote diversity. In its first year of operation, 42% of its students were Black, 37% Hispanic, and 21% 'Other.' Approximately 90% of the students qualified for free lunch (Year One 1989). Twenty years later, in the 2008/09 school year, the diversity remained although the demographics had shifted. The majority was now Latino/Latina (59%) – a crucial point in the account of how 'race' works that we give later in this article. This was followed by 19% African-Americans and 12% White, with the remainder Asian-American and Native-American. Seventy-four percent of the students qualified for free or reduced lunch.

The school, in its previous incarnation, was 'slated to be razed' in 1988, and turned into an 'Exemplary Teaching Center' by the school district (Year One 1989, 68). Valuing the neighborhood's unique diversity, a small group of teachers, parents, and community activists organized to resist this plan, and proposed establishing instead a 'whole language, two-way bilingual, multicultural, site-based-managed school.' The path from proposal to opening the school was not without arduous political struggle, in the face of initially strong resistance from the school-board and district administrators. But the timing was right. The community activism was supported by the success of two political battles being waged in the city at the time, pushing the school-board to eventually back the initiative. The one struggle revolved around allowing site-based management and a whole-language model, two approaches the school-board endorsed. A second source of pressure on the board was the growing criticism of its apparent unwillingness to engage in dialogue with African-American parents and their demands for an independent school district that would be controlled by the city's African-American community. The conjunction of these two struggles led the school-board, fighting for its own political legitimacy, to pass the proposal to establish the school.

The school's two-way bilingualism and, even more in some respects, its overtly critical multicultural curricula and pedagogy are what distinguish it from many others. From the outset, there was a firm conception of the school's mission, expressed in its "Our School Vision" document as follows: to educate students in Spanish and English 'through a program of academic excellence' and to construct a multicultural program founded on an antiracist perspective. A central requirement of the two-way bilingualism model the school adopted is a mixed, preferably balanced, number of native-English-speaking and native-Spanish-speaking students. This not only ensures meaningful exposure to diversity, but, through peer learning, empowers the Spanish-speakers to develop multicultural identity and self-esteem (Skutnabb-Kangas and García 1995) and 'deep academic proficiency and cognitive understanding through their first language to compete successfully with native speakers of the second language,' thereby equalizing the cultural power relations (Baker 2006, 270; Thomas and Collier 2002). The need to balance between Spanish-speaking and English-speaking students eventually led to the busing-in of Spanish-speakers from outside the neighborhood.

Fundamental to the school's identity and mission is sustaining the organic connection and collaboration with parents, the local community, grassroots movements, and social organizations, which grounded the original activism to open the school. As a founding member explained in an interview, there was 'an ideological commitment ... to be accountable to the general population.' In line with its site-based management approach, the school is democratically and collaboratively run by educators, parents, and the community. Various bodies and committees composed of parents, staff, and community members decide jointly on most major matters, including funding, staffing, budget allocation, and school curriculum policy.

Moreover, the school has always sought to generate and facilitate parental participation and representation, never an easy task. A teacher explained the loss of momentum 'once we won the school': 'a lot of parents said, well, now it's the staff's turn to do ... to take responsibility. It was sort of a natural drop-off of involvement.' In order to foster involvement, particularly among African-American and Latino/Latina working-class parents, two paid part-time positions were created for parent coordinators from these communities. Yet diversifying parental representation in school governance remains a challenge. Relative to 'many other inner city schools,' noted a school administrator, 'parent involvement is impressive. But when it comes to decision-making, there's an inequality, a disparity, between middle-class parents of all races, although they tend more to be White.'

The school's approach to curriculum development also reflects its collaborative aims and orientation. The original curriculum was 'an outgrowth of a dynamic process in which parents, teachers, and community members have come together to build a school that serves the needs of an integrated neighborhood and the city as a whole' (Year One 1989, 33). This served as the model for curriculum development at the school. An ongoing organic process, it is vital to the multicultural program, which hinges on dialogue, mutual support, and an integrative approach, but also what has made the program most vulnerable in the struggle for resources and prioritizing. Although the multicultural and bilingualism programs shared 'top billing' in the original vision and agenda, with time their needs – structural, resource, funding – and, notably, objectives grew in ways that led to clashes. This, it will be shown, was generally to the detriment of multiculturalism and anti-racism at the school.

Building multicultural antiracist education

A transformative, critical notion of multiculturalism (Banks and Banks 1997; Ladson-Billings 2004; McLaren 1994) has been central in the school's educational agenda from the proposal stage. The founders embraced a broad vision of multicultural education that goes well beyond human relations, embodying a strong commitment to directly challenging differential power and racism. It also overtly focuses on other categories and forms of difference, such as gender inequities and the politics of sexuality (see Ladson-Billings 2003). The aim is teaching students to not only understand what it means to be antiracist, antibiased, and multicultural, but to put these values into practice: 'It's not just lip-service ... This vision actually drives the curriculum ... And that you are going to take something away from this. Hopefully school doesn't happen in a vacuum.'

In interviews, teachers described this curriculum as infused with lessons about culture and power, identity and community. This echoes Nieto's (2004) conception of multicultural education as far more than 'cultural and linguistic maintenance,' where not only 'issues of difference' are confronted but also 'issues of power and privilege in society. This means challenging racism and other biases as well as inequitable structures, policies, and practices of schools and, ultimately, of society itself' (2004, xxvii). The school addresses these inequities by, as a veteran teacher described, 'taking those issues from under the table and putting them on top of the table to look at and begin to talk about.' This enables students to recognize and contend with their manifestation in their own lives, communities, and cultures and in those of others. Students learn to acknowledge and confront their own biases, preconceptions, and stereotyping and their origins in sources other than 'race' and ethnicity. Ultimately, this multicultural approach understands the school to be 'a social system that consists of highly interrelated parts and variables' and that all of its major components must be substantially impacted to build an institution that grounds itself in the reality, not only the theory, of educational equality and antiracism (Banks and Banks 1997, 26).

This antiracist, multicultural understanding underlies all aspects of the school's curriculum and pedagogy. 'Our whole curriculum I think is based around multicultural, anti-bias, antiracist curriculum. It's kind of integrated and woven into everything that we teach. That's paramount here,' stated a teacher. This was echoed in multiple interviews with teachers and staff: 'It drives what we read, why we read it.'

This has required that the experiences of people of color feature prominently, and the history, literature, art, and music of various groups (not only the food, holidays, and celebrations, which are often the limits of schools' commitments) are integrated into the curriculum in different contexts and ways. The school seeks to thereby impart a transformative, activist message though this curriculum. As a founding educator expressed: 'the ideas and the ideals that they are learning here will be things that the students will take out into the culture, into the main predominantly White culture and maybe make some changes.' This conception of multiculturalism lay at the foundation of the school's original vision statement:

> Multicultural anti-racist education is more than just familiarizing our students with a few facts, faces, and foods of various nationalities who live in our country. Children should develop an 'ethnic literacy' (Banks 1981) in which they understand, analyze and respect their own cultural roots, an understanding of the historical nature of racial oppression in our country and the advantage of multicultural multilingual society. (Year One 1989, 48–49)

As powerful as this statement is, veteran teachers admit that the sweeping and lofty principles do not always offer sufficiently concrete guidelines for coherent and consistent curriculum development: 'The statement is a good starting point, and helps orient new staff and parents,' but is not enough to understand 'how to teach multiculturally' (Peterson 1995, 68). Integral to realizing the school's ambitious vision, it was understood, was a dynamic, 'back and forth' process of curriculum construction and implementation, where teachers said they 'learn from each other ... and from the children.'

Such an approach depends on both collaboration and teachers' independent initiative and creativity. Early on, there was an explicit decision to make only selective use of textbooks and that imposing ready-made materials on teachers would be 'sort of meaningless,' as a veteran noted in an interview. This made teachers ultimately responsible for developing their pedagogy and curriculum, with significant freedom and agency in setting their syllabi and teaching materials and methods. At the same time, teachers were to work closely with one another as well as with parents and the community to develop a basic model and revisit it over the years.

These two aspects of curriculum development have created a strong culture and practice of dialogue, collaboration, and mentoring at the school, as an ongoing routine. As a teacher stated: 'Without ongoing conversation, any curriculum becomes moribund.' Almost all teachers stressed the mutual support and mentoring amongst the teaching staff, in weekly teachers' meetings or informally 'in the lunch room,' as vital for ensuring consistency and coherence in the curriculum: '[There is] unity within all the staff and they're willing to help each other and come up with ideas together, collaborate together, and I think that's very helpful and unique.'

To support teachers, especially newcomers, the original school schedule devoted one full day a week to curriculum planning in each grade level, allowing teachers to meet for team teaching and curriculum development. This was done by scheduling art, music, and gym classes back-to-back to free homeroom teachers to collaborate on planning. Crucial to this, however, was funding for full-time special-subject instructors, which was strongly impacted later on by district budget cuts. Other techniques supplemented this to educate teachers regarding the multicultural, antiracist agenda: 'For instance, the principal has extra meetings with the teachers. The teachers generally work with another staff person at their level who is a veteran teacher. They are certainly provided with materials. They're encouraged to go to workshops.'

Much that has guided the evolution of this approach to curriculum development has been the school's early recognition of the challenge of passing down the founding generation's multicultural, antiracist vision consistently and effectively to 'newcomers.' A founding member explained:

If you are a newcomer, you don't know sort of the party line. You think you kind of have an idea of it. But it has all sorts of nuances and it's reflected in different ways. So we have to really work at making sure that new people are mentored and that we do have staff development, specifically about multiculturalism and antiracism and how the dual-language model works.

To contend with 'unnecessary duplications and omissions' in curricula across classes and grade levels (Peterson 1995, 68), the generalities and ambiguities had to be fleshed out and clearer guidelines provided. The school defined its multicultural program along a continuum (Banks 1981; Miner 1991; Peterson 1995), beginning with teaching the contributions of people of color, moving to non-European cultures, and culminating in a critical thinking phase, where messages from outside – the media, books, textbooks – are critiqued. For coherence in contents and message, four school-wide themes were developed as the overarching framework for teaching multiculturalism at every grade level. These curricular frameworks were aimed at training teachers to better teach transformative multiculturalism and antiracism.

In its binding of multiculturalism to antiracism and its approach to being multicultural education, the school has broken the 'either/or' choice between what Fraser (1997) calls the 'false antitheses' of 'social equality and multiculturalism'; it melds equally redistribution and recognition, understanding that neither alone is sufficient (1997, 3). But as will be shown, powerful pressures arose that undermined the full realization of these admirable ideals and aspirations. The attempt to develop, convey, and concretize the multicultural, antiracist agenda was only partially successful – hampered by the shift in district (and national) ideology towards neoliberal policies and goals and, no less significantly, proving to be not immune to the pervasiveness of the unequal structure of race relations in US society. It is to this that we now turn.

What happened to race?

What happened to race at this antiracist, multicultural school? What can account for its limited success in implementing a truly critical approach to multiculturalism and to equalizing the racial power structure?

This school, like all other public schools, is a site of conflict and tension among different ideologies, interests, and forces. The ascent of the neoliberal agenda in public education impacted budget and resource allocation at the school and forced compromises in its programs and an adjustment of priorities. National policies such as No Child Left Behind (NCLB) and the testing regime it imposed (Apple 2006) proved to be one stream through which neoliberal ideology slowly but steadily entered. The attractiveness of the bilingualism program to the mobility strategies necessary in a capitalistic neoliberal market indelibly harmed the antiracist setting and orientation of the school, as it led to a process of commodification of knowledge. But neoliberalism's frontal attack on transformative, thick democratic education is only one factor in the erosion of the antiracist program and setting at the school. No less significant, and not unrelated, the experience of this school, in its failure to equalize the education experience across the race spectrum, points at the deep-rootedness of structural racial inequality in the United States and the difficulty of removing it from the educational space (Ladson-Billings 2004; see also Apple 2013).

The undermining of overt antiracism at the school occurred on three interconnected planes. The first is the direct impact of district-wide implementation of the neoliberal educational policies of reductive forms of accountability and fiscal 'efficiency.' This led to budget and resource cuts and reallocation, and to a shift to a regime of testing and standards. Second is the commodification process that the school and its bilingualism program underwent, which led to the latter's prioritization and the subordination of the antiracist, critical multicultural program. This is closely connected to the third sphere of impact: the reproduction of structural racial inequality at the school in terms of exclusion of African-Americans and their unique needs as a community, and the general need to equalize the education experience at the school. In all three contexts, the changes were most prominently to the detriment of the African-American community's relationship with the school and its representation there.

The frequent city-wide budget cuts in public education over the last decade impaired significantly the school's ability to realize its original conceptualization of its multicultural program. Although, in being site-based managed, the school had full discretion over how it allocates its budget, it had little control over the total amount of funding it receives from the district or cutbacks in that funding. Moreover, the increasing need to meet district standards and targets was an added pressure in allocating the funding. Thus, when compromises had to be made in the face of cuts, in terms of both resource allocation and choice of resources, tension arose between the cornerstone missions at the school over resources.

One of the central sites of a clash of priorities was in the context of staff cutbacks. Several positions that were vital to sustaining the antiracist program and representation of the African-American community were cut early on when fiscal constraints arose. Most notable were the elimination of the parent coordinators and a significant reduction of paraprofessionals and support staff. The school had originally budgeted for two parent coordinators at the school, one African-American and the other Latina, to liaise with the two less-participating groups in the school's governance. With the loss of funding for these positions, a choice was made to eliminate the African-American coordinator first. This exacerbated the general under-participation and under-serving of the African-American community at the school and reflects the prioritizing of Latino/Latina representation. Unfortunately, the parent coordinator position was not replaced with any other liaising framework with parents. As one teacher noted, this was 'a real blow to our school.' It also points to one of the racializing effects of neoliberal economic decisions. These decisions aggravate racial differences and tensions not only between dominant and subordinate populations but *amongst* subordinated groups as well.

The second significant development was the loss of most of the school's paraprofessionals and assistants over the years. It also lost its full-time special-subject teachers, which led to the elimination of the full day scheduled for grade-level curriculum planning and collaboration. The result was a very real intensification of teachers' work (see Apple 2012). Like so many other teachers in public schools in the United States and elsewhere, teachers described how they were forced to plan their curriculum 'outside of the regular school time' as support 'dwindled and dwindled and dwindled,' in isolation from their peers and those who could guide and train them. The severe impact on curriculum planning time and quality was a central complaint in interviews: 'We have virtually no money for professional development. And we're all overworked, as you can tell, in terms of time. That's an ongoing struggle that we face.' Moreover, early on, the position of program implementor, who oversaw the task of developing and implementing a coherent and comprehensive curriculum, was also eliminated. This was especially critical in the context of the need to ensure consistency and a 'conversation' in the antiracist, multicultural curriculum.

This lack of adequate support for teacher mentoring, dialogue, and collaboration combined with new staff lacking the understanding, theoretically and practically, of how to teach critical multiculturalism – 'We get new staff in who are trained at the universities who don't really know very much about this' – led to variations and inconsistencies in the multicultural curricula among classes and grade levels (see Bhopal and Preston 2012). The 'unevenness' was recognized early on at the school (Peterson 1995) and emerged in both interviews with teachers and classroom observations. Some teachers expressed and taught an expanded and nuanced, multilayered notion of multiculturalism. A first-grade teacher described how she integrates empowerment and racism and sexism as they connect to the children's lives: 'I talk about racism. We talk about sexism. We study women's rights … because they live that. They know … So why am I going to pretend that those things are not issues for first-graders?' Other teachers expressed a narrower understanding, their descriptions focusing on more obvious issues and dimensions of culture. There was no extension of racism to other 'isms' and little evidence of a complex exploration of social justice, power, and other inequities. As Ladson-Billings (2003, 51) notes, 'ethnoracial distinctions [are] a limited way to talk about multiculturalism and multicultural education.' The tension, between an awareness of the multiplicity of ways and forms of oppression and identity and a more limited view, where ethnic and racial differences take center-stage, was evident from the teachers' varying descriptions of the multicultural curriculum and program. In interviews, leaders at the school were clearly reflective and critical about the school's multicultural preparation of new staff members and allocation of resources to ensure coherence and continuity of the vision, with one stating frankly: 'We don't do a good job at it.'

Exacerbating this situation was the introduction of the NCLB testing regime and the focus on standards, test scores, and achievement assessment. In constructing curriculum, teachers were expected to follow district guidelines and meet its targets. Many told of the pressures and frustrations of contending with the conflicting requirements and objectives after the implementation of NCLB. This has hugely impacted the prioritization of time and resources and hampered the meaningful pursuit of antiracism and multiculturalism at the school, as expressed in an interview:

> Many people who come to our school, in terms of teachers – many but not all – know of our beliefs and come because they're attracted to it. However, that's not always the case, and even those who do, their version of social justice or antiracist multiculturalism might be really problematic. Not that mine is perfect, but what we need is conversation. What does that mean in our classroom? What does that mean in our relationship to parents? What does that mean in our relationship to each other? Those things are a challenge in terms of finding time to discuss them because the district is pressuring us to use the time we do have together to talk about test scores.

Class conversion strategies at work

The pressure to conform to the testing, standards, and assessment regime was only one channel through which neoliberalism entered and impacted the school. Less direct was the hegemonization of the school and its bilingual program. The success of the school and the reputation it gained were vital for justifying the district's continued support for its programs. But there was a cost to this: 'Especially as the school has become more popular, we have a long waiting list of middle-class people who want to get in, who tend to be English dominant,' described a veteran administrator. Attracting and serving White, mostly middle-class families also means that the school has to contend with the demands of their commonsense, which is shaped by the material reality they experience and live (see Ball 2003).

This is a crucial point. Bilingualism has its own cultural capital in the global capitalist market. For some parents, command of the Spanish language is an advantage with 'purchasing power.' While some White parents reported sending their children to the school out of full support for the social-justice-oriented, antiracist curricula and agenda, others expressed this as a good 'consumer choice' in a supermarket of commodities, where bilingual education is a means of improving their children's chances in a competitive globalized market and enhancing their cultural capital, as part of a class conversion strategy (see Apple 2004, 2006; Bourdieu 1984). A middle-class, self-identified White mother explained: 'As the world keeps changing more and more, I think that it's important to be bilingual in some way, to be able to function.' Her aspiration for her child to be bilingual is not driven by a commitment to transforming society or reducing racial and cultural biases and inequities. Rather, it reflects the middle-class (White) perception of bilingualism as a means of 'upgrading' oneself, of becoming a 'well-rounded individual' within the dominant hegemonic perspectives. Moreover, this illustrates Reay et al.'s observation of middle-class choice in going 'against the grain' in such settings, as 'directed toward "consuming the desired other" in an act of appropriation' (2007, 1054).

To sustain its success, then, the school has had to accommodate middle-class hegemonic commonsense and demands in maneuvering between its bilingual program and its critical multicultural program. This has been a further factor in its prioritization of bilingualism over the needs and objectives of antiracist, multicultural, equalized education: access, recognition, and representation for cultural and social minoritized groups. In supporting and endorsing bilingualism – making it easier to 'teach,' on the one hand, and a desired commodity, on the other – the school district's neoliberal agenda and the legitimation needs of the local state have created a context in which subordinating antiracist multicultural aspects of the school's life seems a necessary unavoidable compromise. When choices had to be made between ensuring the duality of the bilingual program and transforming race relations, the former won out on almost all fronts.

The absent presence of 'race'

This leads to the third, overarching element of the school's challenges in realizing transformative multiculturalism: its partially unsuccessful prevention of the reproduction of the structures of racial inequality dominating US society and education. This has manifested most prominently in African-American representation in school governance and staffing and the blurring of the group identity of the African-American students.

Not only have attempts to diversify and strengthen parent participation in the school fallen short from the perspective of the African-American community, as we saw above, but the school's professional staff is completely devoid of even one African-American. One teacher sharply criticized the conspicuous absence of African-American teachers at the school as inbuilt racism: 'I don't think that the African-American population is well-served. There's one African-American assistant. Nobody else. How can that be? Only the people who clean or cook. That is huge, a major problem, that we are reproducing.' This 'major problem' points to the role of 'necessary compromises' in the reproduction of class and race power relations of greater US society at the school. African-Americans fill only low-wage positions at the school, at best. The school offers no middle-class, educated, professional role-models for African-American students, but rather only the traditional semi-skilled or unskilled labor roles of cleaning and cooking. This fundamentally undermines one of the school's key founding rationales: challenging oppression and racism in US society in general, but particularly the segregation and discrimination in its own city and in the school itself (see Apple 2013; Lipman 2011).

Again, the needs of the bilingual program were explained by school administrators as producing this marginalization. Priority in hiring teachers was given to bilingual candidates, in a context where it is difficult to find qualified African-American teachers who are fluent in Spanish. Teachers expressed awareness of this deep problem and admitted the choice not to compromise the dual bilingualism at the school by hiring insufficiently bilingual teachers: 'That's a problem [no African-American teachers]. We had a couple in the past, but they have to speak Spanish ... Not making excuses, it's just the way it is.' The result was a failure to recognize and serve African-American students' need for role-models and representation.

Given this, the overriding identity of the school as bilingual partly interrupts the critical dimensions of cultural diversity at the school, trapping it in a sort of bicultural paradox. It creates a dichotomy between Spanish-speaking communities and English-speaking communities as almost exclusively definitive of diversity, 'otherness,' in the school. This has left little room to cultivate a more critical multiculturalism in practice, not only in the program but in the student body itself, in order to recognize in more powerful ways a diversity of cultural groups and communities.

Similar problems arise in the context of politics of recognition and cultural diversity at the school. Many noted in interviews the all-embracing atmosphere of diversity, cultural and otherwise, due to the multicultural and antiracism program, and this was clearly observable in the student artwork on the walls, extracurricular cultural events, and overt discourse in school signs and notices. Yet there is a clear marginalization of non-White, non-Hispanic groups, most particularly the African-American community. African-American enrolment has dramatically declined with time, while White English-speakers and native-Spanish-speakers have been courted and their enrolment has consistently risen. Thus, the needs of two-way bilingualism have effectively stripped the African-American community of its recognition as a distinct political and cultural (including linguistic) group at the school.

The impact of this on linguistic politics has been profound. While not a conscious choice, this has meant that the school erases any cultural aspects to the African-American English dialect, as well as disregarding the community's cultural distinction beyond 'mere' language. In the framework of this Spanish/English dichotomy, the African-American community belongs to (or is considered part of) the majority in terms of first language; they are uncritically put together with Whites who speak Standard English.

This is accompanied by one further factor in the blurring of the African-American community's identity as a distinct cultural group within the school – the need to maintain a balance between native-Spanish-speaking and native-English-speaking students for the two-way bilingualism program to work. This has resulted in a dichotomous – rather than multicultural – approach to diversifying the student body. As the pressures emerged, a prominent concern was how to attract more Spanish-speaking students to balance English-speaking students. Moreover, from a class perspective, attracting a balance of White middle-class students was vital for any real attempt at achieving redistribution and recognition (Fraser 1997). Preventing the reproduction of social and material inequalities requires the production of transformed students (Apple 2013). But transformation must occur at both ends of the spectrum – the privileged and non-privileged/less privileged, the oppressed and oppressors. Thus White, English-speaking, middle-class students are critical for both their own transformation and the transformation of non-White, Spanish-speaking, working-class students.[1] This, again, has come at the expense of African-American students and their place in the school as a distinct group and culture.

Conclusion

There is so much about this school that is worthy of respect and support. But what emerges from our analysis here is a story of complexity and contradictions, a mixture of hope and worry. Even in this school – whose vision, collaborative ethos, and curriculum contents embody recognition, redistribution, and equal representation (Fraser 2010) – inequalities and racializing power relations have been produced in important ways. In these circumstances, what was meant to be a powerful educational challenge to dominance is significantly weakened.

The school is to be commended for its goal of interrupting such relations in the larger society and in the school itself. But the effects of neoliberal policies, the realities of who teaches at the school, the constraints on time and resources, the tensions between the sometimes-contradictory progressive programs, the multiplicity of racialized groups, and the ability of middle-class parents to re-occupy or 'appropriate' (Reay et al. 2007) the space of critical educational reform for their own purposes – all of these and more have created a set of conditions and dynamics that 'interrupt the interruptions.'

In many ways, this school is a powerful example of the impact of the ongoing neoliberal assault, both direct and indirect, not only on public education in general, but most specifically on schools that aim to be counter-hegemonic. This was experienced on a number of levels and in various defining aspects. The school emerges as no less a site of conflict and compromise between different powers and interests – even if all valid and equally desirable from the school's perspective – which has led to concessions most significantly in the sphere of race, representation, inclusion, recognition, and redistribution, with surprising implications for the struggle to equalize social, cultural, and racial power relations.

Promoting social justice and challenging society's power structure are undoubtedly major constituents of the school. This manifests in its structure, governance, and curriculum and pedagogy. The school has had broad success in transforming the public education system in its district and city. Over the years, it has formed important alliances with social groups and movements, other district schools, the teachers union, and progressive activists and scholars, in an effort to introduce more critical multicultural antiracist policies into the public system. This is a story that needs to be told as well.

Alongside these successes, however, the school, like many others in the United States, has had to contend with the major challenges brought on by NCLB. 'Certainly the NCLB and the testing regime and the push to assess districts, to assess schools, to assess students, to assess on the basis of narrow test scores are a huge problem,' a teacher noted. This should remind us that neoliberalism in education is more than mere economic policy and more than an attempt to impose audit cultures on the public sector and the schools within that sector. Neoliberalism seems to be inherently racializing in its assumptions and foundations as well as its effects (Apple 2006, 2013; see also Lipman 2011). In its destruction of what might be best seen as 'thick democracy' and its recreation of the citizen as a consumer, a 'chooser,' it makes full, collective participation by an engaged community more difficult (Apple 2006, 15).

The school in our study exemplifies the depth and breadth of this effect. Daily life in the school is still partly transformative. But the compromises that 'need to be made' and the school's increasing role as a site for middle-class conversion strategies lead to the reproduction of the unequal structure of race relations and a loss of the resources and time needed to maintain the critical work that makes the school a site of counter-hegemonic possibilities.

When the critical multiculturalism program has been set at odds with other fundamental goals or interests pursued by the school, the balancing process has seemed to unevenly weigh against the needs of antiracism. The concessions and compromises that were made – giving up paraprofessionals, but keeping a full-time librarian; choosing a Latino/Latina parent coordinator over an African-American representative – had differentiating effects. The tensions between the conflicting needs of its programs (e.g. sustaining diverse antiracist multiculturalism in and from the neighborhood versus the need to bus-in Spanish-speaking students for two-way bilingualism) had similar hidden effects. Thus the school has had mixed results in challenging racial and social inequalities.

In terms of the politics of official knowledge (Apple 2014), the multicultural antiracist curriculum is no longer uniformly conceived and applied. Some teachers succeed at only expanding the borders of hegemonic domination, failing to challenge it beyond the limited understanding of racism. A deeply counter-hegemonic orientation seems to less fully permeate the life of the school.

This is evident also in the politics of representation. A major shortcoming at the school is its inadequate representation of the African-American community: their unequal representation on the professional staff and in parental participation, and the 'swallowing up' of their culture, language, and identities as a distinct community. Along these two trajectories, the school has paradoxically reinforced the cultural domination, marginalization, and at times exclusion of African-Americans in US society, and has reproduced the unequal and racialized social structure. This was admitted in interviews as a tragic 'price' for the successful implementation of the bilingual agenda. A choice had to be made.

But to call this a 'choice' risks reinstalling neoliberal forms. Why are such 'choices' forced on so many schools? What is the social and economic context of such 'choices'? Who ultimately benefits in the creation and enforcement of such a context?

The school in no way pretends to be a utopian radical school. But it is 'directed toward transcending and fundamentally transforming an unequal and undemocratic society in the here and now' (Tannock, James, and Torres 2011, 941). Given this, we need to ask some crucial questions: in choosing the compromises to be made, who is compromised, at whose expense? Is the social price too heavy, and does it undermine the project as a counter-hegemonic endeavor? Finally, in a context of neoliberal restructuring of the ends and means of schooling, we need to think about what can be done to protect the space that schools like this aim to produce and occupy. Is it inevitable that when faced with the ideological and economic conditions now confronting such schools, these are the only results we should expect? We hope not.

Note
1. Despite the strong correlation between 'race' and class position, we stress that we are not essentializing all Spanish-speakers as lower class, but rather presenting the different ends of the spectrums: White and non-White, English-speakers and Spanish-speakers, middle class and working/lower class.

References

Apple, M. W. 2004. *Ideology and Curriculum*. 3rd ed. New York: Routledge.

Apple, M. W. 2006. *Educating the 'Right' Way: Markets, Standards, God, and Inequality*. 2nd ed. New York: Routledge.

Apple, M. W. 2012. *Education and Power*. Revised Routledge Classic. ed. New York: Routledge.

Apple, M. W. 2013. *Can Education Change Society?* New York: Routledge.

Apple, M. W. 2014. *Official Knowledge*. 3rd ed. New York: Routledge.

Baker, C. 2006. *Foundations of Bilingual Education and Bilingualism*. 4th ed. Clevedon: Multilingual Matters Ltd.

Ball, S. 2003. *Class Strategies and the Education Market*. New York: Routledge-Falmer.

Banks, J. A. 1981. *Multicultural Education. Theory and Practice*. Boston, MA: Allyn & Bacon.

Banks, J. A., and C. A. M. Banks, eds. 1997. *Multicultural Education. Issues and Perspectives*. 3rd ed. Boston, MA: Allyn & Bacon.

Bhopal, K., and J. Preston, eds. 2012. *Intersectionality and 'Race' in Education*. London: Routledge.

Bourdieu, P. 1984. *Distinction: A Social Critique of the Judgment of Taste*. Cambridge, MA: Harvard University Press.

Fraser, N. 1997. *Justice Interruptus*. New York: Routledge.

Fraser, N. 2010. *Scales of Justice*. New York: Columbia University Press.

Hall, S. 1996. "Gramsci's Relevance for the Study of Race and Ethnicity." In *Stuart Hall: Critical Dialogues in Cultural Studies*, edited by D. Morley and K. H. Chen, 411–441. New York: Routledge.

History of Bilingual Education. 1998. *Rethinking Schools* 12 (3): 1–2.

Ladson-Billings, G. 2003. "New Directions in Multicultural Education: Complexities, Boundaries, and Critical Race Theory." In *Handbook of Research on Multicultural Education: Issues and Perspectives*, edited by J. A. Banks and C. A. M. Banks, 50–66. San Francisco: Jossey-Bass.

Ladson-Billings, G. 2004. "Culture versus Citizenship: The Challenge of Racialized Citizenship in the United States." In *Diversity and Citizenship Education*, edited by J. A. Banks, 99–126. San Francisco: Jossey-Bass.

Lipman, P. 2011. *The New Political Economy of Urban Education*. New York: Routledge.

McLaren, P. 1994. "White Terror and Oppositional Agency: Towards a Critical Multiculturalism." In *Multiculturalism. A Critical Reader*, edited by T. H. Goldberg, 45–74. Cambridge, MA: Blackwell.

Meshulam, A. 2011. "What Kind of Alternative? Bilingual, Multicultural Schools, as Counterhegemonic Alternatives Educating for Democracy." PhD diss., University of Wisconsin-Madison.

Mills, C. 1997. *The Racial Contract*. Ithaca, NY: Cornell University Press.

Miner, B. 1991. "Taking Multicultural, Anti-Racist Education Seriously: An Interview with Enid Lee." *Rethinking Schools* 6 (1): 19–22.

Miner, B. 2013. *Lessons from the Heartland: A Turbulent Half-Century of Public Education in an Iconic American City*. New York: The New Press.

Nieto, S. 2004. *Affirming Diversity. The Sociopolitical Context of Multicultural Education*. 4th ed. Boston/New York: Pearson.

Orfield, G. 2009. *Reviving the Goal of an Integrated Society: A 21st Century Challenge*. Los Angeles, CA: The Civil Rights Project/Proyecto Derechos Civiles at UCLA.

Peterson, B. 1995. "A Journey Toward Democracy." In *Democratic Schools*, edited by M. W. Apple and J. A. Beane, 58–82. Alexandria: ASCD.

Reay, D., S. Hollingworth, K. Williams, G. Crozier, F. Jamieson, D. James, and P. Beedell. 2007. "A Darker Shade of Pale?' Whiteness, the Middle Classes and Multi-ethnic Inner City Schooling." *Sociology* 41 (6): 1041–1060.

Skutnabb-Kangas, T., and O. García, eds. 1995. *Multilingualism for All? General Principles*. Lisse, The Netherlands: Swets and Zeitlinger.

Tannock, S., D. James, and C. A. Torres. 2011. "Radical Education and the Common School: A Democratic Alternative. Review Symposium." *British Journal of Sociology of Education* 32 (6): 939–952.

Thomas, P. W., and P. V. Collier. 2002. *A National Study of School Effectiveness for Language Minority Students' Long-Term Academic Achievement*. Santa Cruz, CA: Center for Research on Education, Diversity and Excellence, University of California-Santa Cruz.

Tolan, T. 2003. *Riverwest. A Community History*. Milwaukee, WI: Past Press and COA.

US Census Bureau. 2008. "State & County Quickfacts." Accessed September 5, 2009. http://quickfacts.census.gov/qfd/states/.

Year One. 1989. Unpublished School Document.

Fighting for the 'right to the city': examining spatial injustice in Chicago public school closings

Carl A. Grant, Anna Floch Arcello, Annika M. Konrad and Mary C. Swenson

Department of Curriculum & Instruction and the Department of English, University of Wisconsin-Madison, Madison, WI, USA

This article uses Chicago public school closings as a case study for the rise of mayoral control and the decline of democratic participation – two common responses to stiff competition from global markets – in urban public schools in the United States. In response to the 2013 Chicago decision to close 50 schools and move 30,000 students, this article presents an in-depth look into the history and theory behind the situation. By drawing upon the history of restrictive education and housing policies for African Americans in Chicago and using a 'critical spatial perspective,' the authors argue that school closings are highly counterproductive to the fight for the 'right to the city.' The authors argue for increased democratic participation for students, parents, and community leaders in urban school systems across the globe.

Introduction

The effects of globalization are challenging schools in urban spaces across the globe and, as a consequence, restrictive policies of space and place are perpetuating 'spatial injustice.' Education has become an increasingly important global commodity, with some economists suggesting that knowledge has replaced economists' class denomination of 'land, labor and capital as the chief economic resources' (Branson 1999, 1). Up until the decade of the 1970s, the United States commanded global markets and had the knowledge (e.g. highly skilled work force, technology) to control the world economy; however, this trend shifted in the decades that followed. US cities were not overtly challenged to deal with major advances in technology and communication, stiff competition from China and India, or ongoing demands for new knowledge (Friedman 2005). This desire for global economic competition began to filter into educational settings, and as Friedman states: 'Every young American today would be wise to think of himself or herself competing against every young Chinese, Indian, and Brazilian' (2005, 276). In the 1970s European and Asian economies started to compete with American firms on a global scale, causing them to lose domestic and global market shares, and productivity became stagnant, causing a severe 'crisis of competitiveness' in the United States (Milberg 1994; Wak 2003). This crisis provoked a study of the US educational system by the Reagan administration and the subsequent release of 'A Nation at Risk' that stated:

> Our nation is at risk. Our once unchallenged pre-eminence in commerce, industry, science and technological innovation is being overtaken by competitors throughout the world ... What was unimaginable a generation ago has begun to occur ... other (nations) are matching or surpassing our educational attainments. (National Commission on Excellence in Education 1983, 5)

The report bluntly linked the US crisis of competition to the failure of education, noting that US students were never first or second in international comparisons, and were last seven times in comparison with other industrialized nations (National Commission on Excellence in Education 1983, 8). The report was a national bomb-shell that led to politicians and media blaming the crisis on the low skill levels of American workers, and by implication the poor performance of the school system (Wak 2003).

The impact of mayoral control: turnaround schools and school closings

To respond to this crisis, many urban leaders took control of school systems in an effort to drastically reshape failing schools. Although mayoral control of schools is not a new trend in the United States, it rapidly increased in the 1990s (e.g. Boston in 1991, Chicago in 1995, Baltimore in 1997, Philadelphia in 2001, New York in 2002 and Washington, DC in 2007) (Moscovitch 2010). Turnaround efforts of all kinds, however, have long been attempted in underperforming US schools with varying results (Smarick 2010). For example, numerous research studies have demonstrated that little improvement has been made in failing schools that have been touched by reform efforts such as school restructuring, reconstitution, school size reduction, and certain aspects of the 'No Child Left Behind' legislation (Smarick 2010). Mayoral control of education has specifically introduced reform that deals with: school choice, strict performance accountability, curriculum, charter schools, and school closings. Of all the solutions to the education crisis cited by 'A Nation at Risk,' the closing of schools has created the greatest controversy and pushback.

The basic reasoning behind school closings suggests that students in low-performing schools will benefit from moving to higher performing schools, especially once their schools have been deemed to be failing (Sunderman and Payne 2009, 3). Smarick (2010) argues that closing underperforming schools is a better solution than other reform efforts because the for-profit sector has long succeeded by welcoming failure of businesses so that the successful ones can replace them and transform the market. According to Smarick (2010), there are three main benefits to closing schools: children will benefit by moving out of low-performing schools; the threat of closure will drive schools to perform better; and closing low-performing schools will create opportunities for new, better ones to be formed. Much of the rhetoric used to make pro-school closing arguments emphasizes that closing schools holds adults, rather than children, accountable for educational failures. For example, in a 2006 response to William Ayers and Michael Klonsky, Arne Duncan, the US Secretary of Education, emphasized that the decision to close schools is a moral one because 'the adults involved are held accountable because the school ceases to exist' (Duncan 2006, 458).

Although the general assumptions behind school closings rely on market-based strategies and a moral imperative, the actual data on school closings are not conclusive about the consequences of this reform strategy. The 2009 data from a report prepared by the Consortium on Chicago School Research at the University of Chicago Urban Education Institute attempt to clarify the impact of school closings on displaced students. The Consortium utilizes student outcomes such as reading and mathematics scores, special education referrals, retentions, summer school enrollment, mobility and high school performance in order to determine the positive or negative impact of school closings and 'turn around' schools throughout Chicago (de la Torre and Gwynne 2009, 2). Although the findings do suggest that students who leave closing schools often re-enroll in weaker performing schools, the overall data show that average learning is not impacted in positive or negative ways and that, 'when displaced students reached high school, their on-track rates to graduate were no different than the rates of students who attended schools similar to those that closed' (2009, 2). Although more research needs to be conducted in order to demonstrate the long-range impact of school closings on communities and children, one conclusive finding from the report shows that 42% of students who left shuttered schools continue to be educated in schools with very low academic achievement (2009, 3). Furthermore, although immediate academic achievement measures such as reading and mathematics scores were not impacted negatively, other outcomes such as decreased summer school attendance and frequent changing of school locations continued to occur after students left a closed school and even after they attended a new institution (2009, 19–20). This trend is consistent with the findings from the report, which shows that a 'school closing has negative effects on students' achievement during the announcement year' and that 'achievement for these students returns to its predicted level after one year in their new school' (2009, 25). Although this suggests that perhaps school closings might eventually help students in the long run, other outcomes such as a decreased participation in summer schools and frequent school changing suggest longer-term effects that need to be further examined.

At a glance, these findings might suggest a neutral impact on student achievement; however, the report suggests that more data need to be collected on the individual and community impact of school closings and contradicts the notion that school closings drastically improve a student's academic achievement. The report also highlights that many students continue to fall through the gap between school closings either by withdrawing from summer programs or continuing to change schools consistently after leaving their primary institution. This finding is consistent with data from a recent report from WBEZ in October 2013, which suggests that only 60% of students from Chicago's closed schools showed up at the appropriate new schools (Lutton 2013). In the case of one elementary school, only 12 of the projected 196 students from a nearby closed school showed up for fall enrollment (Lutton 2013). As such, a large group of students remain unaccounted for and/or are showing up in schools and in districts not equipped to handle an influx of students. These data underscore the complexity of the school closing issue, highlighting that there is not one 'quick fix' to improve the educational conditions of students in the poorest and most disadvantaged schools.

In an effort to respond to the inconclusive findings of empirical research on the effects of school closings, this paper examines the ideological, historical, and cultural dimensions of school closing decisions. Many of the ideological and cultural critiques of school closings represented in news media point to the ways school closing decisions reflect a purely market-based model of education and disproportionately affect the lives of students of color. Ayers and Klonsky call school closings a 'mechanical replication process' that creates 'new winners and losers' and privileges private investors and politically connected school leaders, not students (2006, 454–455). In addition, other opponents of school closings point to the fact that these efforts primarily impact the lives of students of color, but fail to directly address the vast racial inequities that persist in US schools. In many of the large urban school districts (e.g. Chicago, Philadelphia, Washington, DC) where mayors took control, schools are predominately black or brown. Because the decision to close a school is typically based on federally mandated test scores, minority and low-income students are most affected by these reform efforts (Sunderman and Payne 2009, 4–5).

What we contribute in this paper, then, is an in-depth theoretical look at the historical, ideological, and cultural milieu surrounding school closing decisions. We argue that the decision to close a school cannot be separated from the sociocultural and historical context surrounding the community in which the school and its students reside. More specifically, we argue that the combination of school closings and the long history of racial segregation in US cities is further deepening legacies of 'spatial injustice' in school systems. As a case study, we examine school reform in Chicago, one of the earlier cities to adopt mayoral control in recent years (1995) and where 50 schools were closed and more than 3500 teachers fired during the 2012/13 school year. In doing so, we pay attention to the continued legacy of racism in the school system, as well as the long history of the segregation of black families to certain areas of the city, which as we will argue has created immense 'spatial injustice.'

The history of Chicago's restrictive educational and housing policies

By recovering the complex history of Chicago's rise as a major city, its deeply rooted segregation policies, and the long legacy of inequitable schooling for black students, we are better suited to understand just how school closings continue to plague black and brown[1] students in Chicago public schools. The US National Center for Educational Statistics reported that over 50% of African American and Latino students are enrolled in schools where students of color make up 75% of the student body. In Chicago, the United States' most segregated city, it is typical for students to attend their entire P/K–12 education without having a classmate of another race (Krauser 2012). The import of the US Supreme Court landmark decision in *Brown vs. Board of Education*, legally ending school segregation throughout the United States, has not come to fruition. In fact, according to Orfield and Lee (2007), schools today are more segregated.

Texts such as *12 Million Black Voices*, written by Richard Wright (1941), help us understand our modern challenges by depicting the stark realities that faced black individuals the moment they arrived in Chicago at the turn of the twentieth century. Wright, a southern transplant to Chicago himself, utilizes images and prose to tell the story of southern migration to northern urban centers and the deplorable conditions that often awaited black settlers. Wright (1941) documents the rapid influx of blacks to Chicago, Philadelphia, and New York. Wright's (1941) work, combining photographs and narration, lays bare the long history of racial tension that still permeates Chicago. This text (among other sociological investigations such as *Black Metropolis*; Drake and Cayton 1962) documents Chicago's rapid growth, and the fraught racial and political boundaries used to segment the city that resulted in concentrated neighborhoods of transplants and hastily thrown together urban and educational policies.

These memories and histories are essential to understanding the complex history of segregation in Chicago, and the ways this history is deeply ingrained in today's neighborhoods and schools. As Pauline Lipman (2011) argues in *The New Political Economy of Urban Education*, Chicago continues to be a microcosm of trends (both positive and negative) in education happening throughout the country and across the globe as cities, mayors, and administrators seek to respond to the 'educational crisis' brought on by globalization. Indeed, as Lipman contends:

> Chicago is where big city mayors go to see how to restructure their school systems ... Chicago is also a prominent case of the transformation of the industrial, Keynesian, racially segregated, city to the entrepreneurial post welfare city. (2011, 19)

Examining how policies of segregation were present from the outset of Chicago's school system helps us to better understand how Chicago arrived at the center of this turmoil. In addition, it is important to trace this history of segregation, overcrowding, and restrictive neighborhood policies in order to better understand just how schools like Mary Macleod Bethune, the focus of the last section of this article, continue to suffer as a result of inherently inequitable education and housing policies.

The impact of segregation and overcrowding in schools

Chicago's current 'educational crisis' is rooted in the politics of segregation since policy-makers began scrambling to attend to the large growth of black students in the late nineteenth and early twentieth centuries. During the 1840s, as fugitive slaves from the South and free blacks from the East arrived and began to move, they became confined to the southern portion of the city, which would come to be known as the Black Belt (Grant and Grant 2013, 35). As a result of this migration, by 1863 the population figures 'had changed drastically for blacks in the city ... their numbers had increased by 286 percent, or from 363 in 1850 to 2916 in 1860 according to the census reports' (Daniel 1980, 148). This pattern of migration created clear racial boundaries between black and white zones in the city of Chicago, and in 1863 the Chicago City Charter was amended to provide separate schools for blacks and whites (Daniel 1980). As the authors of *Black Metropolis* point out, the settlements where black residents lived during this time period were not absorbed into the general population but remained isolated, restricted, and expanding (Drake and Cayton 1962, 17). From the outset, Chicago was marked by violent and restrictive policies towards outsiders. These laws, which sought to respond to the influx of southern blacks, also marked the beginning of educational policies that would favor white students, while systematically punishing students in black and immigrant communities.

Although school segregation was officially outlawed in 1897, from 1840 to 1914, Chicago offered very few civil rights to blacks. Whites in Chicago often resisted giving African Americans rights that came with citizenship of a city. For example, schools that African American children attended were poor in almost every educational area: teaching, material resources, and physical plants. As the black population grew throughout the early twentieth century, the policies of school segregation (although formally outlawed) became even more entrenched as policy-makers continued to attend to the increasing influx of students. Some 50,000 blacks arrived in Chicago between 1910 and 1920 (Drake and Cayton 1962, 58). Between 1920 and 1930 the black population in Chicago increased even more from 109,458 to 233,903, and the number of African American students in segregated schools increased from 6% to 26% (Grant and Grant 2013, 36). This rapid influx was not met with adequate resources. To this day, schools in predominantly black communities have yet to receive the human and financial resources necessary to transform them into high-quality and globally competitive educational settings (Grant and Grant 2013, 36).

Many of the laws that persisted after the official ban on school segregation continued to disenfranchise black students and restrict their access to equitable education. For example, in order to deal with overcrowding in Chicago's black communities and schools, the Chicago public schools instituted controversial methods such as 'double shifts' programs, which had students attending school for only half a day. The *Chicago Defender*, the major black newspaper in Chicago, reported in 1939 that '78% of Negro children spend 40% less time in schools than do children outside of the colored communities in Chicago.'

Historian A. N. Knupfer notes that in 1941 Wendell Phillips High School (a school with an all-black student population) enrolled 3600 students, more than double its capacity. During this time, 20,000 empty seats were available in non-black schools, but 'because of restrictive covenant associations (organizations established to restrict access to housing in white neighborhoods), black children could not transfer to these schools.' It was not until 1957, almost three-quarters of a century after anti-segregation legislation was passed, that a state statute decreed that school officials could not bar black students from attendance (Grant and Grant 2013, 36–37). Although laws were passed as a way to eliminate the policies of segregation and overcrowding in Chicago Public Schools, they often left disjointed and inequitable policies in their place, which continues to have reverberations today. Furthermore, the educational policies had a tremendous impact on the experiences of black students, on school curriculum, and on student identity. One student recalls her school experience in the 1960s:

> I was one of a hundred students that integrated a white school between 1964 and 1968. So during my formative years, freshman through senior high school I was struggling with my identity. I was trying to figure out how I was going to be in this white environment. We lived in the public housing on the east side of the city and I would have to take a bus and go to a school outside of my neighborhood a few miles west [from where I lived]. I [spent] four years trying to figure out whether I'm a little white girl, or … a little black girl; I struggled with my identity' (Grant and Grant 2013, 37).

What this history makes clear is that there were reverberations of racism and discrimination that persisted in Chicago beyond the life of formalized policies and laws.

Restrictive spatial policies

The restrictive and segregated residential policies in Chicago throughout the twentieth century also impacted the access and quality of schools that black students were attending, ensuring that those within the Black Belt remained firmly in place and that they lived in segmented areas separately from whites. As Daniel (1980) details, in 1917 the Chicago Real Estate Board proposed residential policies that owners' societies be created in white neighborhoods against the encroachment of black residential movement and intrusion into white schools (1980, 152). Daniel suggests that the policies and opposition from white neighborhood organizations had an immediate effect, making the black community on the south side 'more densely populated' as 'blacks were consigned to areas no greater than twenty-seven blocks by fourteen blocks, and school segregation was a principal reason for this containment' (1980, 154). Often, the influx of residents into limited black neighborhoods ensured that the houses, which had previously been considered some of the best in the city, quickly fell into disrepair. The residences often housed multiple families at a time with higher rents in black neighborhoods than in white neighborhoods, which had an impact on black students whose parents had to take on multiple jobs to pay for rent, leaving them with little care and oversight (1980, 156). As the densely populated neighborhoods began to grow, so too did crime rates within these areas and overcrowding in schools

By 1920 black secondary students were far behind their white counterparts in school, and a report published that year showed that black students were often three years behind white students (Daniel 1980, 158). The restrictive residential and educational policies had a disastrous effect on students throughout the twentieth century, and remain deeply embedded in Chicago schools up until today. Daniel starkly validates this fact and points to the vicious cycle perpetrated against black students as a result of these policies:

> Many school officials and teachers saw these students, whether northern-born or from the South, as equally unintelligent. To add to this perception, intelligence tests were introduced into the schools. These tests led to vocational tracking and to the isolation of black students into specified course sequences. Vice, a product of a growing Chicago ghetto, haunted black high school students who began to doubt their personal worth and sometimes turned to socially disapproved actions to verify their debasement. (1980, 159)

In this excerpt, Daniel (1980) paints a striking image of life in the black belt, and highlights the ways restrictive residential policies work to create inequitable educational opportunities for those students still living within these neighborhoods. As long as these inherently unequal spatial policies continue to impact the residents of Chicago, so too will school closings, lack of resources, and the intrinsically biased curriculum that students are exposed to throughout the system.

A critical spatial perspective: ideologies behind controlled spaces and places

Inherently unequal spatial policies have continued to segregate cities like Chicago because 'spaces and places' are commonly considered neutral, apolitical features of everyday human life. Spatial theorists such as Edward Soja, Edward Said, and David Harvey help us see how 'spaces and places' are socially constructed concepts derived from particular conceptual lenses. Once we are able to see 'spaces and places' in this light, we can more clearly understand how they serve as vehicles for creating and maintaining inequalities like those rampant in Chicago's history of restrictive residential and educational policies.[2] Edward Soja (2010, 5) argues that all social justice issues are inherently spatial, and all spatial issues are inherently social justice issues. For this reason, it is important to utilize theories of space and place, and their relationship to social justice issues, to see how the recent Chicago school closings are just one more chapter in a long history of systemic racial, economic, and spatial injustice. The following theories allow us to see how spatial policies are not neutral, apolitical decisions, but instead are derived from particular political, class, and racial ideologies. Further, these theories provide a path for imagining a more 'spatially just' approach to school reform

The creation of spatial injustice

The development of large cities has resulted in vast inequalities for the people who live in them (Soja 2010). David Harvey claims that urbanization has always been a 'class phenomenon' because cities arose from 'geographical and social concentrations of a surplus product' and the distribution of those surpluses has been controlled by only a select few (Harvey 2008, first section, para. 3). This 'class phenomenon' has also taken over urban schools in which democratic principles no longer drive the decision-making process, but instead neoliberal ideologies have granted power to those with political and economic control, like city mayors.

In addition to the control of surpluses, Engels (1935) argued that the bourgeoisie has come to control cities through a self-reproducing process of gentrification. In the interest of a 'housing problem,' as Engels puts it, the bourgeoisie approaches the housing problem only to 'continually reproduces the question anew' (as cited in Harvey 2008, Dispossessions section, para.

2). Engels (1935) explains that through gentrification the bourgeoisie performs the same process of disappearing 'the scandalous alleys' and replacing them with 'lavish self-praise' (as cited in Harvey 2008, Dispossessions section, para. 2). The gentrification process only pushes the problem to another location, creating yet another reason for the bourgeoisie to 'solve' the housing problem. The very origin of cities – the concentration of surplus goods – created the opportunity for a select few to control the lives of everyone that lives in them, particularly in the ways that spaces are divided, modified, and populated, as well as the locations of schools and neighborhoods (Engels 1935). In the case of Chicago's history, it is clear that the self-reproducing process of gentrification is a phenomenon that has happened over and over again – first, in the creation of the Black Belt, then in the Chicago Real Estate Board's zoning regulations of the early twentieth century, and now in the displacement of students of color across the city.

Further, postcolonial theory allows us to see how spatial processes like gentrification and school closings require the creation of an 'other' within the city. Said argues that colonization is inherently tied to the political organization of space, and if we think of the political organization of space as colonial, then we are able to reach what Soja calls a 'critical spatial perspective' (as cited in Soja 2010, 36). Said argues that the colonial construction of the 'other' is manifested in the control of all spaces, like classrooms, courthouses, prisons, railway stations, marketplaces, hospitals, boulevards, places of worship, and private homes, as well as larger spaces such as administrative buildings, boundaries, land allocation, and so forth (as cited in Soja 2010, 36–37). While many would not dare to think of the history of spatial policies in Chicago as 'colonial,' Said's theory demonstrates that the political control of spaces, small and large, is inherently colonial because it requires the creation and control of an 'other.' This explains why a full examination of school closings in Chicago, an issue that appears purely economic, requires viewing the control of spaces as intertwined with the creation of a racial, economic, linguistic, or ethnic 'other.'

Soja (2010) outlines a number of more specific means by which spaces are politically controlled, many of which have been widespread in Chicago since the early twentieth century. Tension between public and private property rights, Soja (2010) argues, is a major root cause of spatial injustice. Soja cites the phenomenon of 'security obsessed urbanism,' borrowing Mike Davis' (1990) term, as another reason for systemic spatial injustice in cities. While the rich have always lived behind protective structures, technologies like security systems, spiked park benches, surveillance cameras, and so forth, have created 'a tightly meshed and prisonlike geography punctuated by protective enclosures and overseen by ubiquitous watchful eyes' (Soja 2010, 43). The gated community is the epitome of the divided, protection-obsessed, class-based urban existence in which spaces and public resources are not shared equally among citizens (2010, 43). Soja concludes that the dynamic underlying systemic spatial injustice in cities stems from tension over rights to private and public spaces – our cities are covered with public and private boundaries and we are constantly crossing them. The concept of public space, Soja explains, comes from the idea of the commons, or what he calls 'democratic spaces of collective responsibility' (2010, 45). Soja claims that these zones (e.g. streets, crossroads, buses, train stations, squares, park benches, etc.) are complicated sites:

> of contention between public and private property rights and focal points for social action aimed at assuring residents' rights to the city, in the sense of collective access to the common pool of public resources the city provides. (2010, 46)

Schools, as we explained in the Introduction, have historically been considered 'democratic spaces of collective responsibility,' but as we will argue in the next section, the neoliberal model of education and the resulting school closings has turned schools into economic goods that are meant to be bought and sold without considering the injustices that are unleashed on the individuals who live in and around these spaces.

The achievement of spatial justice

If thinking of 'space and place' as a socially constructed concept allows us to see the spatial injustices that have plagued large cities like Chicago, then how can these theories help us imagine a more just approach to urban spaces, and urban schools in particular? Henri Lefebvre, Harvey, and Soja have theorized what it might mean to achieve spatial justice in cities. Lefebvre's concept of 'right to the city' has been taken up in a variety of ways, but Harvey's conceptualization of 'right to the city' gets at a more specific idea of what it means to achieve spatial justice. Harvey emphasizes that having 'a right to the city' means having the right to change ourselves through the process of changing the city: 'the right to the city is far more than the individual liberty to access urban resources: it is a right to change ourselves by changing the city' (2008, first section, para. 2). Further, Harvey explains that this right must be a collective right, not an individual one, since it requires 'a collective power to reshape the processes of urbanization' (2008, first section, para. 2). Soja contends, however, that in order to fully comprehend what 'right to the city' means, it is imperative to understand the notion of 'socially produced spatial justice and injustice' rather than only thinking about space as 'physical form and background environment' (2010, 105). In other words, examining the 'right to the city' without thinking about all of a city's components makes the concept rather superficial. The remainder of this article, then, takes a 'critical spatial perspective' on school closings in Chicago not by looking at school closings in Chicago as purely economic decisions, but instead by looking at the control of schools and neighborhoods as decisions derived from neoliberal and colonialist ideologies. Further, in the remainder of this article we argue that school closings in Chicago do not grant students and families, particularly those of color, a 'right to the city'; instead, they strip families and students of the right to participate in the democratic decision-making process of shaping the schools in their communities, a principle on which schools in the United States were founded.

The consequences of school closings in Chicago

> Rahm Emanuel thinks that we are all toys. He thinks he can just come into our schools and move all our kids all over gang lines and just say, 'Oh, we can build a building right here. Let's just take this school out. We don't care about these kids.' But it's kids in there. They need – they need safety ... You should be investing in these schools, not closing them. You should be supporting these schools, not closing them. We shall not be moved today! We are going to City Hall. We're deporting Rahm Emanuel. We are not toys. We are not going, not without a fight! Education is a right! That is why we have to fight! (Asean Johnson, third-grade student, protest rally in Chicago, March 2013)

Johnson's quote exemplifies the injustices unleashed on the individuals who live within the urban spaces in Chicago that have been manipulated by neoliberal and colonialist ideologies. We argue that the recent Chicago public school closings, gentrification, and the privatization of public institutions are all moves counterproductive to the fight for the 'right to the city.' These shifts perpetuate the city's legacy of 'spatial injustice' that began in the early nineteenth century with the creation of the Black Belt. Our hope is that by using a 'critical spatial perspective,' we will bring to light the inherent exclusionary nature of these policies, and their potential to deepen educational inequalities in Chicago and other urban schools across the globe.

On 22 May 2013, the Chicago Board of Education voted on and announced the closure of 50 of the city's proposed 54 public schools. This was an unprecedented move impacting 30,000 students, around 90% of whom are African Americans residing in low-income communities. Emanuel pushed for the closures, a continuation of a 'renaissance' in public education initially spearheaded by Chicago's former mayor, Richard Daley, in 2004.[3] In this latest proclamation, Emanuel and Chicago school officials defended the more recent school closings by calling it necessary to 'shutter underused schools to help the district reduce a $1 billion budget deficit' because 'every child [deserves] access to a high-quality education' (Wisniewski 2013). Additionally, proponents project that the city would save more than $560 billion over the next decade, one-half of its projected long-term deficit. This decision 'pitted an array of community complexities against the economics of urban education in the third-largest school district in the [U.S.]' (Yaccino 2013). We argue that neoliberal educational policy instituted by city administrators and mayors around the United States instead dismantles the notion that education is a human right and advances the belief that education is an economic opportunity favoring those with inherited colonial control of urban spaces, thus perpetuating racial and economic divides in cities across the United States and creating an ongoing fight for 'the right to the city.'

Gentrification, in conjunction with mass school closings, both in the name of 'urban revitalization' and of school reform, allow mayors like Emanuel to promote neoliberal educational agendas and maintain class-based urban spaces where resources are not shared equally among citizens. Such practices worsen educational outcomes for those residing in affected areas, serving only to perpetuate what Soja describes as 'socially produced spatial justice and injustice' (2010, 105). In an interview following the Chicago's school board announcement, Diane Ravitch, former Assistant Secretary of Education, highlighted the incongruity of the city's budgetary priorities: 'Rahm Emanuel actually does not have an educational plan, he has an economic development plan' (Goodman 2013). For instance, the city intends to spend some $300 million to renovate a new stadium for the DePaul University basketball team, and renovate certain tourist attractions in the heart of the city, rather than repair its hundreds of deteriorating schools in deprived neighborhoods. In fact, the 'economic development plan' will only further gentrify sections of the city, displacing and dispossessing mostly low-income community members as a consequence. As we articulated earlier, Engels theorized that the process of gentrification is set up only to reproduce itself; this vicious cycle does not benefit anyone but those who already hold urban capital power. Pauline Lipman also critiques closing poor schools and moving students into 'mixed income' schools as a means to improve achievement, increase opportunity, and 'seriously reduce poverty in urban areas' (2011, 75). These promises expose a seriously flawed methodology in the name of school reform. Lipman argues that neoliberal policy makers are actually worsening students' educational outcomes because of the unlikelihood 'that the majority of displaced students in gentrifying areas in Chicago will have access to mixed income schools' (2011, 66). Instead, students will be forced to travel outside their neighborhoods, sometimes through dangerous intersections, '[resulting] in increased mobility and greater neighborhood instability' (Lipman, Person, and KOCO, 2007). According to University of Chicago research, approximately 90% of displaced students, in fact, are not being sent to high-performing schools but rather equally low-performing institutions (Goodman 2013). 'Urban revitalization,' it seems, benefits only those residing outside the immediate sites of disruption, leading us to view Emanuel and his administration's inheritance and utilization of spatial colonial control as vehicles for creating and maintaining inequality in Chicago.

The privatization of public schools and the consequential silencing of certain community voices, particularly those of color, is directly counterproductive to the fight for the 'right to the city,' or 'a collective power to reshape the processes of urbanization.' Apple reminds us that rather than democracy being a political concept, it is 'transformed into a wholly economic concept through voucher and choice plans in education' (2006, 39). Ren2010 is illustrative of this inequitable ideology. The policy promotes school choice and demands an expansion of privately funded charter schools, leaving public deliberation and decision-making – both for parents and teachers – a thing of the past. Specifically, the initiative undermines the locally established and elected Local School Councils in Chicago, comprised mainly of parents and community members who understand the needs of the neighborhoods and schools. Unlike Ren2010, Local School Councils promote a more equitable decision-making process when it comes to local control and 'right to the city,' and Lipman highlights the important role that the coalition plays in democratic life:

> LSC [Local School Council] members are the largest body of elected people of color in the US. The contest over school governance is essentially a struggle around how competence to participate in democratic public life is defined...They develop collective capacities of people to engage in democratic governance and control of community institutions. (2009, 10)

Charter schools, on the other hand, 'governed by appointed boards with no accountability to parents and communities,' clearly weaken this democratic governance of schools (Lipman 2009, 10). As such, charter schools rob parents and community members of their right to an active role in their children's education. Privatizing schools benefits the mayors because it allows them to take over urban schools and fast-track neoliberal initiatives without the 'interference' of democratic deliberation (Lipman 2011, 60–61). This top-down policy is strongly resisted by community groups who wish to maintain schools as 'democratic spaces of collective responsibility.' Harvey reminds us that 'the right to the city is far more than the individual liberty to access urban resources: it is a right to change ourselves by changing the city' (2008, first section, para. 2). Without that right, notions that everyone has access to a high-quality education, despite income, race, gender, sexuality, immigration status, language, disability, or social and emotional issues, become extinct. Silencing these vital voices that fight for an equal stake in education denies students, teachers, and parents the right to their city, and their right to democratic participation in neighborhood schools.

In addition, the fact that 'Schools are closed, phased out, and "turned around" with no real community participation' clearly perpetuates the legacy of oppressive practices in urban spaces, particularly for those living on the margins (Brown, Gutstein, and Lipman 2009; Lipman and Haines 2007). Steven Yaccino of *The New York Times* emphasizes this idea in his article 'Chicago School Closings May Leave Some Communities Without Old Lifelines,' published shortly after the official announcement in May 2013. Yaccino's (2013) discussion of the effects of Mary McLeod Bethune Elementary School's closure on the community represents what is happening to thousands of families coping with the loss of their schools in Chicago, 90% of whom are African American or Latino. These sudden closings impact people like Shawanna Turner, whose third-grade daughter Tzia and kindergarten-aged son Quinten became victims of colonial control when they lost the right to their neighborhood school – one attended by the family for the past two generations. It was 'A place where Turner "[knew] everybody" … [She] knew the parents because [she] went to school with them' (Yaccino 2013). In other words, Bethune School was a part of her identity. Similarly, the story of Alicia Jefferson, whose 13-year-old daughter Leonshay attended the school, illustrates how central a role the school played in their lives: '… teachers at Bethune had assisted her with personal problems, including drug-related issues … her son, Brandon, now in high school, still returns to Bethune to get tutoring from a trusted staff member' (Yaccino 2013). The school itself, named after African American educational pioneer and activist Mary McLeod Bethune, has been a community staple in the Garfield Park neighborhood on Chicago's west side for decades. However, the now shuttered and locked doors prove emblematic of the separation between progress and neoliberal policies, between Said's concept of the colonial and its negative effect on the 'other.' In essence, we argue that policies which destabilize schools, and displace children or their teachers, undermine the important role of public schools as community anchors, 'particularly at a time when the effects of the economic crisis are further destabilizing working class and low-income students and families' (Lipman 2011, 66). Instead of being granted a role in the collective decision-making process of public institutions, the families attached to these schools are treated as second-class citizens who can be picked up and shipped off without serious consequence.

Conclusion: restoring the 'right to the city'

Throughout this article we have highlighted how spatial inequalities have reverberated throughout Chicago's history. From the creation of the Black Belt in the nineteenth century, to the zoning regulations created by the Chicago Real Estate Board in the 1960s, to the recent school closings in 2013, it is abundantly clear that the promises of Brown and 'the right to the city' remain unfulfilled. Our analysis, unlike the deficit-focused arguments of the Chicago Board of Education, shows that real individuals are deeply impacted by these policies and that communities are losing their anchors, their right to democratic participation in the school system, and that their voices are becoming silenced as a result of widely accepted neoliberal models of education. In other words, students and families of color are losing their 'rights to the city,' or their ability to shape and influence the spaces in which their children learn and their communities gather.

Spatial injustice exists in all realms of the city, from education, to housing policies, to the allocation of resources. How we build, promote and grow our cities matters to the individuals living within them, and it is essential that communities are not carved and gutted by these unequal policies, and that individuals are not stripped of the right to shape the spaces in which they live, learn, and work. What we suggest is a push against these policies to maintain more equal access to the 'right to the city.' We support the efforts of parent organizations to preserve community engagement in the democratic decision-making process of public schools.

Notes

1. Brown students have experienced similar conditions to black students in Chicago, but this paper pays attention to the history of African American migration to Chicago and its reverberations. For attention to this area, please see Grant, Manning, and Allweiss (forthcoming) and C. Grant and A. Allweiss' 'Education in Urban Spaces: False Notions about Solutions and Little Attention to Social Justice' under review in *Texas Education Review*.
2. We are deliberate in our theoretical framing because we find that spaces and places are quickly passed over as neutral aspects of human life.
3. Under Ren2010, the Chicago Public Schools sought to create 100 high-performing public schools in designated communities of need by 2010. These schools were to be held accountable for performance through five-year contracts while being given autonomy to create innovative learning environments using one of the following governance structures: charter, contract, or performance.

References

Apple, M. W. 2006. *Educating the "Right" Way: Markets, Standards, God, and Inequality*. New York: Routledge Falmer.

Ayers, W., and M. Klonsky. 2006. "Chicago's Renaissance 2010: The Small Schools Movement Meets the Ownership Society." *The Phi Delta Kappan* 87 (6): 453–457.

Branson, M. S. 1999. *Globalization and Its Implications for Civic Education*. Democracy and Globalization of Politics and the Economy Conference. http://www.civiced.org/papers/papers_oct99_branson.html.

Brown, J., E. Gutstein, and P. Lipman. 2009. "Arne Duncan and the Chicago success story: Myth or reality?" *Rethinking Schools* 23 (3): 10–14.

Daniel, P. T. K. 1980. "A History of Discrimination against Black Students in Chicago Secondary Schools." *History of Education Quarterly* 20 (2): 147–162.

Davis, M. 1990. *City of Quartz: Excavating the Future in Los Angeles*. London: Verso.

de la Torre, M., and J. Gwynne 2009. "When Schools Close: Effects on Displaced Students in Chicago Public Schools, Research Report." *Consortium on Chicago School Research at the University of Chicago*.

Drake, S., and H. Cayton. 1962. *Black Metropolis; a Study of Negro Life in a Northern City*. New York: Harper & Row.

Duncan, A. 2006. "Chicago's Renaissance 2010: Building on School Reform in the Age of Accountability." *Phi Delta Kappan* 87 (6): 457–458.

Engels, F. 1935. *The Housing Question*. New York: International Publishers.

Friedman, T. L. 2005. *The World is Flat*. New York: Farr, Stratus and Giroux.

Goodman, Amy. 2013. *Interview with Diane Ravitch, Aaron Mate, and Jesse Sharkey. Democracy Now! Radio Broadcast*. New York City: Pacifica Radio.

Grant, C. A., and S. A. Grant. 2013. *The Moment: Barack Obama, Jeremiah Wright, and the Firestorm at Trinity United Church of Chris*. New York: Rowman & Littlefield.

Grant, C., K. Manning, and A. Allweiss. forthcoming. "Education in Urban Spaces: What do Media Images that Come From School Closings in Chicago Tell Us About Neoliberal Discourses?" In *Diving In: Commitments and Contradictions in a Radical Teaching Life*, edited by R. Ayers, C. Laura, and I. Nuñez. New York: Teachers College Press.

Harvey, D. 2008. "The Right to the City." *New Left Review. 53*. http://newleftreview.org/II/53/david-harvey-the-right-to-the-city.

Krauser, M. 2012. "Peace and Freedom." johnib.wordpress.com/tag/mike-krauser/.

Lipman, P. 2009. Making Sense of Renaissance 2010 School Policy in Chicago: Race, Class, and the Cultural Politics of Neoliberal Urban Restructuring. Great Cities Institute Working Paper, GCP-09-02, 10.

Lipman, P. 2011. *The New Political Economy of Urban Education: Neoliberalism, Race, and the Right to the City*. New York: Routledge.

Lipman, P., and N. Haines. 2007. "From Education Accountability to Privatization and African American Exclusion – Chicago Public Schools' Renaissance 2010." *Educational Policy* 21 (3): 471–502.

Lipman, P., A. Person, and Kenwood Oakland Community Organization. 2007. *Students as Collateral Damage? A Preliminatry Study of Renaissance 2010 School Closings in the Midsouth*. Chicago, IL: Kenwood Oakland Community Organization. http://www.uic.edu/educ/ceje/index.html.

Lutton, L. 2013. "Only 60 Percent of Students from Chicago's Closed Schools Turn up at 'Welcoming Schools'." WBEZ, Chicago. http://www.wbez.org/news/only-60-percent-students-chicagos-closed-schools-turn-welcoming-schools-108907.

Milberg, W. 1994. "Market Competition and the Failure of Competitiveness Enhancement Policies in the United States." *Journal of Economic Issues* 28 (2): 587–596.

Moscovitch, R., A. R. Sadovnik, J. M. Barr, T. Davidson, T. L. Moore, R. Powell, P. L. Tractenberg, E. Wagman and P. Zha. 2010. *Governance and Urban Improvement: Lessons for New Jersey from Nine Cities*. New Brunswick, NJ: The Institute on Educational Law and Policy, Rutgers University.

National Commission on Excellence in Education. 1983. "A Nation at Risk: The Imperative for Educational Reform." United States Department of Education. http://www2.ed.gov/pubs/NatAtRisk/index.html.

Orfield, G., and C. Lee. 2007. *Historic Reversals, Accelerating Resegregation, and the Need for New Intefration Strategies*. Los Angeles: Civil Rights Projects.

Smarick, A. 2010. "The Turnaround Fallacy." *Education Next.* 10 (1): 20–27.

Soja, E. 2010. *Seeking Spatial Justice.* Minneapolis, MN: University of Minnesota Press.

Sunderman, G. L., and A. Payne 2009. *Does Closing Schools Cause Educational Harm: A Review of Research.* Bethesda, MD: Mid-Atlantic Equity Center.

Wak, L. 2003. "How Globalization Can Cause Fundamental Curriculum Change: An American Perspective." *Journal of Educational Change* 4 (4): 383–418.

Wisniewski, Mary. 2013. "Chicago School Closings: Board Set to Vote on Mass Shutdown Plan." *Reuters*, May 22. http://www.huffingtonpost.com/2013/05/22/chicago-school-closings-board-vote_n_3318108.html.

Wright, R. 1941/2002. *12 Million Black Voices.* New York: Basic Books: Reprinted edition.

Yaccino, S. 2013. "Chicago School Closings May Leave Some Communities without Old Lifelines." *The New York Times,* May 22. http://www.nytimes.com/2013/05/22/education/chicago-communities-wary-of-chicago-school-closures.html?_r=0.

Just imaginary: delimiting social inclusion in higher education

Trevor Gale[a] and Steven Hodge[b]

[a]School of Education, Deakin University, Melbourne, Victoria, Australia; [b]School of Education and Professional Studies, Griffith University, Brisbane, Queensland, Australia

This paper explores the notion of a 'just imaginary' for social inclusion in higher education. It responds to the current strategy of OECD nations to expand higher education and increase graduate numbers, as a way of securing a competitive advantage in the global knowledge economy. The Australian higher education system provides the case for analysis. Three dilemmas for social inclusion policy in this context are identified: questions of sustainability, aspiration and opportunity. The paper argues that while social inclusion policy has 'first-order' effects in higher education, a *just* imaginary is required for more inclusive 'second-order' effects to be realized. It concludes that transformation of the current imaginary will require a more robust theorization of relations between social inclusion and higher education, to give new and unifying meaning to existing practices and to generate new ones. Short of this, social inclusion may be little more than just *imaginary*.

Introduction

Our intention in this paper is to take stock of the current social inclusion agenda in higher education, particularly its expression within OECD nations, and to utilize Australia as a case to illustrate this. We are interested to determine the 'policy effects' (Ball 1993) of current social inclusion policy in higher education, particularly a normative reading of these. We begin from the premise that social inclusion in higher education is now differently legitimated, given a different account of the purposes of higher education itself. This new legitimation fueling higher education's expansion holds out the prospect of a more *just* imaginary (see Taylor 2004) in which 'the trade-off between efficiency and justice no longer holds' (Brown 2003, 142). Yet the policy effect seems to be a social inclusion that is just *imaginary*: a 'collective disillusionment which results from the structural mismatch between aspirations and real probabilities' (Bourdieu 1984, 144).

To elaborate, a new higher education imaginary has emerged in the Asian Century[1] about higher education's role in arresting the declining advantage of OECD nations in the 'rapidly changing profile of the global economy' (Spence 2011, xv), accentuated by the recent global financial crisis (GFC). The strategy, in enlisting higher education, is to supplant the importance of the industrial economy – now dominated by China, India and other rapidly developing nations – with a knowledge economy in which OECD nations claim to excel. The equation is relatively simple, if not simplistic: to be competitive in the global knowledge economy requires more knowledge workers and, particularly, more with higher levels of qualification (a proxy for more and superior knowledge).

The expansion of higher education in OECD nations, from mass to near universal participation (Trow 1974, 2006),[2] is thus informed by a neoliberal logic (Rizvi and Lingard 2010, 2011). Australia provides the classic example. In the wake of the GFC and fairing better than most, Australia has embarked on an 'education revolution' (Rudd 2007) to reposition the nation's workforce for a future more reliant on its citizens' collective human capital (Gillard 2009). Higher education occupies a central place in this strategy, with targets to expand and widen participation (Bradley et al. 2008): for example, 40% of 25–34 year olds are to hold bachelor degrees by 2025. The approach is not particular to Australia. Other nations with similar agendas include, but are not restricted to: the United Kingdom (target: 50% of 30 year olds with a degree by 2010; Department for Education and Skills 2003), Ireland (target: 72% of 17–19 year olds participating in higher education by 2020; Bradley et al. 2008, 20) and the USA (target: 60% of 25–34 year olds to hold college degrees by 2020; Kelly 2010, 2).

The contribution of an expanded higher education project to producing knowledge workers and a competitive edge in the global knowledge economy are becoming the images, stories and legends of a new social imaginary: 'that common understanding that makes possible common practices and a widely shared sense of legitimacy' (Taylor 2004, 23). That is, higher education expansion has been given new importance in our collective mindset. Unlike previous expansion periods, fuelled by the demands of an aspirant middle class or for social justice (see Gale and Tranter 2011), expansion in the current period originates with governments in response to changing global economies and where they want their nations to be positioned within these. In Australia, for example, legitimation for higher education's rapid expansion in the 1970s was primarily Keynesian, informed by a 'politics of expectation' (Fairlie 1973); in the 2000s it is primarily neoliberal, informed by a 'politics of aspiration' (Raco 2009).[3] In the former period, social inclusion was central in the government's rhetoric, even if its policies did not lead to greater representation in higher education of people from marginalized groups. In the current period, social inclusion has again been evoked but this time as central to achieving the nation's economic ambitions. Hence, the Australian Government's current vision is of 'a stronger and fairer Australia' (Australian Government 2009, 5); stronger in terms of:

> a highly educated workforce … to advance the growth of a dynamic knowledge economy … [and fairer by] ensuring that Australians of all backgrounds who have the ability to study at university get the opportunity to do so. (Australian Government 2009, 12)

Similar coupling of social and economic agendas within higher education policy has been evident in the past. It is a familiar strategy among liberal and neoliberal governments to argue the economic importance of social inclusion. However, in the new higher education imaginary – in which nations seek a competitive edge in a global knowledge economy – being 'stronger' is not possible without being 'fairer.' Mass higher education has led to the near saturation of participants from high and mid socioeconomic status (SES) backgrounds. The shift towards universal higher education now requires greater participation of their low-SES peers. It is a transformation more akin to the introduction of compulsory schooling – established to re-orientate and prepare new kinds of (industrial) workers – than to previous periods of higher education expansion. In previous moves towards social inclusion, redressing inequities in the proportional representation of disadvantaged groups in higher education relied on the support of an expansionist agenda (Alon 2009; Gale and Tranter 2011). This time, expansion (from mass to universal participation) is dependent on widening participation.

The theoretical framework of the paper draws on Charles Taylor's (2004) work on 'social imaginaries.' We have already referred to the formation of a 'higher education imaginary' and have singled out the new form of legitimation of social inclusion in higher education policy as contributing to this formation. In our view, shifting from 'first order' to 'second order' policy effects (Ball 1993) in the sphere of higher education involves transformations at the level of the social imaginary. Taylor's analysis of theory-led transformations of imaginaries is central to our argument. We suggest that the changes currently being wrought to the higher education imaginary by neoliberal theorizations are unlikely to foster a just imaginary (if any lasting change can be expected at all).

Three questions focus this paper's empirical analysis: how sustainable is the social inclusion effort in higher education by governments and universities; what aspirations should we have for higher education; and what opportunities are possible for university graduates given near universal participation? Data are derived from Australian higher education, a system dominated by the nation's 37 public universities and by Australian Government political and financial management. Through analyses of three dilemmas for social inclusion in higher education engendered by Australian Government policy, we reveal theorizations of social inclusion that generate limited or contradictory impacts on the imaginary. The first dilemma concerns the sustainability of new 'first order' practices. Our analysis highlights the need to engage with the challenge of surpassing first-order effects and of enabling new practices on the basis of the imaginary of higher education. The dilemma raises the question of the congruence of theorizations of inclusion in policies driving first-order effects and the understandings necessary to sustain second-order effects. The second dilemma concerns the aspiration for higher education of under-represented groups. Our analysis shows that the crude theorization of aspiration embedded in higher education policy fails to comprehend the dimension of imagination in aspiration and highlights the need to embrace diverse epistemologies if under-represented groups are to imagine a place for themselves in higher education. The third dilemma revolves around the paradox of diminishing economic returns through increased participation in higher education. This dilemma points to a crucial issue for the promotion of a just imaginary. Our analysis indicates a contradictory effect of appropriating social inclusion measures to an economic conceptualization of higher education. If a *just* imaginary of higher education emerges over the longer term that is based on an economic rationale for social inclusion, then the diminution of economic returns on participation that is also a longer-term possibility may turn out to be the ultimate treachery of social inclusion policy. The third dilemma points to the urgent need to reconceptualize the rationale for social inclusion or face the prospect of policy effects that are just *imaginary*.

Sustaining social inclusion in a context of waning political will/financial resources

The first dilemma confronting social inclusion policy in higher education is how it can be sustained. While the policy is seen to be having an effect, there are questions in the current political and economic climate about whether this is sufficient to sustain social inclusion in the absence of authorized support. Stephen Ball (1993) has written about the effects of policy being of two orders. First-order effects involve changed practice, whereas second-order effects involve changed relations of dominance. The latter includes a normative reading of the former. Thus, there can be the appearance of change (first-order effects) without it being substantial and/or without the prospect of change being sustained (second-order effects). In our reading, to which we return below, the interplay between these policy effects echoes the connections Taylor (2004) envisages between theory, practice and imaginary.

There is certainly evidence of social inclusion policy in Australian higher education having first-order effects. More Australians, including those previously under-represented, see higher education as a viable destination

(Bowden and Doughney 2010; Gale et al. 2013); more from low-SES backgrounds are gaining access to university (from 31,900 undergraduate commencements in 2008 to 40,200 in 2011; Department of Industry, Innovation, Climate Change, Science, Research and Tertiary Education [DIICCSRTE] 2012); and more low-SES students are qualifying for bachelor degrees (from 13,800 completions in 2008 to 14,800 in 2011; DIICCSRTE 2013b). Yet there are reasons to quibble with these policy outcomes. For example, increased participation is below expectations, particularly in proportional terms (i.e. increased student enrolments, including those from low-SES backgrounds, currently fall short of what is required to meet the 40% and 20% targets; Birrell, Rapson, and Smith 2011; Sellar, Gale, and Parker 2011); the participation is concentrated in particular parts of the sector (i.e. in less prestigious institutions and courses; Gale and Parker 2013); and the increased proportion of bachelor degrees among 25–34 year olds is more to do with migration than the contributions of Australian universities (Australian Bureau of Statistics 2013).[4] Even so, there is little doubt that the Australian Government's social inclusion policy is having an effect in reconfiguring the higher education student population overall.

Still, social inclusion's continued effect depends on continued policy support, in part because to date changes in higher education have been primarily numerical: an accounting of student bodies more than what they embody (i.e. who they are as people). In short, there is little evidence of second-order policy effects of the kind that take seriously the inclusion of different ontologies and epistemologies associated with different kinds of students and their implications for the transformation of higher education itself (Gale 2011). These are not the stated/desired second-order effects of current higher education policy, which is intent on advancing Australia's global economic competitiveness and sustained economic growth. But in their absence, social inclusion remains variable and elusive. Sustaining the effect of social inclusion policy in higher education – currently confined to superficial changes in practice – still requires the political will and financial resourcing of governments. Both of these conditions for social inclusion's sustainability are now in question in Australia, as they are in other OECD nations still experiencing the aftermath of the GFC.

The importance of political will and financial resources for social inclusion policy in Australian higher education came into sharp relief in the context of the recent federal election (September 2013) and the relevant policy positions of the two major opposing parties. Even though the Australian Labor Party approached the election from the position of government and had itself introduced the latest iteration of widening participation in Australian higher education, there were clear signals in the lead up to the election that the will and resources to continue its policy approach were waning. For example, while the government's May 2013 budget statement prior to the election announced (for the first time) a projected 10-year outlook – doubling the usual five-year outlook – it failed to declare funding for university outreach programs beyond 2015; that is, beyond two years. In addition, three months before the election, the relevant government minister – the fourth that year and the sixth in six years – began to unravel the government's commitment to its higher education expansion agenda and, by implication, its commitment to advancing social inclusion to meet its expansionist targets. In his response to the 'tremendous growth' in university student enrolments – a claim tempered by the fact that the growth had not matched the Government's own enrolment projections (Australian Government 2009; Sellar, Gale, and Parker 2011) or its financial calculations (DIICCSRTE 2013a; Trounson 2013) – the Minister floated the prospect that 'given the strength of growth in demand, it is appropriate to [revisit issues of] quality and excellence … to consider refocusing government investment to get the best possible use of public money' (Carr, as cited in Hare and Matchett 2013). At the time there was surprisingly little challenge to the 'growth blowout' claim and unsurprising support for claims of 'risks to quality' (Gallagher, as cited in Hare and Matchett 2013), echoing earlier 'roadmap to mediocrity' (Gallagher 2009) assessments made in response to the government's re-introduction of social inclusion policy in 2009. This was despite clear evidence of rising student retention rates at Australian universities (Harvey and Luckman 2013).

The posturing of the conservative Liberal Party of Australia in the lead up to the election was relatively similar. For the Liberal Party, social inclusion is an ongoing threat to quality; a convenient standpoint in times of fiscal austerity while maintaining 'faith' with the party's neoliberal orientation. For example, in an address at Monash University early in the year of the election, the Shadow Minister announced:

> The Coalition [of conservative parties] is determined to ensure Australian universities have their academic standing protected, so that students can be confident their degrees are taken seriously and their research is considered world class. (Pyne 2013)

At the same time, the Liberal Party leader observed:

> Not everyone needs a university education … reasonable public investment in higher education is not dudding poorer people to help richer people: it's strengthening our human capital in ways that ultimately benefit everyone. (Abbott 2013)

Taken together, there is clear indication in these comments of the Liberal Party's view that reigning in the expansion of student numbers in higher education is no bad thing: in protecting academic reputations and prospering the nation's economy, with 'trickle down' effects for those excluded. Besides, in adjusting budgets from a mining-boom economy to the demands of the GFC, 'what was possible in an era of $20 billion year surpluses is not possible following an era of $50 billion a year deficits' (Abbott 2013).

These are unsurprising responses. They echo the history of social inclusion and higher education policy in Australia (Gale and Tranter 2011) and elsewhere. But it is their repetition that is of interest in this paper, more than the particulars of the accounts. As noted above, social inclusion policy in higher education has been shown to have numerical effects but the sustainability of these often depends on the level of political will and financial resources, which wax and wane over time and (at times) between governments. The very idea that the sustainability of social inclusion is in question draws attention to inadequacies in the current higher education imaginary. To be sustainable, social inclusion needs to become part of what higher education is itself, at the level of the imaginary, so that social inclusion is as sustainable as higher education. At a minimum this will require re-theorizing oppositional relations between quality and social inclusion in higher education (Gale 2011), so that quality without social inclusion is recognized as a diminished quality (Milem 2003). (We return to the need for re-theorizing relations between quality and social inclusion in higher education in the following section.)

There is some way to go in establishing this quality-inclusion nexus within the higher education imaginary. In the lead up to the Australian election and buoyed by the above challenges to the political will and financial resources for social inclusion in higher education, Fred Hilmer, the Vice Chancellor of the University of New South Wales, announced that his university would raise the minimum entry-level score (i.e. the Australian Tertiary Admission Rank) required by applicants to 80 (out of a possible 100), reinforcing that Australia's demand-driven higher education system is in name only. His justification was based in arguments about quality:

> If you are in an undifferentiated group of students and you are getting comments on your work, you get a lot of junk. But if you are in a selective cohort, it will lift the standard of everyone. (Hilmer, as cited in Hare 2013)

The comments here are symbolic more than substantive. Prior to the announcement, only two of the University of New South Wales degree programs accepted students with Australian Tertiary Admission Ranks below 80 and then they were in the high 70s. Moreover, Hilmer's assessment of the detrimental effects of social inclusion on quality bore little connection with the research. In 'a multidisciplinary analysis of the research literature,' Jeffery Milem (2003, 129) has found that heterogeneous university student populations actually exhibit higher levels of academic achievement than homogeneous university student populations, and that the greatest gains are by 'majority students who have previously lacked significant direct exposure to minorities' (Milem 2003, 131–132). The educational benefits for all university students in more diverse cohorts include: 'greater relative gains in critical and active thinking ... greater intellectual engagement and academic motivation ... [and] greater relative gains in intellectual and social self-concept' (Milem 2003, 142). But, as alluded to above, it is not the sheer presence alone of different students that generates this effect. Institutions and their staff who fail to engage with the diversity of their students also fail to see this academic improvement (Association of American Universities 1997). In short, pursuing 'diversity in colleges and universities is not only a matter of social justice but also a matter of promoting educational excellence' (Milem 2003, 126).

Expanding higher education in a context of uncertain interest

A second dilemma facing social inclusion policy in higher education is what aspirations it should engender. In making it possible for more students to participate in higher education, particularly those from under-represented groups, the Australian Government is concerned to foster in students a commensurate desire to participate. Yet it would appear that the value of higher education is not immediately apparent, particularly to those who have been traditionally under-represented (Australian Government 2009).

Aspiration is a relatively recent inclusion in Australian higher education policy. While recognized in the late 1970s as an important condition for university entry, it was considered to be outside the purview of higher education policy until the recent *Review of Australian Higher Education* (Bradley et al. 2008) and the Australian Government's (2009) policy response. In the past, aspiration for higher education was theorized by Anderson (Anderson et al. 1980; Anderson and Vervoon 1983) to be largely a private concern for individuals and families. However, in the current moment, students' aspirations have become an explicit site of policy and institutional intervention, with the intention of 'building the capacity of people from low-SES backgrounds to access higher education' (Australian Government 2012a, 14). Aspiration has also been linked more strongly to availability, in a way not theorized by Anderson. Student aspiration and the availability of places – de-regulated with the removal of government restrictions on student enrolment numbers – are now seen by government as interrelated.

However, the strategy to 'build it and they will come' (*Field of Dreams* 1989) – to expand the supply of higher education in the absence of an identified unmet demand – has not been overly successful. While the 40/20 targets have created new opportunities, in themselves they have not delivered participation in higher education in the quantity required. Progress towards the targets was initially strong but has been slow since and, given current trajectories, there is considerable doubt that they can be achieved (Sellar, Gale, and Parker 2011; Gale and Parker 2013). While the numbers of bachelor's degree students rose sharply in 2009 and 2010 with up to 15,000 new additional students in each year, by 2011 the figure dropped to 6000 additional new students (DIICCSRTE 2010, 2011, 2012). Yet even in the system's 'best' years since the targets were announced (in 2009), these year-on-end additions have fallen well below the 25,000 additional commencing bachelor students required each year in order to reach the government's 40% student attainment target by 2025 (Sellar, Gale, and Parker 2011).

Increasing students' aspirations for higher education is seen to be the way in which to address this problem. Indeed, in government policy discourse, aspiration is a relatively simplistic and individualized concept. People from under-represented groups, particularly those from low-SES backgrounds, are seen to lack or have low aspirations if they do not aspire to go to university (for example, Australian Government 2009). This assumed aspiration deficit is particularly problematic for the Australian Government, with ambitions to increase the proportion of Australians (particularly 25–34 year olds) with a bachelor's degree as a way of improving the nation's capacity to compete in a global knowledge economy. By comparison with other OECD nations, the proportion of Australians with bachelor degrees is quite low (Bradley et al. 2008). The Australian Government's policy solution is to raise, increase or build the aspirations of low-SES people for university study (Australian Government 2009). For example, two current programs at Australian universities – both named 'Aspire' and borrowed from the United Kingdom – seek to '*motivate* students from low SES backgrounds,' '*challenging the traditional attitudes* of people from low SES backgrounds towards higher education' (DIICCSRTE 2013a; emphasis added).

Yet aspiration might not be the problem for students from low-SES backgrounds that the Australian Government and Australian universities imagine it to be. A major problem with the aspiration-deficit account is that the most recent research suggests a large proportion of students from low-SES schools – whether in city or regional/remote areas – do aspire to higher education. For example, a recent survey of over 2000 students from secondary schools in Melbourne's low-SES western suburbs found that around 70% of students from these schools already aspire to go to university (Bowden and Doughney 2010). A survey of 250 school students in Central Queensland – a regional/remote area of significant low-SES concentration – recorded a similar result, with 67% of students recording aspirations to attend university in the future (Gale et al. 2013). These high levels of aspiration for higher education by low-SES students, combined with their below-parity participation in higher education,[5] suggest that the problem is something other than a lack of aspiration for university study.

Considerable research on student aspiration is now in progress (for example, in the United Kingdom see Watts and Bridges 2006; Archer et al. 2007; Brown 2011; Burke 2012; and in Australia see Bok 2010; Gale and Tranter 2011; Smith 2011; Sellar, Gale, and Parker 2011; Sellar 2013; Zipin et al. 2013). One line of inquiry draws attention to students' 'navigational capacities' (Appadurai 2004; Gale and Tranter 2011). For example, the Central Queensland survey shows that a number of students from low-SES backgrounds have diminished navigational capacities – the result of their limited archives of experience (Appadurai 2004; Gale et al. 2013). Their aspirations tend to be informed by a 'tour' knowledge of higher education pathways – reliant on the 'hot' (Ball and Vincent 1998) and sometimes errant knowledge and guidance of others – rather than the 'map' knowledge of their high-SES peers who are 'in the know' (de Certeau 1984; Gale et al. 2013). Appadurai (2004) similarly describes the disadvantaged as having more brittle aspirations, given their sparse aspirational nodes – that is, long-distance journeys between where they are now and where they want to go – and 'extremely weak resources where the terms of recognition are concerned' (2004, 66). This different understanding of aspiration has implications for the objectives and practices of universities, to resource prospective students' navigational capacities and to recognize the value of the sociocultural resources for aspiring they have at hand (Gale et al. 2013).

A second problem with how aspiration is conceived within Australian higher education policy and much practice is that it tends to confine students to populist and ideological conceptions of the 'good life.' These are the out-workings of beliefs and assumptions of the dominant that circulate as natural and commonsense. They are the aspirations with which students often respond when asked 'what do you want to be when you grow up?' They are the responses that students know they should give to such inquiry, the responses deemed to carry the most value. They are what Zipin et al. (2013) refer to as *doxic* aspirations. Students from low-SES backgrounds subscribe to these aspirations and to higher education up to a point. They 'give up' on higher education, suspending 'doxic adherence to the prizes it offers and the values it professes' (Bourdieu 1984, 144) when the distance between prized aspirations and their own biological and historical conditions is too great. The alternative is *habituated* aspirations (Zipin et al. 2013), which re-assert students' social–structural positions in society, particularly their assumed deficits in relation to and by the dominant. Universities contribute to these aspiration 'distinctions' (Bourdieu 1984) by failing to recognize the value and legitimacy of alternative conceptions of the good life (Brown 2011). They contribute to the aspiration 'problem' by assuming that higher education offers the best possible route or even destination, as an unassailable good (Watts and Bridges 2006; Burke 2012; Sellar 2013). (We return to the need for re-theorizing higher education purposes in the following section.)

Thus, while students from low-SES backgrounds aspire to higher education, many conclude that 'this isn't for the likes of us' – spoken in the indicative-imperative mode – simultaneously expressing 'an impossibility and an interdiction' (Bourdieu et al. 1990, 16–17). Higher education effectively excludes their participation because of its doxic tendencies. It is, in Connell's (2007) terms, a social space colonized by and for the Global North. Rendering higher education more socially inclusive necessarily involves unsettling 'the centre–periphery relations in the realm of knowledge' (Connell 2007, viii) through the legitimation of a variety of knowledges and ways of knowing, so that students are able to recognize themselves and hear their own voices (Couldry 2010). Marginson (2009) refers to such inclusions as derived from an 'equity of respect'; for Dei (2010) they are at the heart of re-theorized relations of 'epistemological equity,'[6] indicative of a just imaginary. These are the potential of social inclusion policy in higher education and the first steps for re-theorizing relations between quality and social inclusion.

Increasing opportunities in a context of diminishing returns

A third dilemma for social inclusion policy in higher education is the prospect of its own success. If the Australian Government's current higher education policy settings have the desired effect – at least in a first-order sense, with increased higher education participation and attainment levels in absolute terms as well as in the proportional representation of people from low-SES backgrounds – there will be more graduates qualified to compete for the same or similar pool of higher education rewards, increasing labor and scholastic market competition and thus diminishing opportunities. In Berlant's terms, the effect is a form of 'cruel optimism': 'a relation of attachment to compromised conditions of possibility whose realisation is discovered either to be *im*possible, sheer fantasy, or *too* possible, and toxic' (2007, 33; original emphasis). It 'arises when objects of desire that sustain people's life projects simultaneously undermine them' (Sellar 2013, 247).

Access to the opportunity of participation has long been touted as the prime objective of social inclusion policy in Australian higher education (Gillard 2009), and of social justice more generally (i.e. 'fair equality of opportunity'; Rawls 1993). The benefits for participants are well rehearsed: higher status jobs, increased job security and earnings, lower rates of poverty and unemployment, healthier lifestyles, children with higher cognitive skill levels, and so on (Baum and Payea 2005; WHO 2008). The critique of this simple access agenda is that 'access without support is not opportunity' (Engstrom and Tinto 2008). While it is not the unsettling of center–periphery knowledge relations born of a 'just imaginary' suggested above, the critique does raise the possibility of social inclusion being about more than just access. Social inclusion as support is the apparent foil for anticipated student failings, even if some seem unable to move beyond issues of access. Despite evidence indicating that students from low-SES backgrounds perform well at Australian universities when given the opportunity (for example, Dobson and Skuja 2007; Win and Miller 2005), many in the sector still believe that their inclusion has potential to reduce student quality. For example, the recent Australian Government *Higher Education Base Funding Review* warned:

> The expected enrolment growth in response to government targets and the demand driven system from 2012 is likely to lead to an increase in the numbers of less well prepared students, who may be at greater risk of attrition. (Lomax-Smith, Watson, and Webster 2011, 80)

Similarly informed, others have questioned the value of providing opportunities for students from low-SES backgrounds:

> What's the use of taking more students if there's a big chance they will drop out? It's a waste of money. It's also a shattering experience for students who find they are not able to cope. (Cervini 2012)

The evidence suggests otherwise. Student retention rates at Australian universities are rising (Harvey and Luckman 2013). Some suggest that this is the result of better student support services, particularly in the first year (Kift, as cited in Hare and Trounson 2013). However, the improvement might simply be that student transfers between courses and universities are no longer counted in attrition figures calculated by the Australian Government.

Still, drawing attention to institutional support for students from disadvantaged backgrounds as a matter of social inclusion also points to the broader question of 'access to what?' Epistemological equity is one possible response. Others are the opportunities for graduates beyond higher education. In particular, the global knowledge economy has raised the prospect of opportunities for all. This is a central claim of OECD nations with higher education expansion agendas that 'the demand for knowledge workers will far exceed the numbers now graduating' (Lauder, Brown, and Tholen 2012, 43–44). For example, modeling undertaken by the Australian Workforce and Productivity Agency suggests a 'widening gap between the expected supply of higher level skills and expected industry demand' (2013, 9) of up to 2.8 million knowledge workers. The Australian Workforce and Productivity Agency has thus recommended:

> To meet industry demand and position ourselves as a knowledge economy in the Asian century, it is imperative for qualifications in tertiary education to increase by a minimum of 3 per cent per annum in the years to 2025. (2013, 25)

It is such analysis that has 'led many to believe that we have more opportunities that [*sic*] ever before. … the opportunity to exploit the talents of all, at least in the developed world, is in prospect' (Brown 2003). Yet graduate employment rates in Australia have been declining, from 85% in 2008 to 76% in 2012 (Graduate Careers Australia 2013a), and 'graduates employed in occupations that do not appear to make use of their qualifications are a prominent feature of the labour market of many countries' (Li and Miller 2013, 15). Another is diminishing graduate starting salaries. In 1977 the mean starting salary of Australian university graduates, relative to the annual rate of full-time average weekly earnings, was 100%. In 2012 it was 78% (Graduate Careers Australia 2013b). It is not simply that the number of graduates is increasing or that this increase is not commensurate with increases in jobs that require graduates. The proportion of graduates is also increasing relative to the workforce as a whole, which is leading to shrinking returns. That is, markets reward scarcity (Marginson 2004, 2011). When similar graduates increase in number, even when there is a commensurate increase in positions, their rewards diminish.

University students from low-SES backgrounds, who tend to congregate in particular fields (e.g. teaching, nursing, engineering) with high student volumes (Gale and Parker 2013), are the most vulnerable. They enter university with 'high hopes of what the knowledge economy has to offer, fuelled by the expansion of higher education ... but the labour market cannot keep pace with social expectations of work, rewards and status' (Brown 2003, 150). While now within the grasp of the working classes, higher education qualifications and previously desirable occupations are increasingly devoid of the objective rewards they once guaranteed and, in isolation, offer little more than 'blighted hope or frustrated promise' (Bourdieu 1984, 150). In sum:

> The personal costs incurred in realising our 'opportunities' are increasing because success depends on getting ahead in the competition for tough-entry schools, universities and jobs. Middle-class families are adopting more desperate measures to win a positional advantage. They are having to run faster, for longer, just to stand still (Boudon 1973). Yet if all adopt the same tactics nobody gets ahead. But if one does not play the game, there is little chance of winning. This is the *opportunity trap* as few can afford to opt out of the competition for a livelihood. (Brown 2003, 142; original emphasis)

This is the danger of an instrumental conception of higher education (and of social inclusion), marshaled by OECD nations in hot pursuit of advantage in the knowledge economy. In the absence of a just imaginary, the purposes of higher education default to those of the labor market. As Paul Keating, a previous Australian Prime Minister, once remarked: 'The great access, the great opportunity to participate in this country, is through a job' (*The Australian*, 24 March 1995, 3). Yet the cruel reality is that 'equality of opportunity' (Rawls 1993) in the current configuration of our institutions cannot deliver on its promise (Sen 2009) or, rather, can only deliver for some. A just imaginary requires a re-theorization of social inclusion (as opportunity) and of the purposes of higher education, of the kind proposed by Amartya Sen (2009), particularly the 'opportunity aspect' of his theory of freedom. For Sen, opportunity is the freedom to pursue one's own objectives; that is, the opportunity to 'decide to live as we would like and to promote the ends that we may want to advance' (2009, 228). In this theoretical work, Sen makes a useful distinction between 'narrow' and 'broad' views of opportunity:

> It can be defined only in terms of the opportunity for 'culmination outcomes' (what a person ends up with [e.g. a degree, a job, etc.]), if we see opportunity in that particularly narrow way and regard the existence of options and the freedom of choice to be somehow unimportant. Alternatively, we can define opportunity more broadly – and I believe with greater plausibility – in terms of the achievement of 'comprehensive outcomes,' taking note also of the way the person reaches the culmination situation (for example, whether through his own choice or through the dictates of others [e.g. government policy, school counseling, etc.]). (2009, 230)

A just imaginary requires a theory of higher education that goes beyond narrow conceptions of opportunity, which restrict higher education to an end in itself or even a means to an end (culmination outcomes) with means and ends determined by others. In a broader comprehensive theory of social inclusion, the role of higher education would be not simply to teach students how to be middle class (Bourdieu 1984). It would be to enable the development of capabilities within all students to pursue a life they have reason to value (Sen 2009).

A *just* imaginary of higher education?

We began this paper by arguing that for social inclusion to become entrenched in the institutions and practices of higher education, it must pass beyond the 'first order effects' (Ball 1993) of higher education policy and enter into the higher education imaginary. The framework of our argument is provided by Taylor's (2004) theory of social imaginaries. This theory, which draws on Benedict Anderson's work on 'imagined communities,' was developed to account for the enactment of practices characteristic of modernity. The concept of social imaginary refers to:

> The ways people imagine their social existence, how they fit with others, how things go on between them and their fellows, the expectations that are normally met, and the deeper normative notions and images that underlie these expectations. (Taylor 2004, 23)

The significance of the social imaginary is that 'it is what enables, through making sense of, the practices of a society' (Taylor 2004, 2). We are arguing, then, that the commonsense made of higher education must incorporate social inclusion if the practices of higher education are to be inclusive. We believe that the goal must be a *just* imaginary of higher education.

But in Taylor's (2004) account of social imaginaries the kind of shift or transformation we seek involves a circuitous process that cannot be planned or programmed in any straightforward way. His investigations of the emergence of the imaginaries characteristic of modernity suggest that imaginaries 'mutate' in one of two ways: through the 'penetration' of theory or through the reinterpretation of old practices. The second kind of mutation is not an option here, for it is precisely the old practices of higher education that are problematic, regardless of how they are or can be interpreted. The focus thus must be on the first kind, for which Taylor provides the example of the 'modern moral order' (the sense of obligation to each other) that arises first among intellectual elites in the seventeenth century. As Taylor explains in the case of a theory-driven transformation of the imaginary:

> For the most part, people take up, improvise, or are inducted into new practices. These are made sense of by the new outlook, the one first articulated in the theory; this outlook is the context that gives sense to the practices. Hence the new understanding comes to be accessible to the participants in a way it wasn't before. It begins to define the contours of their world and can eventually come to count as the taken-for-granted shape of things, too obvious to mention. (2004, 29)

As our first dilemma above illustrates, new socially inclusive higher education practices are indeed being initiated. But the 'theory' governing these practices – that social inclusion is entailed by the need for more knowledge workers with higher qualifications – is fundamentally that of neoliberal economics, which suggests that the content of the sense-making by actors who enable these practices (institution staff, students) is going to be conditioned by economic rather than social concerns. If the theory of social inclusion that accompanies the first-order effects of higher education policy is not congruent with the assumptions of a just imaginary, then no transformation of the kind advocated here can be expected. The first dilemma, then, reveals changed practices, but raises the question of how the new practices are being understood by those engaged in them. There is not yet evidence that they are being understood in a way that may pre-empt a just imaginary that counts as the 'taken-for-granted shape of things.'

The second dilemma concerning aspiration supports this conclusion. Continued under-representation in a context of government and institutional support is a clear indicator of the state of the higher education imaginary; that is, first-order effects have not been surpassed. The new practices instituted by policy are not being understood by under-represented groups as benefitting them. But the second dilemma offers more than an index of the mutation of the higher education imaginary. Like the first dilemma, it provides a window on the kind of 'theory' being used by policy-making elites to inform their interventions. In this case, the theorization of aspiration as deficient in under-represented groups, to the extent that it penetrates to the self-understanding of actors engaged in new practices, is incongruent with the understanding of aspiration that would articulate with a just imaginary. We make the point above that theorizations of aspiration which are positive about epistemic diversity are required to move beyond theories of deficit. Until theorizations based on alternative values inform policy and policy-initiated practice, these practices cannot be taken up as practices of a just imaginary.

While the first and second dilemmas reveal theorizations that cannot be effective as supports for a just imaginary, it is the third dilemma that directly undermines its emergence, at least on the basis of the first-order effects of current policy. As long as social inclusion is theorized as benefitting all participants in economic terms, the disillusionment threatened by the narrow conception of opportunity – the paradox of diminishing returns of a higher education due to wider participation – awaits those engaged in the new practices. As Taylor (2004) demonstrates, the process of the transformation of social imaginaries is slow. Even if a just imaginary emerges despite the contradictory theorizations accompanying the introduction of new practices, it will emerge over the longer term, just as the disillusionment to be expected from the reality of eroded rewards of higher education will be of the longer term. The third dilemma points to a cruel trap awaiting participants who have invested on the basis of promised economic rewards, and the need for the images, stories and legends of higher education to be founded on a different basis.

The framework employed in this paper, and the dilemmas analyzed in it, furnish reasons to be pessimistic about the possibility of the emergence of a just imaginary of higher education in the wake of the first-order effects of current social inclusion policy. We regard the transition to 'second order effects' in this context as a question of the formation of 'social imaginaries,' the images and ideas that inform the way people understand and enable practices. Taylor's (2004) research on actual mutations of social imaginaries suggests that theories can shape such transformations. The dilemmas analyzed above exhibit theorizations that either do not or cannot support the emergence of a just imaginary of higher education. We have suggested alternative theorizations that are congruent with a *just* imaginary, but if they do not become disseminated in the self-understanding of actors engaged in new practices of higher education, it may be that these practices and their effects will prove to be just *imaginary*.

Acknowledgements

The authors appreciate the specific comments of Sam Sellar, Stephen Parker and Julie Rowlands on earlier drafts of this paper. They also acknowledge the broader support of The Warrnambool Collective.

Notes

1. The Asian Century refers to the projected dominance of Asian politics and economics in the twenty-first century, assuming current trends persist. As a term it arose in the mid-1980s, in talks between leaders of China and India and a US Senate Committee on Foreign Relations. The term is now used widely in the media and increasingly in government policy (for example, *Australia in the Asian Century* (Australian Government 2012b)). Characterization of the twenty-first century as the Asian Century follows similar depictions of the twentieth century as the American Century and the nineteenth century as the British Century.

2. Martin Trow (1974, 2006) distinguishes between three categories of higher education participation: elite (15% of the population and below), mass (16–50%) and universal (50% and above). Based on these, most OECD nations have reached or are fast approaching universal participation by their citizens in their higher education systems.

3. The 'politics of expectation' is a term coined by Henry Fairlie (a 1960s British political journalist) to describe the politics of US President John F. Kennedy in raising the lifestyle expectations of Americans beyond hope of their fulfillment (as Fairlie and others see it). Mike Raco has more recently suggested that the British welfare state is now characterized by a 'politics of aspiration' in which the hope of better things requires and indeed encourages citizens to be self-reliant.

4. Increasing the participation of Australians in higher education is not the only way in which to increase the proportion of 25-year-old to 34-year-old Australians with bachelor degrees. The target can also be achieved by ensuring that preference is given to potential migrants in possession of a bachelor's degree before entering Australia.

5. Twenty-five percent of the Australian population are from low-SES backgrounds but in 2008 their representation among undergraduates was 16.1%; in 2011 it was 16.8% (DIICCSRTE 2012).

6. Dei (2010) developed 'epistemological equity' as a postcolonial concept. It is an attempt to address 'the question of how to create spaces where multiple knowledges can co-exist in the Western academy' (2010, 98). Here we suggest it has similar potential for asserting the importance of including knowledges derived from working-class or low-SES backgrounds, to disrupt center–periphery relations in the realm of knowledge (Connell 2007) and as part of a more general 'southern theory' of higher education (Connell 2007).

References

Abbott, T. 2013. "Address to Universities Australia Higher Education Conference Canberra, Australia." Wednesday March 28. http://www.liberal.org.au/latest-news/2013/02/28/tony-abbotts-address-universities-australia-higher-education-con ference.

Alon, S. 2009. "The Evolution of Class Inequality in Higher Education: Competition, Exclusion, and Adaptation." *American Sociological Review* 74 (5): 731–755.

Anderson, D. S., R. Boven, P. J. Fensham, and J. P. Powell. 1980. *Students in Australian Higher Education: A Study of Their Social Composition since the Abolition of Fees*. Canberra: AGPS.

Anderson, D. S., and A. E. Vervoorn. 1983. *Access to Privilege: Patterns of Participation in Australian Post-Secondary Education*. Canberra: ANU Press.

Appadurai, A. 2004. "The Capacity to Aspire: Culture and the Terms of Recognition." In *Culture and Public Action*, edited by V. Rao and M. Walton, 59–84. Stanford: Stanford University Press.

Archer, L., S. Hollingworth, and A. Halsall. 2007. "'University's Not for Me – I'm a Nike Person': Urban, Working-Class Young People's Negotiations of 'Style', Identity and Educational Engagement." *Sociology* 41 (2): 219–237.

Association of American Universities. 1997. "On the Importance of Diversity in University Admissions." *New York Times*, 24 April, 27.

Australian Bureau of Statistics [ABS]. 2013. *Snapshot: Migration and the Increase in Bachelor Degrees among People Aged 25–34 Years in Australia*. 4211.0 – Education and Training Newsletter, April, 2013. http://www.abs.gov.au/ausstats/abs@.nsf/Lookup/4211.0main+features30April%202013.

Australian Government. 2009. *Transforming Australia's Higher Education System*. Canberra: DEEWR.

Australian Government. 2012a. *Higher Education Support Act 2003: Other Grants Guidelines (Education) 2012*. Canberra: Commonwealth of Australia. http://www.comlaw.gov.au/Details/F2012L00281.

Australian Government. 2012b. *Australia in the Asian century* (White Paper). Canberra: Commonwealth of Australia.

Australian Workforce and Productivity Agency [AWPA]. 2013. *Future Focus, 2013 National Workforce Development Strategy*. Canberra: Commonwealth of Australia. http://www.awpa.gov.au/our-work/national-workforce-development-strategy/2013-workforce-development-strategy/Documents/FutureFocus2013NWDS.pdf.

Ball, S. J. 1993. "What is Policy? Texts, Trajectories and Toolboxes." *Discourse: Studies in the Cultural Politics of Education* 13 (2): 10–17.

Ball, S. J., and C. Vincent. 1998. "'I Heard It on the Grapevine': 'Hot' Knowledge and School Choice." *British Journal of Sociology of Education* 19 (3): 377–400.

Baum, S., and K. Payea. 2005. *Education Pays 2004: The Benefits of Higher Education for Individuals and Society*. New York: College Board.

Berlant, L. 2007. "Cruel Optimism: On Marx, Loss and the Senses." *New Formations* (63), 33–51.

Birrell, B., V. Rapson, and T. F. Smith. 2011. "The 40 Percent Target Qualified Target: How Feasible?" *People and Place* 18 (4): 13–29.

Bok, J. 2010. "The Capacity to Aspire to Higher Education: 'It's like Making Them Do a Play without a Script'." *Critical Studies in Education* 51 (2): 163–178.

Boudon, R. 1973. *Education, Opportunity, and Social Inequality: Changing Prospects in Western Society*. New York: Wiley.

Bourdieu, P. 1984. *Distinction: A Social Critique of the Judgement of Taste*. Translated by R. Nice. London: Routledge & Kegan Paul.

Bourdieu, P., L. Boltanski, R. Castel, J.-C. Chamboredon, and D. Schnapper. 1990. *Photography: A Middle-Brow Art*. Translated by S. Whiteside. Cambridge: Polity Press.

Bowden, M. P., and J. Doughney. 2010. "Socio-Economic Status, Cultural Diversity and the Aspirations of Secondary Students in the Western Suburbs of Melbourne." *Australia. Higher Education* 59 (1): 115–129.

Bradley, D., P. Noonan, H. Nugent, and B. Scales. 2008. *Review of Australian Higher Education: Final Report*. Canberra: Commonwealth of Australia.

Brown, P. 2003. "The Opportunity Trap: Education and Employment in a Global Economy." *European Educational Research Journal* 2 (1): 141–179.

Brown, G. 2011. "Emotional Geographies of Young People's Aspirations for Adult Life." *Children's Geographies* 9 (1): 7–12.

Burke, P. J. 2012. *The Right to Higher Education: Beyond Widening Participation*. London: Routledge.

de Certeau, M. 1984. *The Practice of Everyday Life*. Translated by S. Rendall. Berkeley: University of California Press.

Cervini, E. 2012. "More Students, but Are They Doomed to Fail?." *The Age*. March 13. http://www.theage.com.au/national/education/blogs/third-degree/more-students-but-are-they-doomed-to-fail-20120312-1uuio.html.

Connell, R. W. 2007. *Southern Theory: The Global Dynamics of Knowledge in Social Science*. Crows Nest, N.S.W: Allen & Unwin.

Couldry, N. 2010. *Why Voice Matters: Culture and Politics after Neoliberalism*. London: SAGE.

Dei, G. J. S. 2010. *Teaching Africa: Towards a Transgressive Pedagogy*. Dordrecht: Springer.

Department for Education and Skills [DfES]. 2003. *The Future of Higher Education (White Paper)*. Norwich, UK: The Stationery Office Limited.

Department of Industry, Innovation, Climate Change, Science, Research and Tertiary Education [DIICCSRTE]. 2010. *Students: Selected Higher Education Statistics, 2009*. http://www.innovation.gov.au/HigherEducation/HigherEducation Statistics/StatisticsPublications/Pages/Students2009FullYear.aspx.

Department of Industry, Innovation, Climate Change, Science, Research and Tertiary Education [DIICCSRTE]. 2011. *Students: Selected Higher Education Statistics, 2010*. http://www.innovation.gov.au/HigherEducation/HigherEducation Statistics/StatisticsPublications/Pages/Student2010FullYearSelectedHigherEducati onStatistics.aspx.

Department of Industry, Innovation, Climate Change, Science, Research and Tertiary Education [DIICCSRTE]. 2012. *Students: Selected Higher Education Statistics, 2011*. http://www.innovation.gov.au/HigherEducation/HigherEducation Statistics/StatisticsPublications/Pages/2011StudentFullYear.aspx.

Department of Industry, Innovation, Climate Change, Science, Research and Tertiary Education [DIICCSRTE]. 2013a. *Higher Education Participation and Partnerships Program*. http://www.innovation.gov.au/HigherEducation/Equity/ HigherEducationParticipationAndPartnershipsProgram/Pages/default.aspx.

Department of Industry, Innovation, Climate Change, Science, Research and Tertiary Education [DIICCSRTE]. 2013b. "Special Data Request."

Dobson, I., and E. Skuja. 2007. "ENTER Scores: An Over-Rated Measure." *Principal Matters* 70: 34–37.

Engstrom, C., and V. Tinto. 2008. "Access without Support is Not Opportunity." *Change* 40 (1): 46–50.

Fairlie, H. 1973. *The Kennedy Promise: The Politics of Expectation*. Garden City, NY: Doubleday.

Field of Dreams. 1989. Directed by Phil Alden Robinson. New York: Universal Studios.

Gale, T. 2011. "Expansion and Equity in Australian Higher Education: Three Propositions for New Relations." *Discourse: Studies in the Cultural Politics of Education* 32 (5): 669–685.

Gale, T., and D. Tranter. 2011. "Social Justice in Australian Higher Education Policy: An Historical and Conceptual Account of Student Participation." *Critical Studies in Education* 52 (1): 29–46.

Gale, T., and S. Parker. 2013. "Widening Participation in Australian Higher Education." Report to the Higher Education Funding Council for England (HEFCE) and the Office of Fair Access (OFFA), England. CFE (Research and Consulting) Ltd, Leicester, UK and Edge Hill University, Lancashire, UK.

Gale, T., S. Parker, P. Rodd, G. Stratton, and T. Sealey with T. Moore. 2013. "Student Aspirations for Higher Education in Central Queensland: A Survey of School Students' Navigational Capacities." Report submitted to CQ University, Australia. Centre for Research in Education Futures and Innovation (CREFI), Deakin University, Melbourne, Australia.

Gallagher, M. 2009. *Bradley's Flawed Vision. the Australian*, February 18. http://www.theaustralian.com.au/higher-education/opinion-analysis/bradleys-flawed-vision/story-e6frgcko-1111118881130.

Gillard, J. 2009. *Universities Australia Conference Speech*. Wednesday March 4. http://ministers.deewr.gov.au/gillard/universities-australia-conference-4-march-2009-speech.

Graduate Careers Australia. 2013a. *GradFiles*. http://www.graduatecareers.com.au/research/researchreports/gradfiles/.

Graduate Careers Australia. 2013b. *Graduate Salaries 2012: A Report on the Earnings of New Australian Graduates in Their First Full-Time Employment*. Melbourne: Graduate Careers Australia. http://www.graduatecareers.com.au/wp-content/uploads/2013/07/Graduate%20Salaries%202012%20%5Bsecured%5D.pdf.

Hare, J. 2013. University of NSW Cuts off Low-Score Students. *The Australian*, July 19. http://www.theaustralian.com.au/national-affairs/university-of-nsw-cuts-off-low-score-students/story-fn59niix-1226681671788.

Hare, J., and S. Matchett. 2013. "Labor Takes Aim at Student Target." *The Australian*, July 2. http://www.theaustralian.com.au/national-affairs/education/labor-takes-aim-at-student-target/story-fn59nlz9-1226672858677.

Hare, J. and A. Trounson. 2013. "Soaring Attrition Fears Not Founded." *The Australian*, July 17. http://www.theaustralian.com.au/higher-education/soaring-attrition-fears-not-founded/story-e6frgcjx-1226680340943.

Harvey, A., and M. Luckman. 2013. How Unis Can Win the Battle of Attrition. *The Australian*, April 17. http://www.theaustralian.com.au/higher-education/opinion/how-unis-can-win-the-battle-of-attrition/story-e6frgcko-1226622004571.

Kelly, P. J. 2010. *Closing the College Attainment Gap between the US and Most Educated Countries, and the Contributions to Be Made by the States*. National Center for Higher Education Management Systems. http://www.nchems.org/pubs/docs/Closing%20the%20U%20S%20%20Degree%20Gap%20NCHEMS%20Final.pdf.

Lauder, H., P. Brown, and G. Tholen. 2012. "The Global Auction Model, Skills Bias Theory and Graduate Incomes: Reflections on Methodology." In *Educating for the Knowledge Economy? Critical Perspectives*, edited by H. Lauder, M. Young, H. Daniels, M. Balarin, and J. Lowe, 43–65. Abingdon: Routledge.

Li, I. W., and P. W. Miller. 2013. "The Absorption of Recent Graduates into the Australian Labour Market: Variations by University Attended and Field of Study." *Australian Economic Review* 46 (1): 14–30.

Lomax-Smith, J., L. Watson, and B. Webster. 2011. *Higher Education Base Funding Review: Final Report*. Canberra: DEEWR.

Marginson, S. 2004. "National and Global Competition in Higher Education." *The Australian Educational Researcher* 31 (2): 1–28.

Marginson, S. 2009. "The Knowledge Economy and Higher Education: A System for Regulating the Value of Knowledge." *Higher Education Management & Policy* 21 (1): 39–53.

Marginson, S. 2011. "Higher Education and Public Good." *Higher Education Quarterly* 65 (4): 411–433.

Milem, J. F. 2003. "The Educational Benefits of Diversity: Evidence from Multiple Sectors." In *Compelling Interest: Examining the Evidence on Racial Dynamics in Colleges and Universities*, edited by M. J. Chang, D. Witt, J. Jones, and K. Hakuta, 126–169. Stanford: Stanford University Press.

Pyne, C. 2013. "The Role of Research and Universities in the Coalition's Productivity Agenda." Address at Monash University, Melbourne, Australia. Tuesday April 30. http://monash.edu/news/show/the-role-of-research-and-universities-in-the-coalitions-productivity-agenda.

Raco, M. 2009. "From Expectations to Aspirations: State Modernisation, Urban Policy, and the Existential Politics of Welfare in the UK." *Political Geography* 28: 436–454.

Rawls, J. 1993. *Political Liberalism*. Columbia, SC: Columbia University Press.

Rizvi, F., and B. Lingard. 2010. *Globalizing Education Policy*. London & New York: Routledge.

Rizvi, F., and B. Lingard. 2011. "Social Equity and the Assemblage of Values in Australian Higher Education." *Cambridge Journal of Education* 41 (1): 5–22.

Rudd, K. 2007. "Australia's Future Growth Challenge. Public Address at Melbourne Graduate School of Education." Tuesday 23 January. http://www.edfac.unimelb.edu.au/news/lectures/20070123KevinRuddAddress/summary.html.

Sellar, S. 2013. "Equity, Markets and the Politics of Aspiration in Australian Higher Education." *Discourse: Studies in the Cultural Politics of Education* 34 (2): 245–258.

Sellar, S., T. Gale, and S. Parker. 2011. "Appreciating Aspirations in Australian Higher Education." *Cambridge Journal of Education* 41 (1): 37–52.

Sen, A. 2009. *The Idea of Justice*. Cambridge, Mass: Belknap Press of Harvard University Press.

Smith, L. 2011. "Experiential 'Hot' Knowledge and Its Influence on Low-SES Students' Capacities to Aspire to Higher Education." *Critical Studies in Education* 52 (2): 165–177.

Spence, M. 2011. *The Next Convergence: The Future of Economic Growth in a Multispeed World*. New York: Farrar, Straus & Giroux.

Taylor, C. 2004. *Modern Social Imaginaries*. Durham: Duke University Press.

Trounson, A. 2013. "Call to Cut Student Intake." *The Australian*, May 15. http://www.pressdisplay.com/pressdisplay/showlink.aspx?bookmarkid=U3HM6X1R7114&preview=article&linkid=4f923b52-160f-4f61-825a-078b11b2bb2e&pdaffid=mqeQZextXQNCwdjgKCmPOw%3d%3d.

Trow, M. 1974. *Problems in the Transition from Elite to Mass Higher Education Policies for Higher Education*, 51–101. Paris: OECD.

Trow, M. 2006. "Reflections on the Transition from Elite to Mass to Universal Access: Forms and Phases of Higher Education in Modern Societies since WWII." In *International Handbook of Higher Education, Part One: Global Themes and Contemporary Challenges*, edited by J. J. F. Forrest and P. G. Altbach, 243–280. Dordrecht: Springer.

Watts, M., and D. Bridges. 2006. "The Value of Non-Participation in Higher Education." *Journal of Education Policy* 21 (3): 267–290.

Win, R., and P. Miller. 2005. "The Effects of Individual and School Factors on University Academic Performance." *Australian Economic Review* 38 (1): 1–18.

World Health Organization. 2008. *The World Health Report 2008 – Primary Health Care: Now More than Even.* Switzerland: World Health Organization.

Zipin, L., S. Sellar, M. Brennan, and T. Gale. 2013. "Educating for Futures in Marginalized Regions: A Sociological Framework for Rethinking and Researching Aspirations." *Educational Philosophy and Theory* 1–20.

Re-articulating social justice as equity in schooling policy: the effects of testing and data infrastructures

Bob Lingard[a], Sam Sellar[a] and Glenn C. Savage[b]

[a]School of Education, The University of Queensland, Brisbane, Australia;
[b]Melbourne Graduate School of Education, The University of Melbourne, Melbourne, Australia

This paper examines the re-articulation of social justice as equity in schooling policy through national and global testing and data infrastructures. It focuses on the Australian National Assessment Program – Literacy and Numeracy (NAPLAN) and the OECD's Programme for International Student Assessment (PISA). We analyse the discursive reconstitution of social justice as equity in Australian and OECD policy, and analyse NAPLAN and PISA as technologies of governance that re-articulate equity as a measure of performance. These re-articulations are set against the extension of neo-social economistic rationalities to all domains of life and the topological production of new spaces of policy and power.

Introduction

The focus of this paper is the re-articulation of the concept of social justice as *equity* in contemporary schooling policy through the creation of national and global testing and data infrastructures. We examine the National Assessment Program – Literacy and Numeracy (NAPLAN) in Australia and the Organisation for Economic Cooperation and Development (OECD) Programme for International Student Assessment (PISA), particularly with respect to their complementarity and functioning as new technologies of governance. While the empirical focus is Australian education policy and the education work of the OECD, our argument has applicability in many national polities and domains of governance across the globe.

The proliferation of testing and new data-driven accountabilities has changed what counts and what is counted as social justice in education.

Social justice has been re-articulated as equity through numerical and comparative expressions of these concepts that untether them from carefully elaborated definitions, such as Nancy Fraser's (1997, 2009) work on the redistributive, recognitive and representative dimensions of social justice, which has been usefully applied to education (Gilbert et al. 2011; Keddie 2012). Current definitions of equity are linked to the introduction of multiple layers of technical and numerical mediation to measure equity, translating life in schools and communities into a series of abstract representations in graphs, grids, league tables and indices. These technologies of governance are facilitated by, and further contribute to, the discursive re-articulation of social justice as equity. This re-articulation reflects the rise of the 'neo-social' (Rose 1999a, 1999b; Savage 2013), which involves an elision of the economic and social domains of governance to recast all aspects of human life in terms of an individual's potential for self-capitalisation in a market society.

Our argument is that social justice and equity are being transformed through the national and global reworking of education into a field of measurement and comparison. Bailey (2013) uses the Foucauldian concept of *dispositif* to refer to both the material and the discursive components of education policy. The concept of *dispositif* challenges readings of Foucault's work that imply there is nothing beyond discourse. Bailey draws on the concept to describe education as an idea – as a conceptual or philosophical construction – and also as a technical and material space that is made legible for governing:

> ... education is considered as always in a process of becoming, constituted in different ways at different times according to the differential multiplicity of forces, discourses and knowledges which act upon and constitute it as both an *idea* and a *material and governable field* of practices, culture and leaning. (Bailey 2013, 6; original emphasis)

We seek to show how both ideas and material spaces and practices of social justice in education are being reciprocally reconstituted in contemporary schooling policy.

Our aim is to open up a set of issues, rather than to provide a definitive account. In doing so, our contribution locates changing social justice conceptions in Australian schooling in relation to global re-spatialisations of education governance (Meyer and Benevot 2013) and the 'becoming topological' of contemporary cultural, political and economic life (Lury, Terranova, and Parisi 2012). After reviewing the emergence of new technologies of governance in education, we trace changing discursive conceptions of social justice as equity in Australian schooling and in the education work of the OECD. We show how in these discursive re-articulations, stronger conceptions of social justice as equality of opportunity in an equal society have given way to weaker conceptions of equity as fairness in a meritocratic society. We then provide an analysis of new topological spaces produced by the technologies of NAPLAN and PISA and their effects on governance of the performance of schools and systems in relation to equity. Finally, we consider some implications of this numbers-driven conception of equity.

New technologies of governance in education

The re-articulation of social justice as equity through test-based accountabilities is linked to what Lyotard (1984) called *performativity*, which Ball (2013) has written about in relation to new technologies of governance in education. In the context of the neo-liberal reworking of education policy and the emergence of the neo-social, comparison has become a central mode of national and global governance (Novoa and Yariv-Mashal 2003), particularly as the state has been restructured in line with new public management principles and new forms of network governance (Ball and Junemann 2012). Policy here can be seen as a network of numbers 'connecting those exercising political power with the persons, processes and problems that they seek to govern' (Rose 1999b, 99). As Rose observes: 'Democratic mentalities of government prioritise and seek to produce a relationship between numerate citizens, numericised civic discourse and numerate evaluations of government' (1999b, 232). He adds:

> a focus on numbers is instructive, for it helps us turn our eyes from grand texts of philosophy to the mundane practices of pedagogy, of accounting, of information and polling, and to the mundane knowledges and 'grey sciences' that support them. (Rose 1999b, 232)

We argue that along with this analytical demand to attend to mundane numerical practices, we are seeing an empirical shift away from philosophical discourses about social justice to a reliance on more data-driven practices of equity. Numbers have become central in contemporary education policy regimes (Ozga 2009; Lingard 2011) and this has weakened the influence of conceptual-discursive accounts of what constitutes social justice in schooling.

These developments have been made possible through the creation of new national and global infrastructures for collecting and analysing data (Anagnostopoulos, Rutledge, and Jacobsen 2013). Sassen (2007) argues that the creation of global infrastructures is a central feature of globalisation and we see global testing as one example. More aspects of everyday life are now being subject to 'datafication' and 'big data' modes of analysis, enabled in part by dramatic increases in computational capacities (Mayer-Schonberger and Cukier 2013). Big data analytics are changing the rationalities at work in quantitative analysis, moving from sampling to mining large datasets and from concerns with causality and understanding towards more pragmatic approaches focused on correlations and predictability. These new rationalities have significant implications for the work of the private sector and governments in and through public policy, including schooling. For example, the repositioning of the education company Pearson as a globally powerful data analytics provider in education is suggestive of the changes this development holds for new public/private partnerships (see Ball 2012, 124–128) and emergent heterarchical organisations of governance in education (Ball and Junemann 2012).

Associated with the shift towards big data, measurement and comparison is what some have described as the becoming topological of culture (Lury, Terranova, and Parisi 2012) resulting from the production of new continuities and discontinuities through metrics, models, calculations and comparisons. These facilitate new global flows and imaginaries (Appadurai 1996), new modes of governmentality (Ruppert 2012) and 'a new order of spatio-temporal continuity for forms of economic, political and cultural life' (Lury, Terranova, and Parisi 2012, 4). This topological turn is distinct from the rescaling of state power, which Brenner (2004) has written about in respect of globalisation and which might be seen as a vertical conceptualisation (Allen and Cochrane 2010). While re-scaling speaks of new multi-scalar politics, the topological sees a new relational politics alongside territorial accounts of space (Allen and Cochrane 2010), which requires changed conceptions of what is near or connected and what is distant or disconnected. Indeed, from a topological perspective, 'power relationships are not so much positioned in space or extended across it, as compose the spaces of which they are a part' (Allen 2011, 284). As Harvey argues, infrastructures such as those constituted by national and international testing programmes 'transform relational fields' (2012, 85) and 'create and sustain dynamic political and moral spaces' (2012, 88). NAPLAN and PISA both operate in terms of this topological rationality, which works through ever-changing spaces of calculative correlations, and which untethers social justice in schooling from implicit values and norms embedded in the cultural and political traditions of particular places.

Social justice as equity: evolutions in Australian education policy

Since the late 1970s, conceptions and practices associated with social justice in education have shifted considerably in Australia and other OECD member countries as a result of changes associated with neo-liberal governance. These changes involve a shift away from strong conceptions of equality of opportunity and redistributive approaches that defined the post-war Keynesian welfare state era, towards market-oriented *neo-social* approaches, which collapse together the social and economic domains of governance and either evacuate or obscure earlier concerns for social justice and equality (see

Savage 2013). The test-driven data infrastructures of PISA and NAPLAN (and their political utilisations) typify this neo-social approach and play a powerful role in reconstituting the conditions of possibility for social justice in education.

Historically, the post-war 1950s and 1960s saw the rapid expansion of Australian public education and the dawn of the mass secondary schooling system (Teese and Polesel 2003). This rapid acceleration continued until the 1980s, fuelled by the baby boom and immigration. These developments ignited debates about historically ingrained educational inequalities, particularly concerning the unequal patterning of educational access and outcomes based on socio-economic status and gender. Until the mid-1970s, Australian education policies were dominated by a commitment to equality of opportunity, seeking to provide young people from diverse backgrounds with 'the same chance' at climbing the 'educational ladder' (Collins and Yates 2011, 109). Redistributive approaches were also enacted through the Whitlam government's Disadvantaged Schools Program, which enhanced the federal role in education through a needs-based, redistributive funding model that worked across the government/non-government school divide.

The educational justice landscape shifted considerably in the late 1970s, following the global breakdown of the Bretton Woods system and the energy crisis recession. During this period, global economic panics gave rise to national education panics and new rationalisations of the relationship between education and the economy emerged. Australia experienced unprecedented levels of youth unemployment, which led to correlative increases in school retention. In contrast to the post-war boom years, school-leavers had bleak economic prospects, due to declining manufacturing industries and the growing competitiveness of entry to white-collar professions. These factors helped fuel the re-imagination of education as a mechanism for investing in human capital and driving economic productivity.

By the early 1980s, global economic concerns had merged with fears about declining educational standards and student achievement across western nations (Ravitch 2010). In 1988 John Dawkins, Australian Commonwealth Minister for Education, released a policy statement entitled 'Strengthening Australia's Schools', which expressed significant anxiety over the education system, arguing that improvements were needed to secure a stronger economic future and these required a stronger federal presence in schooling (Lingard, O'Brien, and Knight 1993). This mirrored international arguments, particularly in the USA, where the 1983 report 'A Nation at Risk' decried the falling quality of educational standards and warned of economic turmoil if schooling systems were not reformed. This coupling of economic and education policy priorities saw debates about justice in Australian education shift to individualistic and market-based rationalities, which framed a fair school system as one that removed barriers for individuals to participate in increasingly competitive school systems (Collins and Yates 2011) and which provided young people with access to pathways that improved their employment prospects in a globalising economy (Keating, Savage, and Polesel 2013).

Since the 1990s, strengthened economic framings of education have seen a new era of equity in education emerge (Savage, Sellar, and Gorur 2013). The concept of equity, drawn from the language of economics, has steadily replaced older terms such as 'equality' or 'justice' in debates about fairness in education. This shift in nomenclature is significant, signalling an important break away from more sophisticated definitions towards meanings and practices that cannot be abstracted from the economic policy agendas in which they are embedded. Social justice has thus been subsumed and transformed into equity by economic rationalities and discourses. Indeed, Australian education policies of recent years have moved towards framing equity as a 'market enhancing mechanism' (Savage 2011), by collapsing notions of educational fairness into a human capital agenda that frames the social and economic domains of governance as intrinsically linked and mutually complementary.

This melting together of social and economic agendas reflects Rose's argument that contemporary governance involves a new approach to the 'capitalization of citizenship' (1999a, 481). Similar to Ong's framing of neo-liberalism as an assemblage of rationalities and technologies centred on 'the optimization of life' (2006, 14), Rose argues that contemporary governance involves a dual focus on the economic and social, thus seeking capitalisation 'of human knowledge, skills and life chances (human capital) and of the social networks and relations that promote economic and personal well-being (social capital)' (1999a, 481). Rose describes the fusion of these domains as a rise of the neo-social (1999b, 145): that is, a rejuvenated interest in facilitating social well-being, but primarily for the sake of fostering greater economic productivity and economic competitiveness within the global economy.

This neo-social approach has been most evident in Australia during the period from 2007 to 2013, when the federal Labor Government promised an 'Education Revolution' that would herald a new era of equity, set within the context of a globally oriented economic policy strategy (see Rudd and Smith 2007; Gillard 2008). The government's commitment to equity became the driving force behind a raft of education reforms, many of which have received bipartisan support through agreements made by the Council of Australian Governments.[1] Central here is the National Education Agreement, which frames inequalities in Year 12 attainment, disparities in literacy and numeracy scores, and underachievement amongst Indigenous Australians as problems that need to be solved for the sake of building greater economic prosperity (Council of Australian Governments 2008, 2009). A similar approach to equity is mirrored in the Melbourne Declaration on Educational Goals for Young Australians (2008) – signed by all State and

Territory education ministers, along with the federal minister and applicable in all Australian schools and systems – which cites the number-one goal for Australian education as the promotion of 'equity and excellence' (Melbourne Declaration on Educational Goals for Young Australians 2008, 7) and frames education as a social and economic investment.

Labor's 'Education Revolution' set in motion policies designed to improve educational achievement and tackle what former Australian Prime Minister Julia Gillard termed 'pockets of disadvantage' (Gorur 2013). An important development was the establishment in 2008 of the Australian Curriculum, Assessment and Reporting Authority (2013), a statutory authority created to oversee the new national agenda. The three primary functions of this Authority were to: develop and administer a national school curriculum; develop and administer national assessments; and to collect, manage and analyse student assessment data and other data relating to schools and comparative school performance (Parliament of Australia 2008). The latter two functions led to the development of NAPLAN and the publication and comparison of testing performance on the My School website. As Gorur (2013) explains, NAPLAN and My School were promoted by the government as central tools for tackling inequities in the Australian education system, by constructing a national data infrastructure for measuring and diagnosing disparities in student achievement. Prior to 2008, young people in Australia were tested using state-wide assessments that varied in the grade levels at which they were conducted and in the instruments used. It was therefore impossible to make credible national comparisons across State systems, because a standardised field of judgement did not exist. NAPLAN claimed to provide the solution to this problem, through the creation of a commensurate space of measurement, which would not only enable inequities in achievement to be measured at a national scale, but would also allow for new interventions to be made into school systems by the federal government.

Equity as fairness and inclusion in the OECD's education work

Recent changes in the Australian national policy field cannot be adequately understood without considering the impact of actors and organisations in the global policy field. The OECD and PISA have had significant influence on the 'Education Revolution' in Australia and on the construction of NAPLAN and My School. The OECD regards equity as important from an economic point of view and it has been central in promoting a neo-social policy agenda in education and shifting discussion away from the language of equality. Reflecting its role as an intergovernmental organisation concerned with economic policy, the OECD argues that equity in education matters because of its economic benefits to nations and the global economy as a whole. Given the recent development of the cross-directorate OECD

Skills Strategy (OECD 2012b), and the related *economisation* of education policy and correlative *educationisation* of economic policy, education work has taken on greater salience within the work of the OECD.

The Organisation's framing of equity is well illustrated by a chapter in a recent report on equity and quality in education entitled 'Investing in Equity in Education Pays Off' (OECD 2012a). The emphasis on equity 'paying off' is explained in terms of the role of equity in building human capital and productivity. For example, the report argues that 'improving equity in education and preventing school failure is cost-beneficial, even more in the context of the current economic crisis' (2012a, 13). It adds: 'Inequitable education policies and practices have a negative impact on individuals and also limit economic and social development' (2012a, 13). Conversely, the OECD laments inequity primarily in terms of economic losses and the wastage of human potential, arguing that economic prosperity is intrinsically linked to social benefits (2007, 31–33). The OECD argues, for example, that the 'costs of inequity and school failure are high for individuals and societies' (2012a, 23), framing 'equitable outcomes' as 'key for both economic prosperity and social cohesion' (2012a, 26):

> Educational failure … imposes high costs on society. Poorly educated people limit economies' capacity to produce, grow and innovate. School failure damages social cohesion and mobility, and imposes additional costs on public budgets to deal with the consequences – higher spending on public health and social support and greater criminality, among others. For all these reasons, improving equity in education and reducing school failure should be a high priority in all OECD education policy agendas. (OECD 2012a, 3)

In weaving together the economic and social, the OECD suggests that a commitment to equity is actually compatible with market efficiency and productivity. Equity is therefore framed as something capable of flourishing in (and enhancing the success of) competitive market-based economies – an argument that opposes a wealth of research suggesting global capitalism and social equality are antagonistic forces and the extent of social inequality limits the extent to which equity can be achieved through schooling (Wilkinson and Pickett 2009). In making this argument, the OECD draws upon a World Bank (2005) report and suggests that 'equity and efficiency are in fact complementary in economic development' (OECD 2007, 33). Indeed, both the OECD and the World Bank set this argument in opposition to classic neo-liberalism, taking aim at free-market economists who argue that the redistribution of resources to the needy helps equity but damages efficiency (World Bank 2005; OECD 2007, 33). Equity is instead framed as central to the pursuit of long-term economic prosperity.

Amidst this neo-social vision, the past decade has seen the OECD develop a definition of equity as fairness and inclusion. Central to this dual definition are three key documents, starting with an OECD-commissioned report prepared in 2003 (Levin 2003). This report avoids a comprehensive definition of equity, yet in a significant move (that has subsequently shaped the OECD's position) it clearly differentiates equity from equality, framing the former as the desirable goal. Levin argues that the aim of policy 'cannot and should not be equality in the sense that everyone is the same or achieves the same outcomes' (2003, 5). Instead, he promotes the view that 'differences in outcomes should not be attributable to differences in areas such as wealth, income, power' (2003, 5). He adds: 'The question is always a practical one, then, of what state or degree of *inequality* is acceptable' (2003, 5; emphasis added). Levin's report also foregrounds the importance of fairness, understood in terms of the 'distribution of opportunity' and access to education so individuals have 'reasonable opportunity to develop their capacities' (2003, 5). This position on equity is developed in two sub-sequent OECD reports: *No More Failures: Ten Steps to Equity in Education* (OECD 2007) and *Equity and Quality in Education: Supporting Disadvantaged Students and Schools* (OECD 2012a). In these documents, fairness is defined by drawing upon notions of equality of opportunity, specifically in terms of ensuring 'personal and social circumstances … are not obstacles to achieving educational potential' (2012a, 9). Inclusion is defined by drawing upon notions of entitlement, in terms of 'ensuring a basic minimum standard of education for all' (2007, 11).

The prime measure informing the OECD's discussions of equity in education is data assembled from PISA. According to the OECD, therefore, issues of (in)equity can be understood via a global infrastructure of performance measurement. Helping students attain higher levels on PISA is seen as a way for nations to invest in producing knowledgeable and highly skilled workers (OECD 2012b). PISA has re-articulated equity within a rationality directed toward measuring and understanding comparative performance and student outcomes. However, this emphasis on measuring and understanding equity in relation to testing and other data conflicts to some extent with the definition of equity as fairness and inclusion. There is an apparent disconnect between the OECD's official definition of equity, which draws on notions of equality of opportunity and entitlement (focusing on system level inputs), and PISA, which promotes an equity of outcomes approach (focusing on system level outputs). Despite these two different equity agendas at play, it is the technical measures that dominate contemporary policy and that are transforming the conditions of possibility for debates about educational justice in Australia and elsewhere.

NAPLAN and My School: new data infrastructures in Australian schooling

The Australian Labor Government's education reform agenda set in motion a strong national approach to Australian schooling (Commonwealth of

Australia 2008), despite the fact that States and Territories have Constitutional responsibility for schooling under Australia's federal political structure. This agenda included the introduction of literacy and numeracy testing through NAPLAN and the reporting of results on the My School website. NAPLAN has been conducted with all students in all schools in Years Three, Five, Seven and Nine since 2008. The programme measures four 'domains' of Reading, Writing, Language Conventions (spelling, grammar and punctuation) and Numeracy. National minimum standards have been established for each year level for each domain. The My School website is a publicly accessible repository of data and is mainly focused on the NAPLAN performance of schools in relation to national minimum standards, average national performance and the performance of subsets of 60 schools that are deemed to be statistically similar. The latter comparison has required the creation of the Index of Community Socio-educational Advantage (ICSEA), which is used as the basis for comparing the performance of a given school against its set of similar schools.

The ICSEA provides a measure of the influence of family background on individual performance at school and is thus described as an index of socio-educational advantage. We suggest that a measure of advantage is not the same as a measure of disadvantage and there is a difference between the least advantaged schools and the most disadvantaged schools. The ICSEA comprises a set of socio-economic status variables and school variables relating to geographic location, the number of students with a language background other than English and the number of Aboriginal and Torres Strait Islander students. The Australian Curriculum, Assessment and Reporting Authority (2013, 1) explains that the ICSEA comprises a 'combination of variables that have the strongest association with student performance on the National Assessment Program – Literacy and Numeracy (NAPLAN) tests'. Each school is attributed a single score on an index with a mean of 1000 and can be compared with similar schools and with all participating schools in Australia. Rose (1999b) makes the salient point that such single numbers hide the multiple categories and other technical and definitional processes that go into the creation of such metrics.

The rationale for using the ICSEA as a basis for comparing schools is that socio-economic background should not affect educational outcomes. Additionally, schools achieving better outcomes with students from similar socio-economic backgrounds ostensibly serve as a basis for identifying and transferring 'best practices' across schools, although there are no formal structural mechanisms currently in place to facilitate such learning. In this regard, observations by political leaders about the role of My School and NAPLAN in policy learning seem to be largely symbolic.

The statistically similar schools comparison does not provide a measure of equity *per se*, but rather provides comparative measures of performance. The policy document introducing these reforms states:

The Australian Government is building a framework in which educational excellence and equity reinforce each other. This combination supports the growth of aspiration, engagement and achievement in every community regardless of its location or income. To do this, we must ensure that the highest quality of teaching and learning is available in every school, and that there are targeted strategies in place to address and overcome the disadvantages that any child may bring to school. (Commonwealth of Australia 2008, 25)

These constructions imply that the amelioration of educational disadvantage lies in the capacities of educators and schools, thus bracketing out any considerations of the extent of broader structural inequalities and forms of poverty within society that have the capacity to deeply impact upon educational achievement (Anyon 2005). Here we can see the statistically similar schools comparisons as controlling for (contextual) variables that are outside the capacities of the school to change and, in so doing, ensuring that it becomes 'impossible for a school or teacher to locate a responsibility outside itself'; a form of governing through responsibilisation (Simons 2013, 13). Power and Frandji (2010) suggest that such approaches imply 'fatalism' towards structural inequality.

As well as measuring the relationship between background and performance, national minimum standards are set for each cohort that sits the test. These minimum standards reflect a concern for inclusion and the view that basic levels of literacy and numeracy competence are required to proceed successfully to the next stage of education and ultimately for full citizenship and a productive working life. This construction could be seen as an entitlement concept of inclusion, similar to the OECD's definition, which is tenuously linked to an entitlement curriculum in the new Foundation-10 Australian Curriculum.

Equity in relation to NAPLAN, then, is defined as both school performance compared with other schools and as the number of students meeting the national minimum standards. Importantly, both constructions imply continuing inequities. For example, improvement on the statistically similar schools measure implies improvement relative to the comparatively inequitable performance of other schools, whilst the very foundations of the ICSEA relies upon the existence of disparate levels of socio-educational advantage (i.e. without inequalities, it would be impossible to create the ICSEA as a technical measure). Furthermore, the target for 80% of the student cohort meeting minimum standards implies that 20% of the student body is *not* expected to meet these standards. Presumably, many of these students will be from the most disadvantaged backgrounds.

Equity and inclusion here are constructed by NAPLAN and My School, at least implicitly, as fairness within a meritocratic school system, in which considerations of the extent of broader social inequality and its impact upon opportunity are not adequately recognised or acknowledged. This point is well made by Wilson and Pickett (2009), who argue it is not only background factors that affect the performance of individual students, but also the extent of inequality within a society. The numerical and comparative reconstitution of equity also limits what counts as factors in the aetiology of educational disadvantage. As demonstrated by Anyon (2005) in relation to economic and social policy, and by Lipman (2013) regarding urban policy, broader public policies and their effects within neo-liberal capitalism have substantial impact on the possibilities of equity and social justice through schooling. Indeed, one could argue that neo-liberal policy has worsened social inequality (Condron 2011, 52).

The data infrastructure associated with the national agenda in Australian schooling has other effects as well. The combined usage of NAPLAN data and the ICSEA on the My School website is reconstituting educational spaces in Australia in at least two ways. First, the My School website lists for each school a set of local schools in the same geographical area, in addition to statistically similar schools that are more geographically dispersed. Comparison against statistically similar schools and against national averages together reconstitute Australian schooling as a national field, despite schooling being the responsibility of States and Territories. Second, this national education space needs to be understood as part of a broader topological functioning of power (Allen 2011). Statistically similar schools are distributed across the nation, eclipsing boundaries between State and Territory systems and government/non-government schools. This measure of comparative performance is connected in a topological sense: that is, otherwise distant and unconnected schools are brought together in a seemingly unproblematic fashion through this mode of comparison. This 'connecting up' of schools necessarily involves dissolving social inequalities, cultural differences, and topographical distances, which differently inform the nature of each school, in order to align all schools in a neat and ordered fashion for the putative purposes of policy diagnosis and intervention. Such 'topological accounts disrupt our sense of what is near and far', loosening our conception of distance (Allen and Cochrane 2010, 1073) and constructing a relational space alongside territorial ones.

We might speak of *local locals* and *non-local locals* in respect of the topographical and topological conceptions of space produced by My School. School context is defined as the sum of the socio-economic contexts of individual students and families. From a topological perspective, context is also constructed through measures of statistical similarity, so that schools in very different geographical, cultural, economic and political locations are seen as sharing the same social and educational context. This is a fundamental reconceptualisation of context and place as a topological space of comparison and governance.

PISA: equity and the education work of the OECD

PISA is the OECD's programme to provide an international comparative measure of the performance of schooling systems and has become increasingly influential since it was first conducted in 2000 (Meyer and Benevot 2013). PISA has also become central to the education work of the OECD, serving as a model for subsequent developments in relation to the assessment of adult skills and the learning outcomes of university education (Sellar and Lingard 2013a). Since 2000, the OECD has conducted PISA every three years across a growing number of member and non-member countries (including sub-national systems such as Shanghai, China), with 64 nations or systems participating in the most recent 2012 assessment. PISA is conducted with a sample of schools in each system, selected to be representative *inter alia* of student socio-economic backgrounds, gender and ethnic backgrounds. PISA measures the capacities of 15 year olds to apply their knowledge at the completion of compulsory schooling, defined as their literacy in the areas of reading, mathematics and science. Unlike the TIMSS and PIRLS tests conducted by the International Association for the Evaluation of Educational Achievement, PISA does not focus on national curricula. We observe here that the PISA implicitly assumes a world culture theory from comparative education regarding the assumed isomorphism of the outcomes of school curricula across the globe (Meyer, Kamens, and Benavot 1992; Ramirez 2012). PISA also requires students to complete a background questionnaire that is used to assess their socio-economic status and their attitudes and behaviours in relation to learning both in and out of school. These data are correlated with performance to measure equity, with weaker correlation suggesting greater equity and *vice versa*.

While PISA supports multiple analyses across a range of areas, the performance of countries and systems is often publicly reported and compared in terms of two measures: quality and equity. Quality here refers to the comparative performance of systems in the different areas tested, and is defined as having a high mean and low standard deviation on the test. In our experience, nations also view quality as a measure of the percentage of students in the top category of performance. Equity is defined in terms of the strength of the correlation between students' socio-economic background and performance (i.e. how much of the variance in performance can be attributed to background factors) and the extent of the 'tail' of relatively poor performance (i.e. standard deviation).

The OECD argues that there is no necessary trade-off between quality and equity: that is, systems can be both high quality and highly equitable (e.g. Finland) and indeed this ought to be the goal of national schooling policy. This is potentially one of the strongest policy implications to be drawn from PISA. Often, however, national responses emphasise quality over equity (Wiseman 2013), failing to acknowledge that improving equity, by weakening the impact of socio-economic background on performance, will drive up mean scores and reduce standard deviations of national performance, thus improving quality scores.

The OECD gives overriding emphasis to policy as the major variable contributing to comparative systemic performance on the dimensions of quality and equity on PISA. Analyses of PISA performance tend to ignore the extent of structural inequality in societies and the contribution of history and culture to both quality and equity measures. For example, the success of Finland has been attributed to highly qualified and autonomous teachers, a comprehensive school system, intellectually demanding pedagogies, lack of high-stakes testing and intelligent forms of accountability (Sahlberg 2011). However, it is important to acknowledge the history and cultural specificities of Finland and its schooling system (Simola 2005), as well as the fact that the global neo-liberal discourse of school reform has not penetrated education policy there to the extent it has in other parts of the world. Finland is also a relatively homogeneous society in ethnic terms and a relatively equal society based on the Gini coefficient of inequality. As with NAPLAN, the solutions to low quality and low equity are seen to lie within schooling systems, their policy regimes and within the remit of schools and teacher pedagogies. As Meyer and Schiller (2013, 210) show, the use of PISA data tends toward 'widespread over-attribution of school outcomes to school-internal factors'. Our position here is a 'both–and' one: that is, structural inequality must be addressed at the same time as reforms in systems, schools and teacher classroom pedagogies are pursued.

Like NAPLAN, PISA produces a re-spatialisation of schooling through topological conceptions of what is near and far in policy terms. First, PISA helps to create a global space of educational measurement and comparison: a single topological space of relations. This contributes to globalisation in the form of extending the imaginaries and gaze of policy-makers, both within the OECD and within nations, to a global scale. The OECD's international performance data are thus simultaneously 'lodged' within the national policy space and the global field (Allen and Cochrane 2010). Second, PISA makes distinct education systems appear proximate and equivalent, at least at the level of the imagined relationships and consistencies between them. Similarly to NAPLAN's elision of differences between schools, PISA elides the geographical, cultural, historical, demographic, political and economic specificities of particular nations and assumes a degree of curricula isomorphism. Finland's status as a global 'poster boy' of PISA success (Sahlberg 2011), and the more recent attention to Shanghai based on its top performance in 2009, are both indicative of this decontextualising and the creation of new commensurate spaces of relationality (Sellar and Lingard 2013b).

Despite the definitional issues noted previously, the OECD's education work does comprise fairness and inclusion dimensions. The fairness dimension, defined in terms of the correlation between social background and performance on PISA, constitutes a meritocratic definition of equity in a hierarchical, perhaps very unequal, society, but open to mobility determined by educational performance (conceived in terms of both what systems and schools do in connection with the motivation and potential of individuals). The inclusion dimension, defined in terms of ensuring that students meet basic minimum standards, is similar to the soft entitlement conception of inclusion that informs NAPLAN. Equity becomes constituted as a 'moving ratio' (Lury, Terranova, and Parisi 2012) between performance and individual socio-economic background within a reconstituted topological space bounded by minimum thresholds of performance. This conception and measurement of equity helps to constitute modes of educational governance that employ correlations 'to form a grid of power which operates in many different ways from many different points' (Ball 2013, 124). As with the case of NAPLAN, equity is re-articulated as a relation between socio-economic background and performance, while implicitly denying the potential impact on performance of the broader social–structural inequalities surrounding schools, or indeed the impacts of broader neo-liberal policies on other dimensions of social and economic life, which in turn influence what happens in and around schools.

Conclusion

We have documented discursive changes within Australian education policy and the OECD's education work: namely, a move from concerns for social justice to a neo-social focus on equity in a meritocratic society. Equity has been reconceived as a market-enhancing mechanism linked to macro-economic policies and investments in producing greater quality and quantities of human capital. We have shown how social justice has been reconstituted as equity through technologies of measurement, comparison and governance associated with PISA, NAPLAN and the My School website. Equity has become a measure of the strength of the correlation between student backgrounds and test performance, set within a framework that assumes a hierarchical and meritocratic society. The material practices of equity created through these new technologies are imbricated with the conceptual shifts in debates about social justice and equity in schooling.

Measures of equity embedded in PISA, NAPLAN and My School emphasise the significance of in-school factors (especially teacher effectiveness) and education policy in addressing the inequities that are documented through new data infrastructures; they bracket out considerations of broader structural inequalities that have grown in the context of neo-liberal policy approaches. We share Henig's view that:

Suspicion that attention to non-school factors – concentrated poverty, social services, housing, and public health – will be used to excuse poor teaching has led to an accountability system narrowly focused on what happens within school buildings; in the process, we are missing opportunities to build more comprehensive data bases that situate accountability for learning within broader social and economic contexts. (2013, xi–xii)

It is significant, however, that Henig's proposed solution is 'more comprehensive data bases'; an argument that illustrates how the contemporary 'policy as numbers' phenomenon tends to encourage technical solutions through 'better' numbers.

Furthermore, we have argued that social justice as equity has been redefined in terms of comparative scores on national and global tests. We noted that numbers are inscription devices and that quantifying equity creates new meanings (Porter 1994). We also pointed out the topological aspects of this trend, because the globe and the nation are reconstituted as commensurate ideational spaces or surfaces of measurement and comparison. This has seen the remaking of national and global spaces as relational in terms of the numerical measurement of equity; a new dimension of relationality that exceeds traditional territorial and topographical conceptions of space.

There is also fatalism towards the degree of social inequality in these metricised ideas and practices of equity (Power and Frandji 2010). Just as there has been growing social and economic inequalities within nations, so too has there been growing inequalities between nations (Rizvi and Lingard 2010), but these facts are ignored in representations of equity in NAPLAN and PISA. For example, the fact that Finland has a low Gini coefficient of inequality is most often ignored in OECD and other policy arguments about why Finland has a high-quality/high-equity system of schooling. Moreover, the statistically similar school measures reported on the My School website require that comparative improvements be made at the expense of another school declining in the comparative measure. This is a zero-sum construction. The minimal performance benchmarks on NAPLAN also provide a weak definition of inclusion, as does the national target of 80% meeting these benchmarks.

Large-scale data infrastructures such as NAPLAN and PISA not only rely upon the measurement and production of difference as a means of understanding difference (difference in both senses defined via a limited measure of performance), but also obscure complex social, cultural, economic and historical factors, which differentially position young people in relation to education and achievement in the first place. Equity measures in contemporary education policy are thus highly reductionist, unable to move beyond a comparative narrative about 'who does better or worse' and thus construct the need to improve test scores as the only sound basis for undertaking educational reform. This most often means that schools serving poor communities need to focus more on improving test scores than those with middle-class clientele, which reduces the likelihood of socially just curriculum provision, narrowing opportunities for young people from poor families to access the high-status capitals necessary for educational success. As Berliner (2007) has argued, the 'technical focus' of measures such as PISA and NAPLAN means policy debates are positioned within a very narrow definition of equity.

There is no doubt, however, that PISA and NAPLAN have served to increase political attention to issues of inequity. PISA has exposed inequities in test outcomes both within and between nations, which are often patterned by socio-economic status, migration, geographical location and gender. In countries such as Australia, PISA has helped put equity back on the political agenda. Australia's former Prime Minister Gillard, for example, expressed a desire to see Australia become one of the 'top 5'nations in PISA, focusing on both quality and equity, and used this aim as a basis for trying to introduce large-scale and historically important redistributive funding increases to the public education system. In turn, PISA has helped drive the development of NAPLAN, which, in turn, has exposed inequities in test outcomes within Australia.

The narrow outcomes-based equity focus of PISA and NAPLAN, therefore, has flow-on effects, with the potential to legitimise political arguments for resourcing programmes that are designed to ameliorate educational disadvantage. Governments promote a globally competitive logic and deploy political rhetoric that reflects an economic imaginary of education, yet the 'actual effects' of the reforms being promoted have the potential to stretch far beyond this reductionist position. We might see this as a form of 'externalisation' (Schriewer 1990) whereby economic and equity rationales can be used by governments to legitimise more progressive social policy positions. This reflects the neo-social mode of governance with investments in educational equity having flow-on social benefits and the potential to address wider problems of entrenched disadvantage.

For those wishing to challenge reductive re-articulations of social justice as equity, it is important not to abandon conceptual and philosophical debates about inequality in education, which can be mobilised as intellectual resources in a contemporary politics of education. For example, drawing upon Fraser's (1997, 2009) framework for justice, equity as constituted by the technologies of PISA and NAPLAN clearly denies a politics of recognition – all young people sit for exactly the same test and equity is deemed to be achieved if and when background factors such as ethnicity do not correlate with performance. Cultural background, therefore, is only recognised in so far as it is framed as a potential barrier to achievement on standardised tests. There is also a denial of representation, as the tests are constructed 'elsewhere', away from the everyday realities of schooling, by psychometricians, with scant input from educators or young people. The redistributive politics inherent in them is also very weak and obscures the effects on educational opportunity of broader social and economic inequalities.

Only by attending to the global and national fields in education policy, and the ways they are imbricated in the becoming topological of cultural, economic and political life, will we be able to better understand the emerging conditions of possibility for equity in education and resuscitate those meanings and practices of equity, or rather social justice, that are being extinguished in the neo-social condition. Perhaps this agenda is not so much about resuscitating older conceptions of social and educational justice, but about inventing new ones that can help to address shortcomings in current and future metrics, while also demonstrating the need for conceptual arguments about dimensions of inequality for which measurement is not an appropriate tool.

Note

1. The Council of Australian Governments is an intergovernmental forum, comprised of the Prime Minister, State Premiers, Territory Chief Ministers and the President of the Australian Local Government Association.

References

Australian Curriculum, Assessment and Reporting Authority (ACARA). 2013. *About ICSEA*. Sydney: ACARA. http://www.acara.edu.au/verve/_resources/Fact_Sheet_-_About_ICSEA.pdf.

Allen, J. 2011. "Topological Twists: Power's Shifting Geographies." *Dialogues in Human Geography* 1 (3): 283–298.

Allen, J., and A. Cochrane. 2010. "Assemblages of State Power: Topological Shifts in the Organsiation of Government and Politics." *Antipode* 42 (5): 1071–1089.

Anagnostopoulos, D., S. Rutledge, and R. Jacobsen, eds. 2013. *The Infrastructure of Accountability: Data Use and the Transformation of American Education*. Cambridge, MA: Harvard Education Press.

Anyon, J. 2005. *Radical Possibilities: Public Policy, Education and a New Social Movement*. New York: Routledge.

Appadurai, A. 1996. *Modernity at Large*. Minneapolis, MN: The University of Minnesota Press.

Bailey, P. L. J. 2013. The Policy Dispositif: Historical Formation and Method. *Journal of Education Policy*. doi: http://dx.doi.org/10.1080/02680939.2013.782512.

Ball, S. J. 2012. *Global Education Inc*. London: Routledge.

Ball, S. J. 2013. *Foucault, Power and Education*. New York: Routledge.

Ball, S. J., and C. Junemann. 2012. *Networks, New Governance and Education*. Bristol: The Policy Press.

Berliner, D. 2007. "Our Impoverished View of Educational Reform." In *Sociology of Education: A Critical Reader*, edited by A. Sadovonik, 487–516. New York: Routledge.

Brenner, N. 2004. *New State Spaces: Urban Governance and the Rescaling of Statehood*. Oxford: Oxford University Press.

Collins, C., and L. Yates. 2011. "Confronting Equity, Retention and Student Diversity." In *Australia's Curriculum Dilemmas*, edited by L. Yates, C. Collins and K. O'Connor, 107–126. Carlton: Melbourne University Press.

Commonwealth of Australia. 2008. *Quality Education: The Case for an Education Revolution in Our Schools*. Canberra: Commonwealth of Australia.

Condron, D. 2011. "Egalitarianism and Educational Excellence: Compatible Goals for Affluent Societies?" *Educational Researcher* 40 (2): 47–55.

Council of Australian Governments (COAG). 2008. *National Education Agreement*. Canberra: Council of Australian Governments.

Council of Australian Governments (COAG). 2009. *National Partnership Agreement on Youth Attainment and Transitions*. Canberra: Council of Australian Governments.

Fraser, N. 1997. "Social Justice in the Age of Identity Politics: Redistribution, Recognition, and Participation." In *Redistribution or Recognition? A Political-Philosophical Exchange*, edited by N. Fraser and A. Honneth, 7–109. London: Verso.

Fraser, N. 2009. *Scales of Justice: Reimagining Political Space in a Globalizing World*. New York: Columbia University Press.

Gilbert, R., A. Keddie, B. Lingard, M. Mills, and P. Renshaw. 2011. *Equity and Education Research, Policy and Practice: A Review*. Carlton: Australian College of Educators.

Gillard, J. 2008. *Equity in the Education Revolution. Speech*. April 4, 2008. http://www.deewr.gov.au/Ministers/Gillard/Media/Speeches/Pages/Article_081022_145840.aspx.

Gorur, R. 2013. "My School, My Market." *Discourse: Studies in the Cultural Politics of Education* 34 (2): 214–230.

Harvey, P. 2012. "The Topological Quality of Infrastructural Relation: An Ethnographic Approach." *Theory, Culture & Society* 29 (4/5): 76–92.

Henig, J. R. 2013. "Foreword." In *The Infrastructure of Accountability: Data Use and the Transformation of American Education*, edited by D. Anagnostopoulos, S. Rutledge and R. Jacobsen, vii–xiii. Cambridge, MA: Harvard Education Press.

Keating, J., G. C. Savage, and J. Polesel. 2013. "Letting Schools off the Hook? Exploring the Role of Australian Secondary Schools in the COAG Year 12 Attainment Agenda." *Journal of Education Policy* 28 (2): 268–286.

Keddie, A. 2012. *Educating for Diversity and Social Justice*. London: Routledge.

Levin, B. 2003. *Approaches to Equity in Policy for Lifelong Learning*. Paris: OECD. http://www.oecd.org/education/educationeconomyandsociety/38692676.pdf.

Lingard, B. 2011. "Policy as Numbers: Accounting for Educational Research." *The Australian Educational Researcher* 38 (4): 355–382.

Lingard, B., P. O'Brien, and J. Knight. 1993. "Strengthening Australia's Schools through Corporate Federalism." *Australian Journal of Education* 37 (3): 231–247.

Lipman, P. 2013. *The New Political Economy of Urban Education: Neoliberalism, Race, and the Right to the City*. New York: Routledge.

Lury, C., L. Parisi, and T. Terranova. 2012. "Introduction: The Becoming Topological of Culture." *Theory, Culture and Society* 29 (4–5): 3–35.

Lyotard, J.-F. 1984. *The Postmodern Condition: A Report on Knowledge*. Minneapolis, MN: University of Minnesota Press.

Mayer-Schonberger, V., and K. Cukier. 2013. *Big Data: A Revolution That Will Transform How We Live, Work and Think*. New York: Houghton, Mifflin, Harcourt.

Meyer, H.-D., and A. Benavot, eds. 2013. *PISA, Power, and Policy: The Emergence of Global Educational Governance*. Oxford: Symposium Books.

Meyer, J., D. Kamens, and A. Benavot. 1992. *School Knowledge for the Masses*. Washington, DC: Falmer Press.

Meyer, H.-D., and K. Schiller. 2013. "Gauging the Role of Non-Educational Effects in Large-Scale Assessments: Socio-Economics, Culture and PISA Outcomes." In *PISA, Power, and Policy: The Emergence of Global Educational Governance*, edited by H-D Meyer and A. Benavot, 207–224. Oxford: Symposium Books.

Novoa, A., and T. Yariv-Mashal. 2003. "Comparative Research in Education: A Mode of Governance or Historical Journey?" *Comparative Education* 39 (4): 5–22.

OECD. 2007. *No More Failures: Ten Steps to Equity in Education*. Paris: OECD Publishing.

OECD. 2012a. Equity and Quality in Education: Supporting Disadvantaged Students and Schools. OECD Publishing. http://dx.doi.org/10.1787/9789264130852-en.

OECD. 2012b. What is Equity in Education? In *Education at a Glance 2012: Highlights*, OECD Publishing. http://dx.doi.org/10.1787/eag_highlights-2012-29-en.

Ong, A. 2006. *Neoliberalism as Exception: Mutations in Citizenship and Sovereignty*. Durham: Duke University Press.

Ozga, J. 2009. "Governing Education through Data in England: From Regulation to Self-Evaluation." *Journal of Education Policy* 24 (2): 149–162.

Parliament of Australia. 2008. *Australian Curriculum, Assessment and Reporting Authority Act 2008*. Canberra: Parliament of Australia.

Porter, T. 1994. "Making Things Quantitative." *Science in Context* 7 (3): 389–407.

Power, S., and D. Frandji. 2010. "Education Markets, the New Politics of Recognition and the Increasing Fatalism towards Inequality." *Journal of Education Policy* 25 (3): 385–396.

Ramirez, F. 2012. "The World Society Perspective: Concepts, Assumptions, and Strategies." *Comparative Education* 48 (4): 423–439.

Ravitch, D. 2010. *The Death and Life of the Great American School System: How Testing and Choice Are Undermining Education*. New York: Basic Books.

Rizvi, F., and B. Lingard. 2010. *Globalizing Education Policy*. London: Routledge.

Rose, N. 1999a. "Inventiveness in Politics." *Economy and Society* 28 (3): 467–493.

Rose, N. 1999b. *Powers of Freedom: Reframing Political Thought*. Cambridge: Cambridge University Press.

Rudd, K., and S. Smith. 2007. *The Australian Economy Needs an Education Revolution: New Directions Paper on the Critical Link between Long Term Prosperity, Productivity Growth and Human Capital Investment*. Canberra: Australian Labor Party.

Ruppert, E. 2012. "The Governmental Topologies of Database Devices." *Theory, Culture and Socciety* 29 (4–5): 116–136.

Sahlberg, P. 2011. *Finnish Lessons*. Cambridge, New York: Teachers' College Press.

Sassen, S. 2007. *Sociology of Globalization*. New York: W.W. Norton.

Savage, G. C. 2011. "When Worlds Collide: Excellent and Equitable Learning Communities? Australia's 'Social Capitalist' Paradox?" *Journal of Education Policy* 26 (1): 33–59.

Savage, G. C. 2013. "Tailored Equities in the Education Market: Flexible Policies and Practices." *Discourse: Studies in the Cultural Politics of Education* 34 (2): 185–201.

Savage, G. C., S. Sellar, and R. Gorur. 2013. "Equity and Marketization: Emerging Policies and Practices in Australian Education." *Discourse: Studies in the Cultural Politics of Education* 34 (2): 1–9.

Schriewer, J. 1990. "The Method of Comparison and the Need for Externalization: Methodological Criteria and Sociological Concepts." In *Theories and Methods in Comparative Education*, edited by J. Schriewer and B. Holmes, 25–83. Frankfurt am Main: Peter Lang.

Sellar, S., and B. Lingard. 2013a. "The Expansion of PISA and New Global Modes of OECD Governance in Education." *British Educational Research Journal.* doi:10.1002/berj.3120.

Sellar, S., and B. Lingard. 2013b. "Looking East: Shanghai, PISA 2009 and the Reconstitution of Reference Societies in the Global Policy Field." *Comparative Education.* 49 (4): 464–485.

Simola, H. 2005. "The Finnish Miracle of PISA: Historical and Sociological Remarks on Teaching and Teacher Education." *Comparative Education* 41 (4): 455–470.

Simons, M. (2013). "Governing Education without Reform: The Power of the Example." Paper presented at Critical Analyses of Educational Reforms Conference, University of Stockholm, 17-19 September.

Teese, R., and J. Polesel. 2003. *Undemocratic Schooling: Equity and Quality in Mass Secondary Education in Australia*. Melbourne: Melbourne University Press.

Wilkinson, R., and K. Pickett. 2009. *The Spirit Level: Why More Equal Societies Almost Always Do Better*. London: Allen Lane.

Wiseman, A. 2013. Policy Responses to PISA in Comparative Perspective. In *PISA, Power, and Policy: The Emergence of Global Educational Governance* edited by H.-D. Meyer and A. Benavot, 303–322. Oxford: Symposium Books.

World Bank. 2005. *World Development Report 2006: Equity and Development*. Washington: The World Bank.

Beyond the education silo? Tackling adolescent secondary education in rural India

Orla Kelly and Jacqueline Bhabha

Harvard School of Public Health, FXB Center for Health and Human Rights, Boston, MA, USA

In this paper we examine the factors contributing to gender inequality in secondary schooling in India by critically reviewing the government's secondary education policy. Drawing on the findings of a study in rural Gujarat, we couple this analysis with an examination of the gendered dynamics that restrict girls' ability to fully benefit from the education infrastructure and initiatives that do exist, using Connell's Gender and Power framework. We propose that an extension of the government's current approach to educational reform, focused primarily on expanding infrastructure may aggravate the gender, class and caste asymmetries at secondary level. Fostering an environment that enables vulnerable adolescent girls to benefit from enhanced educational provisions is essential to realizing their rights and the achievement of an equitable system.

Introduction

> Boys cannot work like girls, for example if our daughter is out of the village for some reason then we call our neighbour's daughter for household work. (Mother, age 38, Village E)

Evidence establishing the significant impact of education on social and economic progress has fuelled global efforts to increase equitable educational access as exemplified in the Education for All (EFA 1990) movement and the United Nations Millennium Development Goals (2000) strategy.[1] These initiatives have resulted in significantly improved educational enrolment rates for both boys and girls, particularly at primary level. While overall access to education has increased, targeted programming within and beyond educational institutions is needed to ensure greater equity across gender (and other) divides, particularly at the secondary level. Data from UNESCO (2012) illustrate the extent of this challenge. A majority (56%) of the world's children live in countries that have achieved gender parity at the primary level, but the proportion drops significantly (29%) at the lower secondary level, and even further (to just 15%) at the upper secondary level. India's secondary education system exemplifies this trend. The country has reportedly achieved near-universal enrolment at the primary level through massive infrastructural development, teacher training and community mobilization. These changes were mandated under the 2009 Right of Children to Free and Compulsory Education Act (SSA), the government's flagship programme for achievement of universalization of elementary education. Retention at the upper primary level and ensuring universal transition to the secondary are among the next big challenges. Other major challenges beyond the scope of this paper include improving education quality and learning outcomes.

According to UNESCO (2011), Indian gross enrolment rates in secondary education now lie at 71% and 66% for males and females respectively, a marked increase compared with enrolment rates 20 years earlier of 51% and 36%. Nonetheless, these figures lie well below those of countries with which India is regularly compared economically.

In March 2009 the Government of India (GOI - the central government of India through which education policy is made) launched *Rashtriya Madhyamik Shiksha Abhiyan* (RMSA), a scheme to overhaul its secondary education system over the next decade. The target of this initiative is universal retention by 2020. While the aims are laudable, to date implementa-

Table 1. Net attendance ratio by class group for all of India.

Grade	Rural female (%)	Rural male (%)	Urban female (%)	Urban male (%)	India female (%)	India male (%)
I–V	83	86	84	86	83	86
VI–VIII	54	59	64	67	56	61
IX–X	35	40	51	52	39	43
XI–XII	19	25	39	39	25	29
Post-High School (formal education)	5	8	14	13	7	9
Post-High School (any type of education)	6	10	21	20	10	13

Note: This is the ratio of the number of persons attending a particular class group (i.e. VI–VIII, IX–X and XI–XII) to the total number of persons in the corresponding age group (i.e. 11–13, 14–15 and 16–17 respectively).
Source: GOI. 2010. "Education in India: 2007–08 – Participation and Expenditure," 64th Round (July 2007–June 2008), Ministry of Statistics and Programme Implementation, GOI, New Delhi.

tion has been sluggish and millions of poor rural children, particularly girls, continue to be pushed out of the school system. As illustrated in Table 1, the discrepancies in attendance rates begin at the upper primary school level (Classes VI–VIII) and become more pronounced as children advance in age.

This stark difference between urban and rural secondary school participation rates is particularly concerning because more than two-thirds (69%) of India's population reside in rural areas (Census 2011). Rural location is a proxy for many contributing socio-economic factors such as low parental literacy rates[2] and economic disadvantage.[3] Further, compared with urban populations, adolescents in rural areas are more likely to have to travel longer distances to school and those schools are likely to be less well equipped (World Bank 2009). As evidenced by the national enrolment statistics in Table 1 and smaller-scale in-depth studies on participation (Siddhu 2011), these economic challenges and infrastructural shortcomings impact girls most severely. In recent years, significant attention has been paid to achieving gender parity in schooling in the name of equity and broader social benefits (Lewis and Lockheed 2006).

In recent decades, significant attention has been paid to addressing gender equality in schooling from a variety of perspectives. Many focused on enumerating enrollment rates highlighting the societal benefits of girls' educational inclusion (World Bank 1995). Others, influenced by the Gender and Development theorists such as Kabeer (1994), focused on the broader societal environment in which girls' educational participation is situated (Leach et al. 2003). More recently, many contemporary gender, education and development experts (Unterhalter and Aikman 2005) have drawn on the work of Sen (1990) and Nussbaum (2004) situating girls' educational participation in the broader capabilities approach. They stress the need to explore both educational provisions and the socio-cultural opportunity structure that can enable or hinder girls' and women's participation. While Connell's framework relates closely to the Gender and Development approach, in this paper we take an interdisciplinary perspective drawing on a combination of insights, theories and perspectives to examine educational inequalities in India today. We aim to probe the factors contributing to gender inequality in secondary schooling by critically reviewing the government's secondary education policy. We couple this analysis with an examination of entrenched gendered, social and cultural norms that restrict girls' ability to fully benefit from the education infrastructure and initiatives that do exist. To illustrate the household and community-level obstacles that inhibit girls' educational progression, we present the findings of a mixed-method study in rural Gujarat. We present our findings using Connell's (1987) Gender and Power framework. We argue that current education policies, restricted as they are to the education silo, cannot reverse entrenched social constraints on reaching the most vulnerable. For education initiatives to succeed, energetic legal, political and social enforcement of prohibitions on child marriage and

sexual harassment are essential. Improvements in secondary school enrolment and performance by adolescent girls are intrinsically linked with
improvements in gender equity in the material and cultural environment surrounding education – family, community, public institutions.

In the next section we provide an overview of current secondary education policy, with a particular focus on the northwest Indian state of Gujarat
where our study was conducted. We outline our study methodology and theoretical framework. Our findings illustrate the contextual and socially
embedded nature of gender inequalities and their impact on a key potential
tool for empowerment, the completion of secondary education. We conclude
with suggested policy interventions to enhance the prospect of a more equitable education system and of female empowerment more generally.

Indian secondary education policy

In the decades since Independence, India has raised education attainment
levels, particularly at the primary level. The current five-year plan, India's
12th, addresses deficits in the quality and supply of secondary education as
a central policy concern. The plan notes the persistence of 'an insufficient
number of public schools, […] poor quality of education offered, and […]
high cost of private senior secondary education' (GOI 2012a, 69).

As was mentioned in the Introduction, the current scheme for universalizing secondary education is the RMSA. The government of India launched
the RMSA in 2009 with the ambitious goal of universalizing access by
2017 and retention by 2020. The RMSA has three overarching goals:
Access, Equity, and Quality. The main priorities of this scheme address
supply-side interventions, namely:

(1) upgrading upper primary schools to secondary schools;
(2) strengthening existing secondary schools;
(3) providing additional classrooms, science laboratories, libraries, com-
    puter rooms, art, craft and culture rooms, toilet blocks and water
    facilities in schools;
(4) providing in-service training for teachers;
(5) providing for major repairs of school buildings and residential quar-
    ters for teachers. (GOI 2012a, Section 21.97, 70)

Part of the planned infrastructural improvement includes construction of
hostels with the capacity to house 100 girls in each of 3479 administrative
blocks deemed 'educationally backward' (defined as having a female literacy rate below the national average) across the country. Girls enrolled in
Classes IX–XII and belonging to low-caste minority communities and families subsisting below the poverty line would be eligible to stay free in hostels.[4] However, according to the Ministry of Human Resource Development

website, construction is still in the early stages and large portions of central government funds have yet to be released pending receipt of revised proposals and spending reports from individual state governments[5]. Administrative delays and under-utilization of funds have been a serious obstacle to progress over the last decade of educational infrastructural development.[6] For example, during the 11th five-year plan, only 32.26% of the outlay for public expenditure directed towards secondary education was actually spent (GOI 2012a, 70). This significant shortfall in spending demonstrates the implementation and absorption challenges facing education reform at the local level. Also, thus far the RMSA only covers public lower secondary schools. Public higher secondary schools (Classes 10–12) and all private secondary schools remain excluded.

In addition to these infrastructural projects, the government also plans to continue its relatively smaller-scale investment in scholarships. To date, there have been two centrally sponsored[7] scholarship schemes, the Incentives to Girls for Secondary Education Scheme and the National Means-cum-Merit Scholarship Scheme. The Incentives to Girls for Secondary Education Scheme provides a one-time Rs 3000 ($60) deposit in a bank account in the name of the female student when she completes upper primary (eighth class) and begins secondary school (ninth class). This deposit can be used once the student completes her lower secondary school examination, two years later. Those eligible to enrol in the scheme are Scheduled Caste or Scheduled Tribe students and those who graduate from special girls-only residential schools provided for students from minority communities and families living below the poverty line. To be successful, such schemes need to provide a financial incentive that encourages families to forgo the economic benefit of adolescent contribution to household income though paid or in-kind labour. This represents a major challenge. Whereas the Girls' Incentive scheme provides Rs 3000 ($60) per year for the two years of lower secondary education, the average daily wage of an unskilled labourer in Gujarat (where the research described below took place) is at least Rs 120 ($2) a day. An adolescent girl can therefore earn Rs 3000 ($60) in 30 days.[8] The financial incentive is therefore too low to offset the opportunity cost of further education.

The other main centrally sponsored initiative is the National Means-cum-Merit Scholarship Scheme. This awards 100,000 scholarships of Rs 6000 ($120) per annum to meritorious students from economically weaker sections of the community. The amount awarded is more substantial than the Incentives to Girls for Secondary Education Scheme. However, vulnerable adolescent school girls have many competing obligations that militate again a concerted focus on their academic work. These pressures combine with the current infrastructural inadequacies of secondary schools to severely limit the chances that marginalized rural adolescent girls would achieve the academic results needed to benefit from this merit-based scholarship scheme. This is evidenced by the fact that only 37% of available scholarships were awarded in 2011/12 (as reported by *The Hindu*, 3 September 2012),[9] despite the millions of families who struggle to cover their children's secondary education.

In the next section we outline the results from our mixed methods study in rural Gujarat, using Connell's Gender and Power framework. The findings illustrate the multi-faceted challenges that many rural girls face in their pursuit of a second level education.

Methodology

Our data are drawn from a multi-year action research education project. The project was a partnership between the Self Employed Women's Association, an Indian national women's trade union with 1.2 million members, and the François Xavier Bagnoud Center for Health and Human Rights at Harvard University. The project was conducted in two phases, a pre-intervention needs assessment followed by an experimental intervention. The needs assessment employed a sequential explanatory design (Creswell 2003) to explore the nature of barriers to educational progression experienced by adolescents in five research villages, situated in rural northwest Gujarat. Primarily agrarian, the villages range in population from 1000 to 2500. The villages were selected using a non-random purposive sample based on socio-economic similarity and a high rate of Self Employed Women's Association membership. Employing a convenience sampling method somewhat limits the generalizability of study findings. However, while the villages were not selected randomly, local experts assured us that the villages were typical of other villages in the block.

The research included a structured survey followed by 15 focus groups of three types: female adolescents in school, female adolescents out of school and the mothers of adolescents. The data collection took place across five villages over a six-month period from July 2010 to January 2011. The results from the first quantitative phase informed the qualitative data collection protocols, allowing for a more in-depth investigation.

Quantitative phase

A total of 752 individuals were randomly selected for interview using a stratified sampling approach. The demographic breakdown of the sample was as follows: 94 males aged 10–13, 94 females aged 10–13, 94 males aged 14–17 and 94 females aged 14–17 ($n = 376$) and 376 female caregivers. Using census data provided by the village administration, lists of households with one or more adolescents were categorized on the basis of adolescent age and gender. Households were randomly selected for participation until the participant quota for each village was met. Survey sample sizes were weighted proportionally to population per village and ranged from 72 to 152. The survey tool was developed by the research team, locally pre-tested and refined through a series of pilots. The tool was divided into two parts. The first part, based on the national sample survey household profile section, was administered to female caregivers. It was designed to gather a personal, economic and educational profile on all members of the household. Data were collected on a total of 2102 individuals. A 10-variable section was developed by the research team to assess caregiver perceptions of school quality, motivations for sending children to school and aspirations for children's futures. The second part was administered to adolescents. This section contained a time log that captured participants' typical daily activities in two-hour blocks across the day, from 6:00 a.m. to 11:00 p.m. In addition, a 10-variable section assessed adolescent perceptions of school quality, their regularity of attendance and their aspirations for the future. The reliability of the survey scale items was established based on both pilot and main survey administration.

Preliminary quantitative findings were presented to the community for comment six months after the initial data collection. The community discussion of the first round of data collection, organized by local Self Employed Women's Association leaders, acted as a recruitment site for the qualitative data collection phase.

Qualitative phase

The qualitative phase of the research included 15 focus groups, three per village. In each village, focus group discussions were held with: girls aged 10–17 enrolled in school; girls aged 10–17 not enrolled in school; and their adult caregivers, 80% of whom were female. Criteria for inclusion in the focus group for adults were a minimum of two years residence in the village and having an adolescent aged 10–17 in one's household. Criteria for inclusion in the focus group for adolescents included age (10–17), gender (girls only) and a minimum of two years' residence in the village. Due to the convenience sampling strategy, the size of the focus groups varied between four and seven persons per village. Trained researchers facilitated group discussions based on five to 10 open-ended questions grounded in the findings of the quantitative research. The discussions centred on participants' attitudes to education, parental and personal aspirations, and barriers to girls' education. They also included perceptions of school infrastructural quality and teacher expertise, and opinions about how to improve attendance in and quality of schools. Focus group discussions were audiotaped and transcribed verbatim. We conducted a thematic analysis of the text data using QSR Nvivo 9 qualitative software for data storage, coding, and theme development. Integrating the quantitative and qualitative data at the intermediate stage, through the focus groups and community feedback, helped the research team to understand the scope of issues and the contours of the quantitative data (Creswell 2003).

Theoretical framework

The findings are presented using Connell's (1987) Gender and Power framework. Connell provides a lens to examine the interplay of 'structure and agency' in the formation of gendered social practices. According to Connell, structure is the constraint on social practice (or agency) produced by a given form of social organization such as family, workplace, community. Connell takes a holistic view of structures. She maintains that structures experienced by women are manifestations of a complex set of economic, cultural, religious and other societal factors that intersect with pre-existing characteristics such as race and class. These factors always include the structures of labour, power and cathexis. 'Labour' includes the segregation of labour markets and the creation of 'men's jobs' and 'women's' jobs (Connell 1987, 96). For Indian rural adolescents, the division of labour within the household is most relevant. 'Power' includes the structures of authority, control and coercion that govern gender roles (1987, 96). Finally, 'cathexis' covers the gendered character of sexual desire within intimate relationships, including marriage (1987, 111). In this model, gender dynamics emerge from the interaction between these structures. A 'structural inventory' specifies the configuration of these three factors. According to Connell, women's experiences are constrained and shaped by the structure of gender relations. The relevant structural inventory, be it a specific institution like the home, workplace, school or street, is its 'gender regime'. In this paper we investigate the gender regime of the primary units of socialization for rural adolescent girls in India: the family home and the local community.

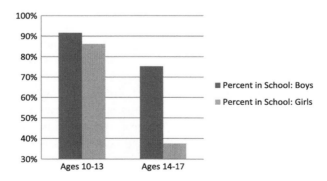

Figure 1.   Self-report enrolment of adolescents by gender and age.

Table 2. Local government school enrolment data.

	Standard	Boys	Girls
Village 1	IX	22	6
	X	20	5
Village 2	IX	24	4
	X	20	1

Findings

In all five villages surveyed the effects of the SSA (primary school education for all) movement were striking: 91% of boys and 86% of girls aged 10–13 self-report attending school. While lower than the national averages, these attendance rates signify a dramatic intergenerational change, as 75% of the mothers and 46% of the fathers in the villages surveyed had never attended school. The data show a dramatic decrease in school attendance as children, particularly girls, progress through adolescence. Only 75% of boys and 38% of girls between 14 and 17 years of age self-report attending school on a regular day (see Figure 1). Of the survey population, 75% would be classified as 'Other Backward Caste', 15% as Scheduled Caste/ Tribe, 8% as Muslims and 2% as other. These mixed-community, agricultural villages with low levels of parental education exemplify the communities that need attention if the advances of the SSA are going to generate an equitable system of education at the secondary level.

The extremely low female attendance figures amongst older adolescents across the five villages are consistent with official enrolment data (Table 2) from the two local lower government secondary schools. In both schools, the enrolment ratio for boys outnumbers girls by more than five to one.

In our survey, gender is a consistently significant predictor of enrolment. When the effects of factors such as age, village and migration are controlled for, boys are 1.4 times more likely to be in school than girls (95% confidence interval = 0.971, 1.836). Using Connell's (1987) Gender and Power framework, we examine some of the underlying social causes of the gender divide in educational participation. We take an inventory of the labour, power and cathexis structures in adolescent girls' households and local communities. The deconstruction of the gender regime allows us to move beyond the 'education silo' and to conceptualize how the gendered power dynamics affect adolescent girls' educational participation as they transition from childhood to womanhood.

Labour

In India, as in many other patriarchal societies, there are firmly established gender roles, according to which girls do household chores and are tasked with care of younger siblings (Sundaram and Vanneman 2008; Kis-Katos 2012). This form of child labour is generally overlooked and considered a normal or natural aspect of a female child's role within the household. Evidence from our study and others in Pakistan (Hazarika and Bedi 2003), Peru (Levison and Karine 1998) and Egypt (Assaad, Levison, and Zibanib 2010) confirms the deleterious effect of domestic burden on educational attainment. To capture the extent to which this was true for this community, the survey contained a log of daily activities: adolescents were asked to report the activities undertaken in two-hour blocks, between 6:00 a.m. and 11:00 p.m. on a regular weekday. This time-use component revealed that only 33% of girls aged 14 and over reported being in school on an average day during the mandated school hours of 11:00 a.m. and 5:00 p.m. (regular school hours). Interestingly, the self-report rate of school enrolment for the same population was 38%, a notable discrepancy in enrolment and attendance. Boys evidenced a much smaller discrepancy between indirect reporting of attendance: 75% of boys reported being enrolled in school, as opposed to 73% reporting attendance through the time-use log. In the morning hours between 9:00 and 11:00 a.m., 57% of girls as opposed to 28% of boys are doing household work. Conversely, during the same period 44% of boys and but only 16% of girls are doing homework. As Table 3 illustrates, many adolescent girls spend their mornings and evenings engaged in household work. The same trend can be seen in the evening hours: 38% of girls are doing chores and 20% are doing homework, as opposed to 11% and 48% respectively for boys.

Similar (although less marked) trends were observed among younger adolescents (ages 10–13). The younger adolescent girls reported higher rates of school enrolment than actual attendance: 87% of girls reported being enrolled in school but only 77% reported attending on a given day. Adolescents aged 10–13, most of whom are in school, have a more equitable distribution of chores by gender. As illustrated in Table 4, 69% of girls are doing housework in the evening hours of 7:00–9:00 p.m. Sixty-two per cent of boys also report contributing to household work during these hours. When compared with Table 3, we see a marked increase in the hours spent by adolescent girls on household work as they progress in age, to the detriment of their education.

The questionnaire asked participants about their perceptions of the primary cause of school drop-out amongst adolescents in the village. Confirming data set out in the tables above, both caretakers and adolescents cited the obligation to perform household chores as the most common reason for school drop-out.

The focus group data also illustrate the lasting and far-reaching impact of these onerous gender-specific responsibilities, as in the quotation at the beginning of the paper:

Table 3. Adolescents' activities during school hours by gender: ages 14–17.

Time /activity	Sleep or rest (%)		Household work (%)		Work (to support family) (%)		School (%)		Craft (%)		Homework (%)		Other (%)	
	Girls	Boys	Girls	Boys	Girls	Boys	Girls	Boys	Girls	Boys	Girls	Boys	Girls	Boys
Morning hours														
9:00–11:00 am	0	3	**57**	28	7	12	3	5	5	0	16	44	12	8
School hours														
11:00 am–1:00 pm	5	1	46	9	9	11	33	73	3	0	0	2	1	4
1:00–3:00 pm	29	6	17	10	7	5	33	72	11	0	0	2	1	3
3:00–5:00 pm	25	7	16	4	11	7	33	73	10	0	1	2	2	6
Evening hours														
5:00–7:00 pm	6	3	38	11	7	11	7	10	10	0	20	48	10	17
7:00–9:00 pm	3	5	80	59	2	1	1	2	2	0	3	12	9	11

Table 4. Adolescents' activities during school hours by gender: ages 10–13.

	Sleep or rest		Household work		Work (to support family)		School		Craft		Homework		Other	
	Girls	Boys	Girls	Boys	Girls	Boys	Girls	Boys	Girls	Boys	Girls	Boys	Girls	Boys
Morning hours														
9:00–11:00 am	0	1	41	27	1	5	7	10	2	0	34	39	15	18
School hours														
11:00 am–1:00 pm	1	1	14	2	0	4	78	90	2	0	3	0	2	3
1:00–3:00 pm	8	2	2	3	2	2	77	88	4	1	3	3	4	1
3:00–5:00 pm	6	2	2	1	4	3	77	87	4	1	3	3	4	3
Evening hours														
5:00–7:00 pm	4	4	29	5	1	1	2	1	0.0	0	50	68	14	21
7:00–9:00 pm	2	3	69	62	0	0	0	0	1	0	14	18	14	17

> Boys cannot work like girls, for example if our daughter is out of the village for some reason then we call our neighbour's daughter for household work. (Mother, Village E)

Clearly labour structures constrain girls' ability to engage in education. In an analysis of the implications of Connell's theory, Maharaj elucidates the long-term implications of these gendered labour structures:

> The gendered division of labour … forecloses a whole range of job options to women: it limits or constrains her economic and other social practices in significant ways. (1995, 52)

In terms of adolescent girls' educational attainment, the time-use data above clearly illustrate the shift in the labour structure that occurs for girls during these crucial pubescent years. While enrolment is high at the upper primary level, participation begins to slip. As girls make the critical transition to secondary school, enrolment drops dramatically. Meanwhile, domestic pressures within the home mount.

Power

The concept of power in Connell's framework includes gendered structures of authority, coercion and control. In our data, adolescent girls' unquestioning submission to parental will and their strong sense of obligation to families emerge as manifestations of the constraining nature of the structure of power. In the interviews, the girls emphasized their sense of obligation and responsibility to the family. This dominant preoccupation seems to supersede any personal ambitions, so that in many cases girls did not even consider completing higher education or embarking on a career:

> Out of duty to her family and family members, girls are leaving school early. It is much easier for parents if there is a girl to do household work and the other reason [for leaving school] is her marriage. (Girl not in school, Village E)

> I had an older sister that had to leave school because my parents were tired and she had to help them. It is her obligation to stay at home to help. (Girl in school, Village C)

> Once a girl reaches a certain age then she must care for her siblings and do her embroidery and go to the fields. It is a girl's responsibility to her parents. (Girl out of school, Village B)

In line with this obedience to parents, girls unquestioningly accept that their parents make all decisions about their life. These decisions range from allocation of daily chores, to marriage, education, mobility and career:

But decisions on education are not made by the society or community, what the parents want is final. (Village B Girl out of school, Village C)

I will be whatever my parents decide I should be, if it is a doctor then I will be a doctor, if they wish for me to stay at home then I will stay at home and that is fine too. (Girl in school, Village C)

Tensions between parents' support in principle for girls' education and their insistence in actuality that girls perform household duties (and thus conform to the structure of labour) resonated throughout the interviews. This tension between notional parental support for their daughters' education and the opportunity costs of freeing up girls from work at home created a precarious balance with a direct impact on the quality of girls' school performance:

[When I was still in school] I always did my homework but I always finished it late at night because after school I had to do household chores too. (Girl not in school, Village E)

The interplay of these restrictive labour and power structures limits young women's voices in deciding their priorities and undermines their potential for educational participation.

Cathexis

Cathexis relates to the socially constructed nature of sexuality and relationships that reflect the dominant interests. According to Maharaj:

'Cathexis' in Connell's terms refers to the structure that constrains and so shapes people's emotional attachments to each other. It refers both to the hegemonic 'limits' placed on practices that constitute emotionally charged social relationships in which the bodily dimension features and to the social practices which challenge such hegemony. (1995, 61)

In the villages surveyed, mixed gendered relationships were referred to only in the context of marriage. Friendships, relationships or even contact between adolescent males and females were outside the bounds of acceptable behaviour. This form of gender segregation is particularly common in rural communities where the male-dominated cultural context affords little contact between the sexes (Verma and Mahendra 2004). In the exchanges relating to marriage, girls spoke of it as a looming destiny over which they had little or no control. In the survey, early marriage emerged as the second most commonly cited factor after performance of household chores for female school drop-out. The impact of the structure of cathexis on girls' educational attainment also emerged in the focus group data:

Girls leave the school at an early stage because when they are to be married, we often refuse to educate them. However if their in-laws want to educate them then we don't say no. (Mother, Village D)

Another reason for female school dropout is the girl's marriage. Once she is married then she becomes totally busy with household work and cannot even think of education. (Girl out of school, Village C)

These quotes illustrate the extent to which the structures of labour, power and cathexis intertwine to limit a girl's agency and educational participation. Adolescent girls are powerless to challenge the authority of their parents and in-laws. The labour and power restrictions in the family home prepare girls for life as an obedient, domesticated wife.

This fear and distrust of sexual relationships with men (whether forced or consensual) emerged as a substantial barrier to continued education. When mothers were asked how they would feel about their daughter leaving the village for secondary school, they responded:

When our daughter goes to school or goes to do any other work, we are afraid very much because the time is not good. (Mother, Village C)

My mother said that she would worry that I would have to walk alone for long distances because school is 25 to 30 kilometers away and the bus is irregular. (Girl not in school, Village D)

Clearly, parents associated continued education with an increased risk of sexual violence. In many exchanges, men were portrayed as menacing forces from which young women were to be protected. Out-of-school adolescents in Village E were asked why girls are not allowed to go beyond the village for school. After a long silence, suggesting that this prohibition had never been challenged, the girls explained:

In the past about five girls were gone to Radhanpur [the local town] to study but all five ran away with boys, so parents are afraid to send girls now. They believe if their girls run away with boys they lose their prestige in the society. (Girl in school, Village E)

They think that once we leave the village we will have affairs with boys and marry them, so they won't send us beyond the village to study. (Girl in school, Village E)

Increasing investment to raise the number of schools in these areas should have positive impact on educational participation as girls will not have to travel so far outside the village. However, beyond access there are other factors at play. According to parents, continued education increased the risk that girls would challenge the constraints of the prevailing social order and start romantic relationships with adolescent boys. Within this conservative rural community, a love marriage would result in great shame for both the girl and her family. The structure of cathexis radically restricted girls' movement and participation in public life, affecting their engagement in education.

The data from the our research project demonstrate how underlying power structures of labour, power and cathexis impact education for rural adolescent girls. Improvements in educational provision will only be of benefit to marginalized girls in communities such as these if they are integrated with other structural changes.

Discussion

Indian government secondary education policy is primarily aimed at achieving universal enrolment by increasing and upgrading school facilities and expanding stipend programmes. But will this be enough to bring marginalized rural girls into the fold of secondary education, given the underlying power constraints that many rural girls are negotiating at home?

An interesting attempt to move beyond the education silo and take on the structures of labour, power and cathexis that inhibit adolescent girls' advancement, is the girls-only residential school movement. This movement began in the non-governmental organization sector and has since been adopted by government. As previously discussed, part of the central government's plans to increase enrolment is the construction of 3479 hostels for rural girls from poor communities. This approach does hold promise for increasing access for the most marginalized as it removes them from the confining gender structures within the home. According to the Ministry of Human Resource Development,[10] the aim of girls' hostels is to ensure girls are not deterred by distance to schools, parents' financial conditions and 'other societal factors'. The programme is an extension of the *Kasturba Gandhi Balika Vidyalayas* scheme,[11] which is a residential school model at the primary level. A 2008 national review (GOI 2008) of the *Kasturba Gandhi Balika Vidyalayas* scheme found that, despite implementation challenges, the scheme has effectively raised enrolment and retention rates in selected educationally backward blocks of the country. It was:

> well received by parents and the community and has the potential to respond to the educational needs of out-of-school girls in the 11+age. In particular, it is of immense value in areas where girls drop out after primary schools because of distance or of terrain. (GOI 2008, 3)

Evaluations of the impact of hostel schemes on rural girls' education at the secondary level are still in the early stages. Of course such a radical course of action presents significant implementation challenges. As yet, many large questions remain unanswered. One clear concern is whether scaling a scheme of this nature would be economically and operationally viable considering India is home to over 100 million adolescent girls. The social and political challenges involved in persuading families to send their girls away without fear of reputational impact are also significant. A longitudinal study to assess how these girls reintegrate into their communities once they have finished their education would also be an important element of evaluation.

Conditional cash transfers for girls' school attendance found to be effective in other contexts (Barrera-Osorio et al. 2008; Kane 2004) are another method of disrupting the gender inequitable *status quo*. But just as scholarship schemes, discussed earlier, have proved difficult to implement effectively in rural India, so stipends also have had a low take-up rate, indicating serious problems in implementation. An evaluation of a government initiative 'to raise the status of the girl child' in Gujarat, carried out by the Planning Commission, the International Institute for Population Sciences and the United Nations Population Fund, highlighted some of the many challenges. They include considerable delays on the part of the banks charged with disbursing the grants, non-cooperation between implementing agencies, demands from above poverty line families for similar funds, and overburdened local government service providers (Sekher 2010). The report recommended simplification of schemes by cutting down on the number of conditionalities and registration procedures. Perhaps similar measures could be taken with regards to education initiatives, particularly given the low education levels of many parents in poor rural communities.

While it is impossible for governments to intervene directly in the underlying power structures in adolescent girls' homes, the lack of enforcement of laws to protect against the ubiquitous practicandre of child marriage amounts to tacit complicity with the inequitable cathexis construction. Nearly one-half (47%) of young women in India marry before the legal age of 18, and this figure rises to 53% in rural areas (UNFPA 2012). By the age of 20, 63% of Indian women are married (Moore et al. 2009). Current legal provisions compound the problem as child marriages are voidable only when children or guardians seek annulment of the marriage. Burdensome and impractical reporting provisions undermine the Prevention of Child Marriage Act's intended purpose. As a result, according to a government report (GOI 2012b) only 113 cases of child marriage were reported under the Act in 2012. This figure is disturbingly low since UNICEF (2011) reports that nearly one-half (43%) of women aged 20–24 are married before the age of 18. Early marriage stands in direct opposition to continued education. As noted by Aikman and Unterhalter (2007), equality entails the removal of deeply embedded obstacles and structures of power and exclusion, such as discriminatory laws, customs, practices, and institutional processes, all of which undermine opportunities and outcomes in education.

Other smaller-scale research and intervention initiatives have examined the effects targeting different elements of the labour, power and cathexis structures that girls are negotiating. Illustrating the effect of targeting the structure of labour outside the home, Jensen (2010) found that securing white-collar jobs (e.g. in call centres) for female secondary school graduates positively impacted female schools attendance at all levels. Similarly, Beaman et al. (2012) found that rigorous enforcement of a government quota system that reserved places for women in local government jobs also increased educational attainment amongst girls.

Other initiatives have effectively targeted the threatening aspects of cathexis structures in the public sphere by initiating safe transport schemes and harsh punishment for those who sexually harass girls on their journey to school (Bennell, Hyde, and Swainson 2002).

Bajaj (2011) found that curricular innovation addressing gender roles, human rights principles and non-discrimination norms seeded changes in attitudes, gender stereotypes and role expectations that have transformative potential for addressing adolescent girls' domestic burden.

Other initiatives include long-term mentorship and psycho-social support (Save the Children 2009), and teacher incentives (Muralidharan and Sundararaman 2011). UNESCO (2005) found that community mobilization initiatives by government that complement the work of non-profit organizations positively affected educational participation and the quality of that education. Given the extent to which the life course of adolescents is determined by parental will and community norms, education initiatives that target community norms and structures as a whole beyond the education silo are a critical policy development area.

Conclusion

In this article we have explored the nuanced causes of the low rates of educational attainment of rural adolescent girls by critically evaluating current government secondary education policy and deconstructing the underlying power dynamics that young women face in their homes. Our findings suggest an urgent need for a more radical approach to girls' educational opportunity if the most marginalized are to be reached. At present, initiatives are hampered by implementation challenges and a narrow sectoral approach that neglects the multiple dimensions relevant to progress. Using Connell's Gender and Power framework as a lens we have explored the constrained gender regimes to which rural adolescent girls are subject. Girls are expected to conform to strict notions of femininity that involve sole responsibility for an extensive roster of household chores, unquestioning acquiescence to parental will and repressed sexuality in preparation for similar roles as dutiful wife in the marital home. These structures heavily restrict their educational prospects, their control over personal decision-making and their overall life trajectories. Essential policies aimed at promoting educational opportunity by positively affecting social structure such as banning child marriage remain weakly enforced, despite their particular significance for secondary school enrolment and gender equality in educational access.

Consistent with other recent scholarship, such as the comprehensive report on education research by the Brookings Institute (2010), we strongly propose a more innovative and holistic approach to education at every level. In the absence of significant changes to the social structures to which adolescent girls are subject, government schemes to strengthen girls' educational access to secondary education will not yield decisive results. The RMSA alone and other education schemes contained within an education silo cannot, despite their positive goals, unleash the full potential of India's rural adolescent girls.

Funding

Funding support was provided by the FXB Center for Health and Human Rights, HSBC Bank, the Self Employed Women's Association and the Sir Ratan Tata Trust. Data collected as part of an action research collaboration with the Self Employed Women's Association.

Notes

1. Millennium Development Goal 2: achieve universal primary education, with the target of ensuring that all boys and girls complete a full course of primary schooling by 2015. Millennium Development Goal 3: promote gender equality and empower women, with the target of eliminating gender disparities in primary and secondary education by 2005, and in all levels of education by 2015. The Millennium Development Goals complement other international declarations on gender equality in education, formulated but not yet realized: the 1995 Beijing Platform for Action for gender equality and the 2000 Dakar Education For All Framework of Action.
2. In rural areas, male and female literacy rates lie at 79% and 59% respectively, compared with 90% and 80% for urban dwellers (Census 2011).
3. In 2012 average rural monthly per-capita expenditure was Rs 1281.45 ($25), as opposed to Rs 2401.68 ($46) in urban India (68th National Sample Statistics Office 2012).
4. Girls belonging to Scheduled Caste, Scheduled Tribe, Other Backward Caste minority communities and below poverty line families studying in Classes IX–XII in a recognized school (run by any authority, State, District or non-governmental organization) in deemed Educationally Backward Blocks (EBBs) with a valid certificate from a school headmaster are eligible to stay in the hostels. At least 50% of the girls admitted to the hostels should belong to Scheduled Caste, Scheduled Tribe, Other Backward Caste, and minority communities.
5. See http://mhrd.gov.in/sites/upload_files/mhrd/files/Updation_of_website_on_31.12.2013.pdf (accessed 27 January 2014)
6. During the 11th five-year plan period, public expenditure directed towards secondary education was increased as a percentage of gross domestic product from 0.78% in 2007/08 to 1.05% in 2011/12. About one-half of the central

government's expenditure was incurred for higher education, and the remainder for elementary (39%) and secondary (12%) education. In the State sector, about 75% of education expenditure is for school education, of which 44% is on elementary education and 30% on secondary education.

7. Similar smaller-scale schemes are available through the Department of Social of Justice and empowerment and at state level. In Gujarat, for example, see http://sje.gujarat.gov.in/ddcw/showpage.aspx?contentid=1490&lang=English.

8. As of January 31st, 2014 on the Paycheck website http://www.paycheck.in/main/salary/minimumwages/gujarat.

9. See http://www.thehindu.com/news/national/centre-to-enhance-income-criteria-to-help-more-students-under-scholarship-scheme/article3851640.ece.

10. See http://mhrd.gov.in/girls_hostel accessed January 27, 2014.

11. *Kasturba Gandhi Balika Vidyalayas*, named after Mahatma Gandhi's wife, was launched in 2004. The schools are residential and completely free of charge for girls at the upper primary level covering Classes VI–VIII. Seventy-five per cent of the seats in these residential schools are reserved for girls of the above communities while the rest are available for upper-caste girls whose families are below the poverty line.

References

Aikman, S., and E. Unterhalter. 2007. "Gender Equality in Schools." In *Practising Gender Equality in Education*, edited by S. Aikman and E. Unterhalter, 18–27. Oxfam: Programme Insights Series. Oxford.

Assaad, R., D. Levison, and N. Zibanib. 2010. "The Effect of Domestic Work on Girls' Schooling: Evidence from Egypt." *Feminist Economics*. 16 (1): 79–128.

Bajaj, M. 2011. *Schooling for Social Change: The Rise and Impact of Human Rights Education in India*. New York: Continuum Publishers.

Barrera-Osorio, F., M. Bertrand, L. Linden, and F. Perez-Calle. 2008. "Conditional Cash Transfers in Education: Design Features, Peer and Sibling Effects Evidence from a Randomized Experiment in Colombia." *World Bank Policy Research Working Paper 4580*, Washington.

Beaman, L., E. Duflo, R. Pande, and P. Topalova. 2012. "Female Leadership Raises Aspirations and Educational Attainment for Girls: A Policy Experiment in India." *Science* 335: 382.

Bennell, P., K. Hyde, and N. Swainson. 2002. *The Impact of the HIV/AIDS Epidemic on the Education Sector in Sub-Saharan Africa*. Brighton: Centre for International Education, University of Sussex.

Brookings Institute. 2010. *A Global Compact on Learning Taking Action on Education in Developing Countries*. Washington, DC: Center for Universal Education.

Connell, R. W. 1987. *Gender and Power: Society, the Person and Sexual Politics*. Stanford: Stanford University Press.

Creswell, J. 2003. *Research Design: Qualitative, Quantitative, and Mixed Methods Approaches*. 2nd ed. Thousand Oaks, CA: Sage.

EFA. 1990. "World Bank Education for All Goals." http://web.worldbank.org/WBSITE/EXTERNAL/TOPICS/EXTEDUCATION/0,,contentMDK:20374062~menuPK:540090~pagePK:148956~piPK:216618~theSitePK:282386,00.html

GOI. 2008. National Evaluation – Ii Kasturba Gandhi Balika Vidhyalaya (KGBV) VERSION 2, 9 FEBRUARY 2008. http://ssa.nic.in/page_portletlinks?folder name=research-studies.

GOI. 2010. "Education in India: 2007–08 – Participation and Expenditure," 64th Round (July 2007–June 2008), Ministry of Statistics and Programme Implementation, GOI, New Delhi.

GOI. 2011. Census. http://censusindia.gov.in/2011-common/censusdataonline.html

GOI. 2012a. 12th 5 Year Plan- Report. http://planningcommission.gov.in/plans/plan rel/12thplan/pdf/vol_3.pdf.

GOI. 2012b. "Children in India 2012 – A Statistical Appraisal," *Social Statistics Division, – Ministry of Statistics and Programme Implementation*, New Delhi.

Hazarika, G., and A. S. Bedi. 2003. "Schooling Costs and Child Work in Rural Pakistan." *Journal of Development Studies* 39 (5): 29–64.

Jensen, R. T. 2010. "The (Perceived) Returns to Education and the Demand for Schooling." *Quarterly Journal of Economics* 125: 515–548.

Kabeer, N. 1994. *Reversed Realities*. London: Verso.

Kane, E. 2004. *"Girls' Education in Africa: What Do We Know about Strategies That Work?"* Africa Region Human Development Working Paper 73, Washington.

Kis-Katos, K. 2012. "Gender Differences in Work-schooling Decisions in Rural North India." *Review of Economics of the Household* 10 (4): 491–519.

Leach, F., V. Fiscian, E. Kadzamira, E. Lemani, and P. Machakanja. 2003. *An Investigative Study of the Abuse of Girls in African Schools*. London: DFID.

Levison, D., and S. M. Karine. 1998. "Household Work as a Deterrent to Schooling: An Analysis of Adolescent Girls in Peru." *Journal of Developing Areas* 32 (3): 339–356.

Maharaj, Z. 1995. "A Social Theory of Gender: Connell's Gender and Power." *Feminist Review* 49 (1): 50–65.

Moore, A. M., S. Singh, U. Ram, L. Remez, and S. Audam. 2009. *Adolescent Marriage and Childbearing in India: Current Situation and Recent Trends*. New York: Guttmacher Institute.

Muralidharan, K., and V. Sundararaman. 2011. "Teacher Performance Pay: Experimental Evidence from India." *The Journal of Political Economy*. University of Chicago Press 119 (1), 39–77.

National Sample Statistics Office. 2012. *Level and Pattern of Consumer Expenditure NSS 68th Round (July 2011 – June 2012)* NSS Report No. 555(68 /1.O/1).

Nussbaum, M. 2004. "Women's Education: A Global Challenge." *Signs* 29 (2): 325–355.

Save the Children. 2009. *Strengthening Girls' Voices: Empowering Girls in Malawi Technical Brief*. Westport, CT: Save the Children.

Sekher, T. V. 2010. *"Special Financial Incentive Schemes for the Girl Child in India: A Review of Select Schemes."* International Institute for Population Sciences, Mumbai for The Planning Commission Government of India in collaboration with United Nations Population Fund, Mumbai. http://www.unfpa.org/gender/docs/sexselection/UNFPA_Publication-39772.pdf.

Sen, A. 1990. *Development as Freedom*. Oxford: Oxford University Press.

Siddhu, G. 2011. "Who Makes It to Secondary School? Determinants of Transition to Secondary Schools in Rural India." *International Journal of Educational Development* 31: 394–401.

Sundaram, A., and R. Vanneman. 2008. "Gender Differentials in Literacy in India: The Intriguing Relationship with Women's Labor Force Participation." *World Development* 36 (1): 128–143.

UNESCO. 2005. *Winning People's Will for Girl Child Education: Community 5 Mobilisation for Gender Equality in Basic Education*. United Nations Educational, Scientific and Cultural Organisation: Kathmandu.

UNESCO. 2011. "UIS Statistics in Brief: Profiles: Education (All Levels) Profile – India 2010." Institute for Statistics. http://stats.uis.unesco.org/unesco/TableView er/document.aspx?ReportId=121&IF_Language=eng&BR_Country=3560.

UNESCO. 2012. *World Atlas of Gender Equality in Education*. Paris: UNESCO. http://unesdoc.unesco.org/images/0021/002155/215522e.pdf

UNFPA. 2012. *Marrying Too Young: End Child Marriage*. New York: United Nations Population Fund.

UNICEF. 2011. "Child Marriage Information Sheet." UNICEF India. http://www. unicef.org/india/Child_Marriage_Fact_Sheet_Nov2011_final.pdf.

United Nations Millennium Development Goals. 2000. http://www.un.org/millenni umgoals/.

Unterhalter, E., and S. Aikman, eds. 2005. "Beyond Access: Transforming Policy and Practice for Gender Equality in Education." Oxfam 2005. http://policy-practice.ox fam.org.uk/publications/beyond-access-transforming-policy-and-practice-for-gender-equality-in-education-115410.

Verma, R. K., and V. S. Mahendra. 2004. "Construction of Masculinity in India: A Gender and Sexual Health Perspective." *Indian Journal of Family Welfare* 50: 71–78.

World Bank. 1995. *Priorities and Strategies in Education*. Washington, DC: World Bank.

World Bank. 2009. "Secondary Education in India: Universalizing Opportunity. Vol. 1 of Secondary Education in India; Universalizing Opportunity." Washington, DC: World Bank. http://documents.worldbank.org/curated/en/2009/01/10567129/secondary-education-india-universalizing-opportunity-vol-1-2.

Pakistani and Bangladeshi young men: re-racialization, class and masculinity within the neo-liberal school

Mairtin Mac an Ghaill[a] and Chris Haywood[b]

[a]Newman University, Birmingham, UK; [b]Media and Cultural Studies, Newcastle University, Newcastle-upon-Tyne, UK

This article explores Pakistani and Bangladeshi young men's experiences of schooling to examine what inclusion/exclusion means to them. Qualitative research was undertaken with 48 Pakistani and Bangladeshi young men living in areas of the West Midlands, England. The young men highlighted three key areas: the emergence of a schooling regime operating through neo-liberal principles, the recognition of class difference between themselves and teachers, and their awareness of how racialization operated through codes of masculinity. In conclusion, it is argued that research on issues of inclusion/exclusion should be cautious when interpreting new forms of class identity through conventional categories of ethnicity.

Introduction

In this paper we engage with the shifting understandings of inclusion and exclusion within schooling, in which Pakistani and Bangladeshi working-class young men are currently experiencing intensified forms of monitoring and surveillance, as part of a 'suspect community' (Kundnani 2009; UK Government 2009; Hickman et al. 2012).[1] Faas' (2010) *Negotiating Political Identities: Multi-ethnic Schools and Youth in Europe* locates the British changing landscape around ethnic and national belonging within a wider European perspective. Historically, within a British context, state schooling strategically has been projected as a primary institution in which the multi-cultural society would be lived out (Tomlinson 2008; Gewirtz and Cribb 2009). Within a contemporary context, Shain (2011, 16) maintains that 'education is central to current discourses of radicalisation and extremism' that are projected onto young Muslim men. Hence its continuing strategic significance, in a period marked by the central government's claim of the emergence of the 'enemy within' and the end of multi-culturalism as a means of attaining inclusion in civil society (Fekete 2004; Choudhurry 2007). Civil society in this instance carries with it a market rationality, where students are 'the active agent of their own self-interest within a competitive world' (Bradbury, McGimpsey, and Santori 2013, 249). The implication is that neo-liberal discourses based on achieving social justice and recognizing cultural diversity have been politically discarded to facilitate new forms of citizenship. As Wright (2012, 291) has suggested, parents, teachers and students must re-fashion themselves into educational citizens that are 'rational, responsible and of high esteem', while '[T] those unwilling to conform to the neoliberal image of the citizen are cast as part of the problem and are consequently penalised and excluded'.

It is within the context of the recalibration of neo-liberal discourses that contemporary forms of Muslim masculinities are being assembled, (dis)identified with and lived out. Unlike much conventional social science research that makes young Muslim students the object of analysis, our starting point is to critically examine the representational positioning of the schooling of a 'suspect community', involving the emergence of a specific regulatory regime operating within particular late-modern educational classifications, subjectification and divisions (Hickman et al. 2012). An important aim of the paper, in understanding how inclusion and exclusion manifests itself in this context, is to explore Pakistani and Bangladeshi young men through an alternative representational space; a space that enables the research participants to reflect on a range of generationally specific social and cultural exclusions that are significantly mediated through and by the education system. More specifically, it focuses on young Pakistani and Bangladeshi men's experiences of neo-liberal discourses to examine how inclusion/exclusion is being experienced in light of the movement of schools away from a local shared community sensibility towards an institution positioned as a global performative academy (Qureshi 2004). A second aim of this paper is to examine how these young men's identities are intersected through class and how class difference operates as a method of ethnic coding. Finally, exclusion is examined in relation to the young men's experience of marginalization through gender, more specifically through the (dis)identifications with 'Muslim masculinities'. Underpinning these aims is an argument that a 'post-race' neo-liberal regulatory regime intersects with attempts by schools to contain and produce Pakistani and Bangladeshi young men by attempting to fix them into a reified singular category of religion. Therefore, as achievement and academic success become reframed through notions of individualized responsibility, the paper examines the young men's experience of schools' exclusionary practice of reifying religion as an ethnic category. As Mills and Keddie (2010, 214) point out: 'neo-liberalism with its focus on individualization tends to attribute disproportionate blame on particular groups of boys who already tend to be marginalised by race, ethnicity, class and sexuality'.

The above aims are contextualized by current British educational policy. An archaeology of the field of policy might identify a shift from assimilation (1960s), through integration (1970s) to multi-culturalism/anti-racism (1980s). This is not to suggest a simple mapping of each policy ideology onto each decade. Rather, these ideologies were in tension with an emerging emphasis that played out differentially across different regions. During the last two decades we can identify a return to assimilation through the implementation of a neo-liberal policy regulatory regime across public institutions, including education, highlighted in New Labour's adoption of a community cohesion strategy. The election of the New Labour government marked a significant move away from the earlier Conservative government's assimilationist stance on race, as exemplified in the Education Reform Act of 1988. Of major significance was New Labour's commitment to publishing the McPherson Report that examined the murder of the young black man Stephen Lawrence. This Report, together with the passing of the Race Relations (Amendment) Act of 2000, emphasized recognition of institutional racism, with a legal requirement for educational institutions to develop race equality policies. There are different accounts of how successful this was across different regions (Department for Education and Skills 2007a; Tomlinson 2008). However, the disturbances in northern towns in 2001 signalled a shift away from materialist accounts of racist schooling to an emphasis on community cohesion, which intensified following the 9/11 attacks and the London bombings in July 2005. More specifically, these policy changes have both helped shape and been a response to a shifting dominant public representation of Pakistani and Bangladeshi young men from an ascribed image as *law-abiding citizens* to the current image of *dangerous brown men* (Bhattacharrya 2008), who are a threat to the British nation (Shain 2011). At a theoretical and policy level, a key discursive shift has emerged, with the projection of the category religion displacing the category ethnicity as the primary marker of Muslims' public identity. In turn, this has been accompanied by the re-racialization of the Muslim community. As Anthias and Yuval-Davis have claimed:

> Since the 'Rushdie Affair', the exclusion of minority religions from the national collectivity has started a process of racialization that especially relates to Muslims. People who used to be known for the place of origin, or even as 'people of colour' have become identified by their assumed religion. The racist stereotype of the 'Paki' has become the racist stereotype of the 'Muslim fundamentalist'. (1993, 55)

The shifting emphasis from neo-liberal discourses that attempted to promote community cohesion to neo-liberal regimes that view diversity as problematic to citizenship is evident in forms of legislation such as the Prevention of Violent Extremism (McGhee 2012). Sian, Law, and Sayyid (2012) highlight how a toolkit designed for schools to prevent extremism specifically targets young Muslim (men). This toolkit places teachers at the centre of surveillance and monitoring through an Islamophobic discourse that elides racial extremism with religion. It is within this context that Muslim young men as a 'suspect community' are subject to an exclusionary discourse that is constituted through the deployment of neo-liberal pedagogy, racial profiling and religious fundamentalism.

Theorizing the performative culture of the neo-liberal school, (re-) racialization and class

To explore how shifting understandings of inclusion and exclusion are experienced by young Pakistani and Bangladeshi young men and the positions they inhabit within late-modern post-colonial urban schools, we bring together two theoretically led frames: critical discussions of the performative culture of neo-liberal schooling, and the fragmentation of theories of racialization and the disappearance of class. It is the tensions embedded within these disparate and expansive frames that facilitate an understanding of often contradictory and fragile identifications within these young men's subjectivities. Thus, these identifications are located within local (regional) post-colonial urban spaces, marked by fracturing classes, fragmenting genders, plural sexualities and new ethnicities, that in turn are embedded within a 'bigger picture' of globally inflected socio-economic austerity, increasing inequalities, the diversity and/or fragmentation of racial politics and accompanying processes of re-racialization (Mac an Ghaill 1994; Shain 2003; Mirza 2009).

In light of the complexity and the range of ways in which young men's identifications are located, one of the ways in which inclusion/exclusion can be understood is through a notion of neo-liberalism. Neo-liberalism operates at a number of levels, but two key areas for consideration focus on how nation-states cultivate values such as competition, entrepreneurialism and individual responsibility through educational policies and how, at more local levels, individuals are responding to the deployment of such values (Apple, Kenway, and Singh 2005; Torres 2009; Rizvi and Engel 2009). It is argued that neo-liberal processes provide a context in which:

> The value of knowledge is now linked to a crude instrumentalism, and the only mode of education that seems to matter is one that enthusiastically endorses learning marketable skills, embracing a survival of the fittest ethic, and defining the good life solely through accumulation and disposing of the latest consumer goods. (Giroux 2012, 43)

The implication of this is that neo-liberalism creates the discourses through which academic achievement and failure become understood and, in so doing, shape social and cultural interpretations of students' behaviours. As Stromquist and Monkman (2000) suggest, knowledge within a neo-liberal context becomes a commodity, and as a result pedagogy is imbricated within marketplace relations. Within England, a results-driven performance begins to dictate the quality, worth and value of a person that in turn becomes measured within a context of competitiveness and the fulfilment of state-ascribed standards. The implication is that the effectiveness of the tea-cher/student relationship becomes the responsibility of the individual learner. As a result, achievement becomes located at the level of the individual and it is suggested that race/ethnicity become less educationally significant.

The contextualization of schools through a neo-liberal agenda of per-formativity is involved in a contested internal politics about (racialized) 'winners' and losers' – who is included and who is excluded across the cur-riculum, pedagogy and assessment (Qureshi 2004). The last 10 years has seen the term Islamophobia emerge as the dominant explanation of Muslim social and cultural exclusions. For some commentators, anti-Islamophobia mobilization is a response to the under-theorization of the concept of racial-ization that does not address the issue of 'faith-hate' (McGhee 2005). For others, the concept serves to disconnect Muslim communities from a wider anti-racist movement and the historical benefits of a broader understanding of racialization (see Commission on British Muslims and Islamophobia 1997; Halliday 1999; Bhattacharya 2008). Currently, in carrying out empiri-cal work that recognizes changing notions of inclusion and exclusion, an effect of the fracturing of the theorizing of racialization is the difficulty in making sense of the 're-racialization' of young Pakistani and Bangladeshi young men, as a conceptual and pedagogical issue. In other words, being aware of the social and cultural complexities generated by neo-liberal condi-tions, raises questions about generating an adequate shared educational or political explanation to make sense of 'complex racial times' in the class-room. Rather, what we need, in exploring Pakistani and Bangladeshi young men's schooling biographies, is an understanding of the specific regulatory regime and local institutional dynamics of a highly fragmented field of education (Tomlinson 2008).

The second theoretical framing acknowledges the institutional reconfigura-tion of ethnicity and racialized identities. Importantly, as Bhattacharyya (2013, 38) argues: '… the concept of racial neoliberalism suggests that racial politics is remade in particular ways in the time of neoliberal economics and state practices – yet key aspects of this racial neoliberalism predate the ascent of neoliberal economics'. The internal fracturing of racial politics, as part of a broader questioning of new social movement theory, has emerged in response to what Stuart Hall (1992) refers to as a contemporary key political question of how we live with difference. An earlier (materialist) anti-racist position enabled us to identify the systematic discrimination experienced by black and Asian students across the curriculum, pedagogy and assessment (Mirza 1992).

As Anthias and Yuval-Davis (1993, 65) illustrate, in the 1970s and 1980s class was the central analytical concept in understanding inclusion and exclusion within British society. Similarly, in academic work on education it was argued that a class analysis of the racially structured British society was more adequate than the 'race-relations' approach in explaining black youths' position in the schooling system (Mirza 1992; Mac an Ghaill 1988).

The materialist position focusing on a black–white dualism, with its emphasis on colour racism, was conceptually challenged by a (post-structuralist) cultural politics of difference position that defines racism beyond colour as the marker of exclusion to include: religion, culture and migration. This approach suggests that a racial politics that uses a black/white dichotomy is deemed to operate through homogeneity, tight boundaries and cultural fixity. It is seen to exclude a wider range of minority ethnic, religious and national communities, fails to address the issue of subjectivity (the who am I and who are we questions), and denies the complexity of racial politics that needs to address the inter-sectionality of social differences around class, gender, sexuality, disability, and so forth (Anthias 2008; Mirza 2009). In contrast, a cultural politics of difference position claims to address a more complex explanation of racist practices and political mobilizations. For example, from an educational perspective, Rattansi (1992, 28) suggests, research operating within such a position provides a more complex picture of contradictory teacher–student interactions varying within and between schools, which in turn result in a range of responses from male and female students. The tension between these positions remains in play with the more recent emergence of neo-liberalism, explored above.

In this paper we argue that neo-liberalism and class and (re-)racialization provide ways of reading and understanding Pakistani and Bangladeshi young men's experiences of exclusion/inclusion in educational contexts. At different moments within their narratives, a simplistic reductionism to one particular frame fails to capture the complexity of what it feels like to be growing up in England. This also has particular methodological implications that we now discuss.

Pakistani and Bangladeshi young men's narratives: methods and methodological autonomy

Our earlier work with a younger generation of Pakistani and Bangladeshi young men, in Newcastle, London and Birmingham, makes clear their geographically specific local experiences of growing up in a rapidly changing Britain (Mac an Ghaill 1994; Mac an Ghaill and Haywood 2005). In other words, the young men in this Birmingham-based sample inhabit specific lifestyles within a spatial context of diverse social trajectories among a changing Muslim diaspora in Britain. This includes acknowledging young

Muslim men's generationally specific reclamation of the concept Muslim as a self-referent, the re-articulation of class and gender-based being and belonging, the cultural politics of Islam and the media-projected visibility of their community as a 'home-produced' anti-British ethnicity. Within this context, such communities are highly diverse; and as a qualitative and explorative study, the paper does not seek inductive validity by suggesting that the participants represent the experiences of the broader Muslim male population of the area or the general population. Instead, as Crouch and McKenzie argue:

> Rather than being systematically selected instances of specific categories of attitudes and responses, here respondents embody and represent meaningful experience-structure links. Put differently, our respondents are 'cases', or instances of states, rather than (just) individuals who are bearers of certain designated properties (or 'variables'). (2006, 493)

Therefore, it is the exploration of the young men's meaningful experiences that was a key objective of the research design. Carrying out this research has presented major theoretical and methodological issues to ensure we do not re-inscribe young men as a social problem for the state, and more specifically an institutional problem for schools. Importantly, the research process was set out to enable the research participants to inhabit an alternative representational space that provides insightful narratives about the complexity of inhabiting subject positions within secondary state schooling.

During a three year period (2008–2011) we have recorded the experiences of 48 Pakistani (*n* = 30) and Bangladeshi (*n* = 18) self-identified Muslim young men living in areas experiencing high levels of poverty and unemployment. Aged 16–21, we use the young men's narratives of schooling to engage with issues of inclusion and exclusion. The majority of the young men (*n* = 38) attended local secondary schools, sixth-form colleges and further education colleges. Group and life-history interviews provided the framework through which to explore a range of critical incidents experienced by these young men. The group interviews were carried out at local community centres and the life-history interviews were carried out in a variety of places, including at youth and community organizations and local cafes. These interviews lasted around 45–90 minutes and provided insight into growing up, family, schooling, social life and local community. The interview groups contained a mix of Bangladeshi and Pakistani young men, as indicated by their names, who shared not only intimate friendships but were part of a broader social community that included attending the same youth and community organizations and colleges, sharing the same employers and participating together in leisure activities. Furthermore, although they were diverse individuals, in terms of ethnicity, age, past experience and social status with different current experiences of being in education, work/training or unemployed, they held a shared critical reflexivity of their schooling experiences as Muslim students.

While carrying out empirical work with young people, we were introduced to two young men who were politically involved in the local area. In turn, they introduced us to other young people and this subsequently led to further snowballing of other friends, family and community representatives (Patton 1990). Access was greatly enabled by our being known for our social commitment to the local area, working with families in the local community. These interviews were supplemented by a range of other research strategies that included observations, informal conversations and interviews with parents and local community representatives (Alvesson and Skoldberg 2000), as part of a wider critical ethnography on the impact of globally inflected change upon the local formation of diasporic young men's subjectivity and identity (Appadurai 1991; Harvey 2003).[2] The datasets from each of the methods was subject to thematic analysis (Braun and Clarke 2006) that enabled us to explore '… the underlying ideas, constructions, and discourses that shape or inform the semantic content of the data' (Ussher et al. 2013, 3). The subsequent analysis was taken back to the young people themselves not simply as a form of 'face validity' but also as a way of exploring the practical and political implications of the findings. All interviews throughout the study were anonymized and the research participants were given pseudonyms to protect their confidentiality.

From the local community school to the global performative culture of the neo-liberal school

In this section, we explore Pakistani and Bangladeshi student's experiences of exclusion/inclusion through neo-liberal restructuring of education. The performative culture of the neo-liberal school can be understood as being subject to a series of state interventions that promote competition, entrepreneurialism and deregulation (Davies and Bansel 2007). Furthermore, schools are tasked with generating knowledge and skills that can be traded by students in the global marketplace. Becoming the 'right' kind of student enables and facilitates educational success. Arnot and Mac an Ghaill (2007) in their anthology on gender and education, illustrate the cumulative effects of the constant intensified restructuring of schooling over the last few decades. They write:

> Behind recent research on gender and education lies the conundrums associated with the restructuring of educational institutions and the governance, the changing curriculum, the differential patterns of educational performance, the transformation of teachers' work and shifting community, family and work relations. (Arnot and Mac an Ghaill 2007, 1)

In turn, contemporary schooling is embedded within major social and cultural transformations, of which it is a key institutional actor (Gewirtz and Cribb 2009). The latter transformations include: new patterns in the international division of labour, the changing nature of the nation-state and the associated assumed crisis in Anglo-ethnicity, new labour processes and local labour markets, within the context of de-industrialization and de-regulation, new educational and work technologies, increased state regulation of youth, advanced global communication systems and diverse family forms (Brah et al. 1999).

One of the important issues discussed by the students focused on how exclusion was articulated in relation to institutional performativity. This means that there is not a displacement of categories of racialization and their attendant exclusionary effects, but rather a re-racialization through performativity. Most interestingly, they suggested that schools through everyday curricular and pedagogical practices draw upon Muslim as a racialized category. Furthermore, they suggest that the specific teacher–student interactions that they experience are generated by constant government-led institutional changes. In developing their narratives of education around issues of inclusion and exclusion, they provided a comparative analysis based on their families' earlier experiences of local community schooling and a review of their own schooling biographies:

Imran: Like the other day, when that group of kids were all talking, some saying that school is really Islamophobic cos the teachers really hate Muslims and the others were saying no that's not true.
M.M: What do you mean?
Imran: Other kids weren't sure if you could call the teachers Islamophobic or racist or something big like that. But what Ajaz says now seems more true. It's not like teachers thinking, you're a Muslim so I'm going to discriminate against you. It's nothing planned or anything. The way teachers treat pupils is just ordinary stuff, just like every day stuff, like they don't really care about kids. They'd probably treat all kids like this, maybe a bit worse cos they're Muslim. I agree with Ajaz.

For Imran, exclusion operates through racial/religious categories, and he highlights the complexities of identifying the subjectivities of young Muslims. The discussion on the appropriateness of classifying exclusion as Islamaphobia or racism highlights the ambivalence within young people of how to make sense of their experiences. Part of the issue is to move away from the assumption that these young people have 'settled' understandings about their own identifications and their experiences of exclusionary practices. Crucially, these young men did not reduce exclusion to a singular notion of racism or Islamaphobia but, rather, how that exclusion is articulated became linked to specific educational processes. In the context of this section, the framing of exclusion intersects with neo-liberal educational policies. To explore this in more detail, further questions were asked that highlighted a regulatory shift in how the school engaged with young people:

M.M: Why do you think the teachers are like this?

Wasim: When I started at secondary school and definitely at primary, going to school was like a community and the teachers were an important part of that community. But everything's changed, all the league tables, tests, all the time tests, tests, academies, everything. It's run just like a business.

M.M: So, what was your school like?

Wasim: You're a customer, but everyone knows business isn't about caring about people. And, Muslim customers would be at the bottom. Like in the past for our parents the racist stuff was about the 'Paki' corner shop, now the racist stuff is the Muslim school. Who'd wanna go there? Who'd wanna teach there, it's seen as the lowest. Like you go there and no chance of getting a job. Employers, they'll look at what school you're from and say, no thanks.

The implication of the discussion above is that their inclusion/exclusion as Pakistani and Bangladeshi young men has become reconfigured outside anti-racist theories that frame race through black/white dichotomies. Rather, performance and achievement become de-racialized in one moment, while in another the religious identity of Muslim has become a re-racialized source of exclusion. In this sense, exclusion becomes articulated across multiple discourses, which have been facilitated through a reconstitution of notions of the 'good' teacher, student and parent (Baltodano 2012). We can see from the above extract that the notion of the 'good school' is being redefined. This has been further reinforced by an historical legacy of the authoritarian popularism of the New Right moralists' marginalization of the established post-war social democratic account of social justice that has been to play down the notion of the 'social subject' and the accompanying significance of categories such as class, gender, race/ethnicity and sexuality. The new regime has reconstructed 'social' practices within a neo-liberal political framework. As a result, attempts have been made to reconfigure the labour process of teaching and learning within the context of a wider audit/performative culture with an attendant discursive reductionist repertoire of economic cost/benefit (Ball 2000). In turn, this has the effect of aligning a neo-liberal concept of the *schooling self*, with the emergence of the *entrepreneurial self*, suggesting that individual subjects are responsible for their own academic 'under-achievement' (Walkerdine 2003). This new schooling regime differentially affects different social groups. So, for example, the disproportionate high levels of academic under-achievement among Pakistani and Bangladeshi students is primarily explained in terms of an assumed cultural deficit model of the (Muslim) students' learning identities that is directly connected to their home lives (Garner and Bhattacharyya

2011). The students below understand that, despite the rhetoric of all students being treated the same, social differentiation continues. The reconfiguration of schools into academies, for example, serves to increase feelings of marginalization:

M.M: So what happens in schools now?
Wasim: Whether, you're a good pupil or a bad pupil, it doesn't matter to teachers. It's just a job. Collect all the clever ones together, the ones they see as clever and then just forget the rest, cos in the business world what the teachers do with the clever pupils by getting them to improve will show up on the league tables.
Sajid: When you leave school and you talk to some of the teachers, they'll tell you, it's all about their cvs. Things like league tables, they're not about the kids, the kids getting jobs. They're about the teachers' careers.
Asif: Like they're not going to let too many Muslims like us into academies, are they?
M.M: How does that affect pupils round here?
Sajid: Teachers aren't now rewarded for looking after kids in a general way, like supporting them, like encouraging them if the work is hard. I don't think they'd even know, if a pupil was doing bad work, if it was because they found the work hard or were just lazy.
Asif: I think they get paid for sorting kids out into difference levels. Like you're the clever ones, like we were told and you lot aren't the clever ones. But teachers, especially the younger teachers don't even know anything about us. Like out mates were just as clever as we were, even more ability, really clever, but they were slotted into the not clever, the failing group.
Azam: This is normal for loads of Muslim kids. You can't really blame the teachers. It's just the way it is.

These young men recognize that the schooling processes underpinned by an ideology of performativity continue to use cultural differences as a mechanism for segregation. It is suggested that the neo-liberal regulatory regime of the 'performative school' is of central constitutive significance in the conceptual manufacturing of British Muslim students. The fixing of this social group works through Muslim-specific discursive mechanisms of control imposed upon young Muslim men, alongside wider institutional processes that operate against the interests of working-class young people. For example, Shain (2011, 21) powerfully illustrates how: 'recent policies have implicated educational institutions in the surveillance, monitoring and containment of populations identified as problematic'. At the same time, the de-regulation of state schooling has resulted in a new stratification with the emergence of a diverse range of institutions, including academies, voluntary-aided, community and free schools. This fragmentation has been accompanied by a new internal hierarchy of schools, with widening selection of students that has differentiated class and racial effects on different regions (*The Observer* 2013). This is occurring at the same time as inner-city schooling is officially seen as a central element of a projected doxic social spatialization in which young working-class people are positioned (Reay 2004). Therefore, the next section recognizes the ideological implication of neo-liberal discourses in the context of class differentiation as a constituent of these young men's experience of inclusion/exclusion.

Class difference, neo-liberalism and young Muslims

The last decade has witnessed a fundamental shift in dominant British political and media discourses that have positioned the Muslim community, and more specifically young Muslim men and women, as a major social problem for the state (Bhattacharya 2008). They are projected as having broken the multi-cultural social contract that emerged during the 1970s around a notion of ethnic integration. Their projected refusal to integrate has manifested itself in pervasive images of a traditional religious community living a self-segregating, anti-modern existence that is alien to a British way of life. Importantly, it is not Muslims *per se* who are seen as a threat to social cohesion; rather, it is young (non-)working-class men (and women). Currently, at a time when commentators speak of a post-racial politics, there is much evidence of the historical continuity of racially inflected, class-based structural constraints on Pakistani and Bangladeshi working-class young men. Their collective profile includes the highest levels of unemployment and over-representation in low-skilled employment, over-representation in prisons, over-representation in poor housing, high levels of poor health and lowest levels of social mobility (Garner and Bhattacharyya 2011; Laird et al. 2007). A key contradiction is being developed around inclusion/exclusion within schools. Their social and economic vulnerability is somewhat in contrast with an assertive English nationalism, involving a forging of a renewed British identity and an accompanying re-racialization of Muslims that have emerged.

Recently, within conditions of socio-economic austerity, increasing inequalities and regional socio-economic disparities, the success of UKIP in local elections provides evidence of this emerging new nationalism. Furthermore, following the murder of Drummer Lee Digby, there has been an increase in anti-Muslim attacks; 'forty percent of Muslim attacks recorded by *Tell Mama UK* (a monitoring group), last year were linked to English Defence League sympathisers' (Shabi 2013, 10). The emergence of this assertive English nationalism provides the most explicit evidence of how different communities within Britain are impelled to live with different social realities. The increasing fear of an (imagined) all pervasive Muslim Fundamentalism articulated through English nationalism is captured by Majid and Asif, as they discuss social exclusion:

Majid: Can you imagine if white people had to live with a threat from rac-
           ist groups, can you imagine it? It would be top of the news every
           day. But Muslim people in this country live with this every day.
           And you're not worried just for yourself but if your mother or sister
           or if the old people are going out. And the media love to stir it up
           every time there's something from Afghanistan, Iraq, just all the
           time talking about extremists and we don't even know any extrem-
           ists. We're just trying to get on with our lives.
Asif: The trouble is, it's worst than just the EDL or the BNP. It's just part
           of the violence of living in this country, its normal. My uncle said
           that when they came from Bangladesh in the 70s, they did not
           really settle because they thought they might be kicked out at any
           time. Then things got a bit better and they thought it'd be OK for
           us been born here. But now it's worse than ever. Something is
           reported on the news and anyone who looks like a Muslim walking
           down the road can be attacked.

Class restructuring in Britain is being played out within the context of
austerity and accompanying socio-economic divisions, which, as the students indicate above, differentially impact on racialized diasporian groups,
such as Pakistani and Bangladeshi communities. More specifically, reading
through the research literature, a main government and academic image of
Pakistani and Bangladeshi students is that of under-achievement, with Pakistani and Bangladeshi male students, in terms of ethnicity, faith group, class
and gender, placed at the bottom of league tables on academic school performance (Department for Education and Skills 2007b; Office for National
Statistics 2012; Birmingham City Council 2013). A decade ago, Archer
(2003) made the argument about the continuing impact of socio-economic
inequalities on the education of Muslim boys, that the young men in our
study suggest has intensified.

Farzana Shain (2011) provides one of the most sustained critical expla-
nations of contemporary Muslim boys' experiences in England, arguing for
a more theoretically sophisticated approach that includes the development of
a socio-economic dimension. She adopts a Gramscian analysis emphasizing
the articulation of multiple structures of race, gender and class with socio-
economic and political relations of domination and subordination (Gramsci
1970). She maintains that:

Gramsci's framework recognises that young people are located within material
contexts that structure and limit the structure of possibilities for agency and
action. This entails the recognition of the role of historical forces-in this case
colonialism and imperialism-in shaping the class locations and settlements of
Muslim communities in areas of England that has suffered most from economic decline. These settlement patterns have had a lasting legacy in terms of
the types of schooling and educational and employment opportunities available. Pakistani and Bangladeshi communities find themselves located in some
of the most materially deprived wards in the country. (Shain 2011, 50)

In our research, the young men's narratives serve to critique the dominant culturalist explanation that the state, including institutional sites, such as schooling and policing, ascribes to them (Faas 2010). Rather, they are experiencing generationally specific material conditions, in which securing masculine subjectivities is a complex process that conceptually cannot be contained within the singular identity category of religion. Throughout the research there was evidence of a range of contemporary fragmented male subjectivities, social trajectories and cultural belonging. So, for example, for some of these working-class students there was an intense consciousness of how their divided lives from that of their teachers is materially structured, enacted and performed each school day (Qureshi 2004). Thus, while in the previous section discourses of religion and ethnicity were articulated through neo-liberal regulations, in a similar way class difference was generated by teachers who actively distancing themselves from Pakistani and Bangladeshi working-class communities.

> Imitiaz: I used to think it was all because we were Muslim that the teachers were really different to us, but becoming mates with some of the white kids here, I can see things differently. Teachers are just posh people. They don't live here in this area and our white mates are definitely closer to us than they are to them.
>
> Tamim: Maybe the teachers have more problems with the white kids, because they're white, but the teachers know they're nothing like them.

In the above conversation, they highlight the racialization of class difference. According to Jacobowitz (2004, 7) this racialization refers to 'what we might call the displacement of class differences onto racial differences'. In this context, middle class becomes a code for whiteness, with young Bangladeshi and Pakistani men often developing friendships with young white working-class men living in the same neighbourhood. In effect, social inequality brought together young men from a range of ethnic backgrounds that was often articulated through a shared sense of difference from and enacted forms of resistance to middle-class teachers. Thus, normative whiteness and middle-classness become fused and projected onto the bodies of teachers. Importantly for these young men, whiteness and middle class become synonymous and are underpinned by an entrepreneurial self that is aligned to individualized choice. As Farooq points out:

> Teachers wouldn't dare live in this area. Of course they would never send their kids to the same school as us. They live in posh areas, white areas, so really they're segregating not us?

This fusion of whiteness and class becomes emblematic of the exclusions that are a consequence of a shift in the meaning of social justice and citizenship. More specifically, this is a shift from an inclusive schooling premised on social justice and a recognition and acceptance of diversity, to one where diversity is not tolerated. Furthermore, as we illustrate in the next section, social justice is not only positioned as a threat to social equity but, in the context of contemporary England, it is being elided with the promotion of a terrorist threat (Khiabany and Williamson 2012). In summary, we have argued that these young men are identifying the shift from community-based schools to that of Academies located within a globalized economy. They highlight how such ideologies of citizenship tended to hide the racialization of class differentiation. In the final section below, we explore how masculinity can be used to understand Pakistani and Bangladeshi young men's experience of inclusion/exclusion in the schooling context.

The emerging figure of the Muslim male student: from (the local) feminization to (the global) masculine cultural warrior

In an earlier period, policy, academic and teacher discourses operated with an oppositional logic that valorized the ascribed cultural unity of the Asian community, with Asian male students projected as 'pro-school' in contrast to 'anti-school' African-Caribbean students (Mirza 1992; Mac an Ghaill 1988). Adopting a discourse of cultural deficit, the differential educational performance of Asian and African-Caribbean young people, informed by a quasi-anthropological perspective, was frequently explained in terms of the assumed pathological structure of the African-Caribbean family and kinship organization (Benson 1996). In contrast, the assumed cultural unity of the Asian extended family network, with religion as a key positive signifier, was imagined as providing the necessary support for a younger generation (Lawrence 1982). However, there were contradictory elements in the discursive construction of each minority ethnic group, without which a racial classification could not form a system of knowledge. For example, simultaneously within gender discourses circulating across the school, Asians were assumed to be culturally recidivist, with Asian young men positioned by teachers as the most sexist of male students, emerging out of the assumed regressive gender/sexual practices of the intensely patriarchal Asian community. At the same time, within the gendered politics of the playground, Asian young men were ascribed the lowest ethnic masculinity, with terms of abuse – for example, 'Paki' – carrying not simply a racial connotation but at the same moment connoting a gender meaning. Deriving from an imperial legacy of Orientalist discourses, this was part of a wider ascription of institutional processes of feminization that served to position them as 'non-proper' men (Said 1993; Harvey 2003; Haywood and Mac an Ghaill 2003).

Exploring the current conceptual manufacturing of the Muslim male student, for the Pakistani and Bangladeshi young men in this study, as suggested in the Introduction, a central feature of their lives are schools' attempted institutional containment of them within the singular category of religion. This has major effects in limiting the range of positions that can be occupied as a young Muslim man within schools, which is informed by a wider societal 're-categorisation of various ethnic (Mirpuri, Bangladeshi, Pakistani) groups into religious (Muslim) ones' (Shain 2011, 15). For the young men in our study, there is now an intensified global surveillance, local cultural pathologization and multiple forms of social and racial exclusion of their social lives that operates within this re-categorization. Here, they identify the specific ways in which its logic is played out within a schooling arena. More specifically, they were aware of the history of the racialized gendered positioning of earlier generations, outlined above, which contrasted with their current ascription as the '(global) bad boys' within schools.

Yasin: You know the police put up these big cameras round here to spy on us. That's one way of doing it and teachers do it in their way. Like we say in a more hidden way, but it's like they're suspicious of us, all the time.

Tareq: It's true but they do it in their own way. I think they would mostly say they're not racist, not Islamophobic coz they probably don't think that we're bombers or terrorists. But they have their own ways of keeping you in a box.

Waqar: Basically, they see us as trouble. We're the bad boys. I remember in our school earlier on it was the black boys who the teachers picked on most but then it slowly changed and it was us.

M.M: So, what has changed?

Waqar: My cousins say that Asian pupils used to be seen as really weak, but now Muslims are seen as the strongest, like we're seen as like warriors.

Farooq: Yes, it's that but it's more than that. If you're a Muslim pupil, then they think you're always as a Muslim, whatever you're doing, P.E., walking in the playground, coming into the class, everything. They wouldn't think that about a Sikh or a black kid and never about a white kid. We're just marked out.

Ali: Yeah, as trouble makers.

Farooq: No. Not necessarily trouble makers. We're seen in a different way than any other group, any other group of pupils. But you're right that most Muslim kids know that if you scratch the surface then white people, teachers, even the good ones, the nice ones, see you in a certain sort of way. You can never escape.

Kashif: Do you understand? In the past the word 'Paki' was the stereotype. Now people say Muslims are called terrorists but the real stereotype now is to be called a Muslim. So how are you supposed to behave in school?

Javed: That is very true.

A key issue that emerges here is the question of how a socially constructed phenomenon, such as religion, becomes fixed as an apparently stable unitary category. Adopting a post-colonial analysis, we suggest that schools alongside other institutions currently attempt to administer, regulate and reify unstable social categories, such as religion, ethnicity, gender and sexuality (see Mirza 2009). Most particularly, the administration, regulation and reification of the boundaries of these categories are institutionalized through the inter-related social and discursive practices of staffroom, class-room and playground micro-cultures. In relation to young men, Muslim masculinity has been an alternative space where the State is attempting to re-claim a safe ethnic identity. Dwyer et al. (2008) highlight the different primary resources through which Pakistani men articulate their masculini-ties. They discuss 'religious masculinities', 'middle class masculinities', 'rebellious masculinities' and 'ambivalent masculinities' (often a combina-tion of middle-class and rebellious masculinities) to capture the diversity of masculine styles taken up by men in their study. They use these character-izations of masculinity:

> because it allows us to highlight what we believe are significant insights; par-ticularly the different ways in which class operates, how religious identities are mobilised in different ways, and how young men with similar educational backgrounds may negotiate different choices. (Dwyer et al. 2008, 121)

The accounts below suggest a fluid process of (dis)identification with young people taking up particular understandings of Muslim identities that facili-tate different masculinities at different times. As indicated in the previous section, it is not self-evident how young people understand the notion of Muslim or indeed how this is a constituting feature of their 'masculinities'. In the context of schools and the young people in this research, a major theme that emerges from the students' narratives is the disjuncture between teachers and students in how they mobilize the concept of Muslim. From the students' perspective, this mobilization consists of students reclaiming the concept of Muslim as a collective self-referent and recognizing teachers' racialized ascription of the term Muslim that ultimately serves to contain and explain student subjectivities. Teachers were seen as operating with a highly reductive understanding of religion that assumed a homogeneous image of Muslims. In contrast, in the young men's self-representations, reclaiming the concept of Muslim did not necessarily mean an increase in religious identity or ethnic behaviour. Most importantly, the research partici-pants illustrate throughout this article that the school's institutional attempt to contain young Muslim men by fixing them into a reified singular radical-ized category of religious identity denies them the social power of self-authorization.

> Shabbir: I think teachers see a Muslim and straight away think about reli-gion. But most kids in our school are not really very religious. It's

just the same like any other group, like the Sikhs. A few are very
religious, but most are just ordinary, getting on with their lives.

Sajid: Teachers are probably confused by Muslims, cos the media show
all these extremists, but Islam is not like other religions, like Chris-
tianity, there is no central system governing ordinary Muslims. So
it's the opposite to what they think. We're not all brainwashed into
acting the same.

Asif: Sometimes you'd like to explain to a teacher, there's no such thing
as *a* Muslim. We're all individuals. But I don't think they'd understand, do you?

Abdul: Yes, definitely teachers are weird, especially with Muslim girls at
school. If teachers saw a Muslim girl with traditional clothes as well
as any modern fashion, you would hear them saying, look at her,
wearing the fashionable clothes when she's supposed to be a Muslim. It's like they're the police and they're saying you're supposed
to be a traditionalist Muslim girl, why don't you act like one. It's
weird, it's like they're offended, so they feel they have to force her
back into their stereotype of what a proper Muslim is.

Parvez: It's because teachers don't really know Muslims. So, they'll have
these strange stereotypes of them been oppressed and forced to wear
the veil and all that. It's like we've to act out what they think we are.

We need further research on the young men's active involvement in the
reconfiguration of the meaning of being Muslim by reclaiming the concept
as a collective self-referent. For example, some of the Pakistani and
Bangladeshi young men in our research emphasized the positive aspects of
publicly identifying as Muslim in a society that exhibits high levels of
faith-hate.

Shoaib: I sometimes think that for the teachers, the real issue is that they
look at Muslims, and cos there's a lot at our school and we're
strong and look after each other, they can't pick on us. Like you
look at the white kids, there's not many of them and they get
picked on more than us by some teachers. Even the black kids don't
stick together like they used to and they get picked out as well.

M.M: So, Muslims get the best treatment?

Shoaib: No, nothing like that. We get a lot of bad stuff as well. But I'm saying there's a good side to being Muslim, like we won't get racist
stuff cos we are seen to be strong. And our parents were seen to be
weak, so they got attacked and beaten up, even at school. We are
under more pressure from the racists now but they know Muslims
can't now be messed with.

Broader dominant representations of young Asian/Muslim men projected
across the state, media and popular culture are mediated within public institutions, alongside specific institutionally produced internal school representations. This has included a diverse range of cultural archetypes within the
changing social formations of early and late modernity – the age of global
migration (Lash 1994). There is a long history of British schooling

employing 'containing' categories that frame the possibilities of knowing and understanding Asian/Muslim male students. In turn, established educational research rationalities serve to rigidly catalogue the lives of these young men. Of particular significance in understanding the emergence of the figure of the Asian/Muslim male student has been the institutional deployment of key analytical categories, namely culture, community and religion, that are implicitly assumed to be ahistorical, unitary, universal and thus unchanging. As Westwood (1990, 59) notes: 'Discourses of registers of masculinity are worked out in a variety of spaces'. Therefore, the fear of Muslim young men does not simplistically operate outside the school; rather, these representations are produced and located within the school itself and most recently played out within the context of the 'war on terror' (Ramji 2007). As Shain explains, linking the contradictions of the cohesion policies and the Coalition government's most recent appeals to Britishness and empire:

> Britishness tests, citizenship ceremonies, and Britishness taught on the school curriculum, could be read from this perspective as offering one way of hanging onto a sense of national identity in the face of pressure to compete as a global player. However, these 'inclusive' politics of community cohesion also represent the 'softer' consensual face of a series of coercive measures designed to contain and manage problem populations (Burnett 2009). (Shain 2011, 35)

The formation of appropriate forms of Britishness resonates with a previous moment in British history, where English (masculinities) become recoded through ascendant registers of Britishness, in response to the catalyst of civil war and the Act of the Union (Colley 1992; Kumar 2003). At present, current initiatives, suggested by Shain above, resonate a similar process of colonization and the designation of safe and dangerous young British men through school-based regimes of masculinity.

Conclusion

The historical reconfiguration of race/ethnicity in English schools through policy initiatives has resulted in a number of disparate intellectual interventions. The theoretical tensions and convergences between perspectives such as anti-racism, multi-culturalism and post-colonialism facilitate a productive context to systematically engage with recent government strategy to address inclusion/exclusion in young Muslim men's lives. This engagement has enabled the recognition that Pakistani and Bangladeshi young men's experiences of schooling are being shaped by recent neo-liberal based policy initiatives. Alongside this, their experience of inclusion/exclusion within the school context is also inflected by a broader cultural turn that involves the reconfiguration of Muslim as sign of religious membership to one of Muslim as an ethnic identity. One of the findings of the research highlighted how the shift to institutional performativity helped provide a context for ambivalence in young men about how inclusion/exclusion operated. They demonstrate that there is no settled understanding of why exclusion is taking place. They often oscillated between exclusion as Islamophobia or racialization. At the same time, they recognize that as an individualized entrepreneurial (neo-liberal) self is promoted, their academic failure becomes reducible to their (Muslim) family backgrounds. Alongside this, the research illustrated how the racialization of inclusion and exclusion operated through class dynamics. In the school context, teachers' embodied whiteness became a space wherein class difference could be displaced. Finally, the research identified how young Pakistani and Bangladeshi young men are now being framed through particular notions of Muslim masculinity. The dominant inclusionary narratives about minority ethnic young men as victims are often juxtaposed with discourses that position these same young men as tough, aggressive and misogynistic. Thus, Pakistani and Bangladeshi young men highlight how schools use Muslim identity as a gendered construct that is indicative of a particular threatening masculinity. In conclusion, the increasing ambivalence surrounding race/ethnicity and the growing visibility of a neo-conservative nationalism that impels an absolute cultural (moral) difference means that categories of same and other are moving into sharper distinction. Theorizing how such distinctions operate and are deployed in schooling spaces is an increasingly necessary intervention in understanding contemporary racial/ethnic relations and the attendant practices of inclusion and exclusion.

Notes

1. Paddy Hillyard (2003) originally used the concept to capture the experiences of the Prevention of Terrorism Acts among the Irish diaspora in Britain during the 1970s and 1980s. More recently, Mary Hickman adopted the concept to carry out a comparative analysis of the intense state surveillance and criminalization of the Irish and Muslim communities with reference to current discourses of integration and social cohesion (Hickman et al. 2012).
2. See Popoviciu, Haywood, and Mac an Ghaill (2006) for further explanation of critical ethnography. A main focus here is to use critical theories, including feminism and post-colonial analysis, to interrogate diasporic working-class young men's subjectivity and identity formation, with a specific focus on capturing their meanings at a time of rapid local and global change.

References

Alvesson, M., and K. Skoldberg. 2000. *Reflexive Methodology: New Vistas for Qualitative Research*. London: Sage.

Anthias, F. (2008). "Thinking through the Lens of Translocational Positionality: An Intersectionality Frame for Understanding Identity and Belonging." *Translocations: Migration and Social Change* 4 (1): 5–20.

Anthias, F., and N. Yuval-Davies. 1993. *Racialized Boundaries: Race, Nation, Gender, Colour and Class and the Anti-Racist Struggle*. London: Routledge.

Appadurai, A. 1991. "Global Ethnoscapes: Notes and Queries for a Transnational Anthropology." In *Recapturing Anthropology: Working in the Present*, edited by R. G. Fox, 191–211. Santa Fe, CA: School of American Research.

Apple, M. W., J. Kenway, and M. Singh. 2005. "Globalizing Educaton: Perspectives from above and below." In *Globalizing Education: Policies, Pedagogies, and Politics*, edited by M. W. Apple, J. Kenway, and M. Singh, 1–31. New York: Peter Lang.

Archer, L. 2003. *'Race', Masculinity and Schooling: Muslim Boys and Education*. Maidenhead: Open University Press.

Arnot, M. and M. Mac an Ghaill. 2007. "(Re)Contextualising Gender Studies in Education." In *The RoutledgeFalmer Reader in Gender and Education*, edited by M. Arnot and M. Mac an Ghaill. London: Routledge.

Ball, S. J. 2000. "Performativities and Fabrications in the Education Economy: Towards the Performative Society?" *The Australian Educational Researcher* 27 (2): 1–23.

Baltodano, M. 2012. "Neoliberalism and the Demise of Public Education: The Corporalization of Schools of Education." *International Journal of Qualitative Studies in Education* 25 (4): 487–507.

Bauman, Z. 2000. *Liquid Modernity*. Cambridge: Polity.

Benson, S. 1996. "Asians Have Culture, West Indians Have Problems: Discourses of Race inside and outside of Anthropology." In *Culture, Identity and Politics*, edited by T. Ranger, Y. Samad, and O. Stuart, 47–56. Aldershot: Avebury.

Bhattacharya, G. 2008. *Dangerous Brown Men: Exploiting Sex, Violence and Feminism in the War on Terror*. London: Zed.

Bhattacharyya, G. 2013. "Racial Neoliberal Britain?" In *The State of Race*, edited by N. Kapoor, V. Kalra, and J. Rhodes, 31–49. London: Palgrave Macmillan.

Birmingham City Council. 2013. "Ethnic Groups: Population and Census." http://www.birmingham.gov.uk.

Bradbury, A., I. McGimpsey, and D. Santori. 2013. "Revising Rationality: The Use of 'Nudge' Approaches in Neoliberal Education Policy." *Journal of Education Policy* 28 (2): 247–267.

Brah, A., M. J. Hickman, and M. Mac an Ghaill, eds. 1999. *Global Futures: Migration, Environment and Globalization*. London: Macmillan.

Braun, V., and V. Clarke. 2006. "Using Thematic Analysis in Psychology." *Qualitative Research in Psychology* 3 (2): 77–101.

Burnett, J. 2009. "Racism and the State: Authoritarianism and Coercion." In *State, Power and Crime*, edited by R. Coleman, J. Sim, S. Tombs, and D. Whyte, 49–62. London: Sage.

Choudhurry, T. 2007. *The Role of Muslim Identity Politics in Radicalisation (a Study in Progress)*. London: Department of Communities and Local Government.

Colley, L. 1992. "Britishness and Europeanness: Who Are the British Anyway?" *Journal of British Studies* 31 (4): 309–329.

Commission on British Muslims and Islamophobia. 1997. *Islamophobia: A Challenge for Us All*. London: Runnymede Trust.

Crouch, M., and H. McKenzie. 2006. "The Logic of Small Samples in Interview-Based Qualitative Research." *Social Science Information* 45 (4): 483–499.

Davies, B., and P. Bansel. 2007. "Neoliberalism and Education." *International Journal of Qualitative Studies in Education* 20 (3): 247–259.

Department for Education and Skills. 2007a. *Diversity and Citizenship Curriculum Review*. London: Department for Children, Schools and Families.

Department for Education and Skills. 2007b. *Gender and Education: The Evidence on Pupils in England Research Information*. London: Department for Education and Skills.

Dwyer, C., B. Shah, and G. Sanghera. 2008. "'From Cricket Lover to Terror Suspect' – Challenging Representations of Young British Muslim Men." *Gender, Place and Culture: A Journal of Feminist Geography* 15 (2): 117–136.

Faas, D. 2010. *Negotiating Political Identities: Multi-ethnic Schools and Youth in Europe*. Farnham: Ashgate.

Fekete, L. 2004. "Anti-Muslim Racism and the European Security State." *Race and Class* 43: 95–103.

Garner, S., and G. Bhattacharyya. 2011. *Poverty, Ethnicity and Place*. York: Joseph Rowntree Foundation.

Gewirtz, S. and A. Cribb. 2009. *Understanding Education: A Sociological Perspective* (Cambridge, Polity).

Giroux, H. 2012. "The Post-9/11 Militarization of Higher Education and the Popular Culture of Depravity: Threats to the Future of American Democracy." *International Journal of Sociology of Education* 1 (1): 27–53.

Gramsci, A. 1970. *Selections from the Prison Notebooks*. London: Lawrence and Wishart.

Hall, S. 1992. "The Question of Cultural Identity." In *Modernity and Its Futures*, edited by S. Hall, D. Held, and T. McGrew. Cambridge: Polity.

Halliday, F. 1999. "Islamophobia' Reconsidered." *Ethnic and Racial Studies* 22 (5): 892–902.

Harvey, D. 2003. *The New Imperialism*. Oxford: Oxford University Press.

Haywood, C., and M. Mac an Ghaill. 2003. *Men and Masculinities: Theory, Research and Social Practice*. Buckingham: Open University Press.

Hickman, M., L. Thomas, H. Nickels and S. Silvestri. 2012. "Social Cohesion and the Notion of 'Suspect Communities': A Study of the Experiences and Impacts of Being 'Suspect' for Irish Communities and Muslim Communities." *Critical Studies on Terrorism* 5 (1): 86–106.

Hillyard, P. 2003. *Suspect Community: People's Experiences of the Prevention of Terrorism Act in Britain*. London: Pluto Press.

Jacobowitz, S. 2004. "Hellenism, Hebraism, and the Eugenics of Culture in E. M. Forster's *Howards End*." CLCWeb: Comparative Literature and Culture 6 (4): 1–10. http://dx.doi.org/10.7771/1481-4374.1250.

Khiabany, G., and M. Williamson. 2012. "Terror, Culture and Anti-Muslim Racism." In *Media and Terrorism: Global Perspectives*, edited by D. Thussu and D. Freedman, 134–151. London: Sage.

Kumar, K. 2003. *The Making of English National Identity*. Cambridge: Cambridge University Press.

Kundnani, A. 2009. *Spooked! How Not to Prevent Violent Extremism*. London: Institute of Race Relations.

Laird, L. D., M. M. Amer, E. D. Barnett, and L. L. Barnes. 2007. "Muslim Patients and Health Disparities in the UK and the US." *Archives of Disease in Childhood*. 92 (10): 922–926.

Lash, S. 1994. "Reflexivity and Its Doubles: Students, Aesthetics, Community." In *Reflexive Modernization*, edited by U. Beck, A. Giddens, and S. Lash, 110–174. Cambridge: Polity Press.

Lawrence, E. 1982. "In the Abundance of Water the Fool is Thirsty: Sociology and Black Pathology." In *The Empire Strikes Back: Race and Racism in 70s Britain*, edited by the Centre for Contemporary Cultural Studies, 93–141. London: Hutchinson.

Mac an Ghaill, M. 1988. *Young Gifted and Black: Teacher-student Relations in the Schooling of Black Youth*. Milton Keynes: Open University Press.

Mac an Ghaill, M. 1994. *The Making of Men: Masculinities, Sexualities and Schooling*. Buckingham: Open University Press.

Mac an Ghaill, M., and C. Haywood. 2005. *Young Bangladeshi in the North East: A Study of Ethnic (In) Visibility*. York: Joseph Rowntree Foundation.

McGhee, D. 2005. *Intolerant Britain? Hate, Citizenship and Difference*. Maidenhead: Open University Press.

McGhee, D. 2012. "Responding to the Post 9/11 Challenges Facing 'Post-secular Societies': Critical Reflections on Habermas's Dialogic Solutions." *Ethnicities* 13 (1): 68–85.

Mills, M., and A. Keddie. 2010. "Cultural Reductionism and the Media: Polarising Discourses around Schools, Violence and Masculinity in an Age of Terror." *Oxford Review of Education* 36 (4): 427–444.

Mirza, H. S. 1992. *Young, Female and Black*. London: Routledge.

Mirza, H. S. 2009. *Race, Gender and Educational Desire: Why Black Women Succeed and Fail*. London: Routledge.

Office for National Statistics. 2012. 2011 Census: Religion (Detailed), Local Authorities in England and Wales, Table QS210EW. http://www.ons.gov.uk.

Patton, M. 1990. *Qualitative Evaluation and Research Methods*. Newbury Park: Sage.

Popoviciu, L., C. Haywood, and M. Mac an Ghaill. 2006. "The Promise of Post-structuralist Methodology: Ethnographic Representation of Education and Masculinity." *Ethnography and Education* 1 (3): 393–412.

Qureshi, K. 2004. "Respected and Respectable: The Centrality of 'Performance' and 'Audiences' in the (Re)Production and Potential Revision of Gendered Ethnicities." *Particip@Tions* 1 (2). http://www.participations.org/volume%201/issue%202/1_02_qureshi_article.htm.

Ramji, H. 2007. "Dynamics of Religion and Gender amongst Young British Muslims." *Sociology* 41 (6): 1171–1189.

Rattansi, A. 1992. "Changing the Subject: Racism, Culture and Education." In *Race, Culture and Difference*, edited by J. Donald and A. Rattansi, 11–49. London: Sage.

Reay, D. 2004. "'Mostly Roughs and Toughs': Social Class, Race and Representation in Inner City Schooling." *Sociology* 38 (5): 1005–1023.

Rizvi, F., and L. C. Engel. 2009. "Neo-liberal Globalization, Educational Policy, and the Struggle for Social Justice." In *The Handbook of Social Justice in Education*, edited by W. Ayers, T. Quinn, and D. Stovall, 529–541. Lanham, MD: Rowman & Littlefield Publishers.

Said, E. W. 1993. *Culture and Imperialism*. London: Vintage.

Shabi, R. 2013. "Tolerance is Never a Given. It Must Be Defended." *The Guardian*, Wednesday 3rd July, p. 10.

Shain, F. 2003. *The Schooling and Identity of Asian Girls*. Stoke on Trent: Trentham Books.

Shain, F. 2011. *The New Folk Devils: Muslim Boys and Education in England*. Stoke on Trent: Trentham Books.

Sian, K. I. Law and S. Sayyid. 2012. *Debates on Difference and Integration in Education: Muslims in the UK*. Centre for Ethnicity and Racism Studies, University of Leeds. http://www.ces.uc.pt/projectos/tolerace/media/WP4/WorkingPapers%204_UK.pdf.

Stromquist, N. P. and K. Monkman. 2000. "Defining Globalization and Assessing Its Implications on Knowledge and Education." In *Globalization and Education: Integration and Contestation across Cultures*, edited by N. P. Stromquist and K. Monkman, 3–25. Lanham, MD: Rowman and Littlefield.

The Observer. 2013. "Should Schools Set Their Own Term Dates?" *The New Review*, Sunday 7 July, p. 7.

Tomlinson, S. 2008. *Race and Education: Policy and Politics in Education*. Maidenhead: Open University Press.

Torres, C. A. 2009. *Education and Neoliberal Globalization*. New York: Routledge.

UK Government. 2009. *The United Kingdom's Strategy for Countering International Terrorism*. Home Office. London: The Stationery Office.

Ussher, J. M., M. Sandoval, J. Perz, W. K. T. Wong, and P. Butow. 2013. "The Gendered Construction and Experience of Difficulties and Rewards in Cancer Care, Qualitative Health Research." http://qhr.sagepub.com/content/early/2013/04/03/1049732313484197.

Walkerdine, V. 2003. "Reclassifying Upward Mobility: Femininity and the Neo-Liberal Subject." *Gender and Education* 15 (3): 237–248.

Westwood, S. 1990. "Racism, Masculinity and the Politics of Space." In *Men, Masculinities and Social Theory*, edited by J. Hearn and D. H. J. Morgan, 84–95. London: Unwin and Hyman.

Wright, A. 2012. "Fantasies of Empowerment: Mapping Neo-Liberal Discourse in the Coalition Government's Schools Policy." *Journal of Education Policy* 27 (3): 279–294.

Disability and inclusive education in times of austerity

Wayne Veck

Department of Education Studies, University of Winchester, Winchester, UK

When communities fall into decline, disabled people can find themselves alone and invisible in a society of indifferent individuals. Arendt offers an account of such a time in her discussion of the rise of a society of mass labouring and consuming. Bauman's insights into the fragmentation of life, in which established norms, traditional ties and customs fade and solid institutions liquefy, are equally pertinent. Together, Arendt and Bauman point to the conditions and demands that have given rise to the present policy of austerity, current approaches to the education and care of the disabled and the rejection of inclusive education.

Introduction

Times of austerity are, also, times of contradiction. The current UK Government, a coalition of Conservatives and Liberal Democrats, has implemented cuts to both the benefits and social services that assist disabled people in line with policies of austerity, and it has advanced an approach to the education of disabled young people that explicitly rejects what it considers to be a 'bias towards inclusion' in schooling (DfE 2011, 2). All the while, these policies are presented as part of the government's vision for a society in which disabled people in particular, and local communities in general, are 'empowered' to gain independence. How are we to make sense of this contradiction? Two answers have been offered. In the first, the language of 'empowerment' is taken to be rhetoric, utilised to obscure governmental impotency in the face of a global economic downturn. Thus, Tomlinson writes:

> In the current global recession governments find it easier to focus on individual deficiencies and the removal of welfare payments rather than more costly strategies of reorganising educational institutions to support all young people in their preparation for adulthood. (2012, 283)

The second answer sees talk of 'empowerment' as masking not only economic necessity, but also ideological intent, wherein 'ideology' is taken to denote an unbending and partial way of approaching and accounting for reality (Eagleton 1991). Wolff (2010) argues that there exist 'some alternative "reasonable" kinds of austerity', including serious 'efforts to collect income taxes from U.S.-based multinational corporations'. His point is that (even) if governments have no choice but to enforce austerity, it does not then follow that austerity itself is something other than a series of choices. While Amartya Sen (2012) has written of how, together, these choices constitute a single, 'ill-chosen cult of austerity'. The former UK Prime Minister, Gordon Brown (2012), has used equally pointed language to denounce Europe's leaders for their 'obsession with imposing a swift and deep austerity' and for 'holding dogmatically to a policy of ever more austerity despite all the evidence of stagnation'. Continuing this line of critique, Blyth (2013, 230) argues that the failures of the current form of austerity in Europe could have been foreseen by anyone equated with the 'previous intellectual and natural history' of this 'dangerous idea', and that the consequences of the 'epistemic arrogance and ideological insistence' of European policy-makers 'have been, and continue to be, horrendous'.

Zygmunt Bauman (2011, 23) sees, in responses to the present recession, evidence of an ideological prioritising of those with capital over those living in impoverished conditions that has resulted in governments cutting the benefits of the most deprived while all the time guaranteeing a 'sort of "welfare state" for the rich'. Likewise, Beck has observed:

> Resistance is building not just in Athens but also throughout Europe as a whole to a policy aimed at overcoming the crisis by redistributing wealth *from bottom to top* in accordance with the principle of state socialism for the banks and the affluent, neo-liberalism for the middle classes and the poor. (2013, 7; original emphasis)

No wonder, then, that Labonté (2012, 260) declares 'the austerity agenda has less to do with economics or even good fiscal management than with ideology', that Meacher (2012), a Labour Party Member of Parliament, proclaims 'Britain today is being crucified on a cross of ideology', and that Stuckler and Basu (2013, 140), concluding their comprehensive study of the consequences of contemporary policies of austerity, insist 'Ultimately austerity has failed because it is unsupported by sound logic or data. It is an economic ideology'.

This article, while not seeking to question the validity of these perspectives, nevertheless advances the argument that current approaches to the education and care of disabled people, along with present policies of austerity, which have become a global phenomenon, can be understood only in relation to the decline of both actual community and the concrete hope for its existence. The article is divided into three sections, each of which attempts to offer insight into this decline and its consequences. The first section considers Hannah Arendt's discussion of a crisis in authority in education in 1950s America, which she connects to 'the conditions of mass society', a society of mass labouring and consuming (Arendt 1993, 191), to elucidate the estrangement of both disabled people and those who care for and teach them, from what she names our 'common world' (Arendt 1998). The second section turns to Bauman's (2005a, 313) analysis of what he defines as our 'liquid-modern condition'. In conjunction with Arendt's insights, this exploration points to the ways in which both present policies of austerity and contemporary understandings of and approaches to disability are sourced by the same mass indifference that characterises a society in which individuals labour and consume alongside each other without turning to each other in care and responsibility. The final section addresses Arendt's (1971a) discussion of thinking in an attempt to illuminate possibilities for inclusive education.

Austerity, care and inclusive education in a labouring and consuming society

The principle of 'empowerment' manifests itself in current UK policy documents in two forms. First, there is a positive assertion of the correlation between personalised care and education and the advancement of freedom of choice and independence. Second, there is a damning appraisal of the ways in which institutions and systems can impede the autonomy of disabled individuals and their families. In line with care schemes emerging in countries throughout the West (Jones et al. 2012), the Coalition Government has pledged to provide the parents of children with impairments with the opportunity to have a personal budget by the end of 2014, so that they, supported by a trained key worker, might be granted 'greater control over their child's support' (DfE 2012, 25). This pledge was announced in the Coalition government's (DfE 2011) Green Paper on special education and disability, where it was presented as a central component of a new Education, Health and Care Plan, also to be introduced by the end of 2014. This Plan, drawing upon the 'ambitions' of individual families for their child from birth until the age of 25, will replace the current assessment of special educational need (SEN) and will incorporate all support offered across education, health and social care (DfE 2011, 5). A personal Education, Health and Care Plan and the option of a personal budget are presented as effective ways of securing independence or 'personalisation' (DH 2010, 8), which will enable 'parents to have a much greater say in the way their child is supported and give them a clear role in designing a personalised package of support for their child and family' (DfE 2011, 47). Significantly, the Coalition Government are committed to ensuring that parents have 'real choice over their child's education' (DfE 2011, 5), and in particular the choice between 'mainstream' and 'special' schooling. Alongside budgetary control, this choice is identified as pivotal in securing autonomy for parents and guardians over the care, education and support their children receive.

Despite their insistence that this focus on parental choice in special education represents a major component of a 'new approach to special educational needs and disability' (DfE 2011, 2012), the Coalition Government's policy is hardly novel. Indeed, in their 1997 Green Paper *Excellence for All Children: Meeting Special Educational Needs*, the then New Labour government insisted that while they wanted 'children with SEN to be educated in mainstream schools wherever possible', they would 'maintain parents' present right to express a preference for a special school place for their child' and ensure that 'parents of children with SEN have an increasing degree of real choice' (DfEE 1997, 25). The claim that offering the parents of disabled children 'personalised' support is somehow original is equally dubious. Indeed, New Labour's *Every Child Matters*, for example, claims that by way of introducing 'direct payments, which enable local authorities to give families the funds to buy the help they need, the Government is giving parents more choice over how they receive services' (DfES 2003, 42). Most significantly, the idea that the Coalition Government's policy on disability and special education constitutes a break with the past rests on the assumption that there was a substantive and lasting commitment by New Labour to inclusive education. Tomlinson (2005, 154) has noted that by the second term of New Labour's governance, 'gaps between policy rhetoric and practical reality' became 'more evident, particularly between a rhetoric of "inclusion" and a school system that increasingly separated different groups'. It is worth noting here that New Labour, despite signing the United Nation's Convention on the Rights of Persons with Disabilities in 2007 and formally confirming it in 2009, stipulated the following reservation to Article 24 of the Convention (which calls for all governments to promote 'an inclusive education system at all levels and lifelong learning'; UN 2006, 160):

> The United Kingdom reserves the right for disabled children to be educated outside their local community where more appropriate education provision is available elsewhere. Nevertheless, parents of disabled children have the same opportunity as other parents to state a preference for the school at which they wish their child to be educated. (UN 2006, 10)

The Coalition Government's continuation of this commitment to parental choice and financial control, alongside its suspicion that institutions and systems might hinder such choice and independence, are presented as part of a wider approach to social policy that David Cameron has encapsulated under the name of the 'Big Society'. The 'Big Society' is, in Cameron's (2010) rhetoric, 'a huge culture change' that will empower people to 'feel both free and powerful enough to help themselves and their own communities', so that they need not 'always turn to officials, local authorities or central government for answers to the problems they face'. Such juxtapositions abound in the Coalition's social policy documents, where the potential of 'a big and open society' is differentiated from the state (DH 2010, 21), 'empowerment of local communities' from 'disempowering governments' (DfCLG 2010, 7), and 'the skills and expertise of people across the country' from a government that 'on its own cannot fix every problem' (Cabinet Office 2010).

Beresford (2013a, 2013b) has, along with his colleagues (Slasberg, Beresford, and Schofield 2012), illuminated a significant distinction between *direct payments* and *personal budgets*. Where direct payments were advocated by disabled activists in the 1980s and are based on 'the philosophy of independent living, which meant that the payments should meet the costs of support that would enable the individual disabled person to live on as equal terms as possible to a non-disabled person' (Slasberg, Beresford, and Schofield 2012, 1029), personalisation in general and the practice of offering personal budgets in particular have been informed by a 'consumerist philosophy' (Beresford 2013a). It is Beresford's (2013b) view that, far from offering disabled people a source for adequate support, the finance provided for personal budgets derives from 'existing and inadequate funding, top-sliced for administration and allocated on a points basis'. As a consequence, a 'consumerist rather than empowerment based approach' has been adopted that leaves disabled people particularly exposed in times of austerity, 'where what most service users are actually experiencing is damage to their rights and quality of life' (Beresford 2013b). The emphasis on the values of 'control and choice' in both education and care have obscured the values of those disabled activists who, when calling for direct payments, were seeking qualitative changes to their lives as citizens, and not merely quantitative alterations to their lives as individual consumers (Beresford 2009; Slasberg, Beresford, and Schofield 2012). To be presented with a multitude of choices and to have secured the feeling of being in control of these choices is to have achieved the ideal of the consumer, but not of the activist aiming at the transformation of the lives of disabled people and their communities. Thus, Beresford (2009, 2) connects what he names 'the rhetoric of personalisation', a defining feature of special education and care throughout the West (and again, not an innovation of the current UK Government), to 'a process of rebadging, where the language of consumerism and control does little more than overlay arrangements that remain essentially the same'. Others, like Lingard and Sellar (2012, 59), detect a submerged plot lurking behind 'the Big Society narrative at the heart of Cameronism', one that centres on 'the predominant prescription of consumer choice', and is, as many others still have noted, indifferent to wider societal difficulties and inequalities (see Catney et al. 2013; Fergusson 2012; Labonté 2012; Lister and Bennett 2010; North 2011; Wainwright 2010).

It is impossible to access the implications of these concerns about consumer choice in relation to the care and education of disabled people without understanding how this care and education came to be objects of consumption in the first place. 'It is frequently said that we live in a consumers' society', Arendt (1998, 126) notes, before adding her own observation that 'since ... labor and consumption are but two stages of the same process, imposed upon man by the necessity of life, this is only another way of saying that we live in a society of laborers'. To declare both that the parents of children with impairments have become consumers of education and that disabled adults are consumers of their care is, equally, to say that the providers of these services – the educators and carers – are labourers.

Arendt (1998) locates the meaning of labour within the things it produces, things that serve no other use than the maintenance of separate bodies. In the production of things to be used up, disposed of and consumed by distinct individuals, labourers, the *animal laborans*, are estranged not only from each other but also from any form of activity that aims to produce objects that might take on a form that bypasses what are, for Arendt (1998), the twin characteristics of labour: necessity and futility. But where 'labor leaves no permanent trace' (1998, 90), work, the activity of the *homo faber*, transcends both impermanence and necessity by producing objects that contribute to the enduring construction of a world that is both common to all people and which survives on past the mortal existence of each of its individual contributors. Moreover, work is always purposive activity, directed to a concrete end or *telos*, and is thus quite distinct from '*laboring*' that 'always moves in the same circle, which is prescribed by the biological process of the living organism' (1998, 98; original emphasis).

Arendt further differentiates the aims of labour and work – the production of things for consumption and the production of objects that contribute to the persistence of a common world – from what she names 'the 'products' of action and speech, which together constitute the fabric of human relationships' (1998, 95). It is Arendt's view that action and speech, in contrast to mere behaviour, allow the individual to reveal their distinctness by way of making an appearance within and a contribution to the public realm, which is 'the world itself, in so far as it is common to all of us' (1998, 52). But the act and the spoken word are endowed with this potential only by virtue of the fact that they are heard and witnessed. It was the 'fundamental insight' of the Greeks, Arendt (1971a, 140) contends, to realise 'that whatever appears is there to be seen, that the very concept of appearance demands a spectator, and that therefore to see and to behold are activities of the highest rank'. Deeds and speech persist beyond the moment of action and utterance, and through them an actor is able to divulge, in Arendt's (1998, 180–181) language, 'who' they are becoming, their 'unique and distinct identity', as opposed to merely 'what' they are. But this is only because of the spectator who, having gifted their attention to the other person, goes on to keep some form of record of what they have seen and heard (Arendt 1998).

If the worker produces objects that might retain a usefulness which endures beyond the life of the worker and the actor produces deeds and speech that, if they are attended to and recorded, can obtain an immortal place within common culture and the tapestry of human affairs, then labour, producing the things that sustain life, is utterly incapable of transcending the boundaries of the private and immediate experience of the individuals engaged in consuming its products. When labouring, we are estranged from acting and speaking in the public realm, the common world. When consuming, we are entirely incapable of realising our distinctively human abilities to give witness to others and to give voice to what we have witnessed. It follows that, with the emergence of a mass society, 'where the most private of all human activities, laboring, has become public and has been permitted to establish its own common realm' (Arendt 1998, 112), public spaces of action and speech have been lost and human lives have come to be demarcated by immediacy and privacy.

It is within this context that we might begin to make sense of a policy of austerity which involves cutting the benefits of people living in poverty and people with impairments. If I look to another person and see neither a potential spectator, who might witness my acts and hear my words, nor an actor, to whom I might attend, then when the services that sustain the welfare of this other person and provide them with opportunities to participate in public life are cut I do not feel that my life has to any extent been diminished. Moreover, it is in this same context, this same loss of our concrete sense of our interdependency, of being part of 'the "web" of human relationships' (Arendt 1998, 183), that Arendt's (1993) account of what she names a 'crisis in education' is situated. Arendt's account unfolds as a tale of a twofold alienation. First, Arendt claims that education is estranged from its responsibility to the world. Second, education has lost sight of what, Arendt (1993) describes as its 'essence', which is *natality*, the potential that each child, by virtue of being born, possesses to make a new and distinct difference to the world. To educate young people is, in Arendt's (1993) view, to be perpetually between the established world, which owes its survival to the rising generation, and young people, who require protection from this world if they are to be prepared to make a difference to it. But living in the midst of 'world alienation' (Arendt 1998), in a society where 'consumption takes the place of all the truly relating activities' (Arendt 1994, 21), both teachers and parents are likely to 'refuse to assume responsibility for the world into which they have brought the children' (Arendt 1993, 190). To address young people with an indifference to the world is to be entirely estranged from the distinctive responsibility of the educator, which incorporates both an acceptance of culpability for what has come to pass between persons and a willingness to represent the world to young people. It is this responsibility that, for Arendt (1993), endows the educator with an authority that immediately distinguishes them from a teacher, who owes their authority to their qualifications and knowledge of the world.

Coinciding with the loss of the educator's authority, there has, in Arendt's view, been an elevation of pedagogy to a specialist activity, to what she calls 'a science of teaching', which is 'wholly emancipated from the actual material to be taught' (1993, 182). Within the confines of this 'science', what matters is merely *how* one teaches and not *what* one teaches. What, then, might be said when the education of children with certain identified impairments is conceived as a specialist activity, to be conducted by specialist practitioners, and when the authority of these professionals derives neither from their knowledge of, nor from the responsibility they have taken for, the world, but rather from their specialist expertise? For an answer we need look no further than to one of the 'key reforms' announced in the UK's Green Paper (DfE 2011), a 'local offer' to be provided by local authorities that will outline all the support which will be offered to any young person who has been given an Education, Health and Care Plan. The Coalition Government's 2012 report on special education and disability describes the 'additional or different provision schools make for children with SEN' guaranteed by this 'local offer', including assurances that 'the curriculum offers breadth and balance and is tailored to meet children's individual needs', 'teaching is adapted to meet children's SEN', and 'arrangements are made to secure specialist expertise' (DfE 2012, 46). Once again, there is nothing 'new' about either this attempt to create a 'science' of teaching children 'with SEN' or the accompanying separation of pedagogy into two distinct branches, one for 'mainstream' schooling and the other for special education. The consequence of this ongoing quest to devise specialist pedagogy for young people classified as 'special' is, for the educator, a growing estrangement from the responsibility that is the source of their authority. This is their responsibility for the world that is common and to the essential newness of *all* young people that demands that they are simultaneously protected from and prepared to act within the world. Estranged from this responsibility, the educator is rendered less and less capable of including young people in an education that will, in turn, prepare them for their future inclusion into the world.

Luff et al. encapsulate their appraisal of recent approaches to care in education in the United Kingdom in the following words:

> Over the years, increasing government preoccupation with care has resulted in a shift from general concerns of the well-being of all learners to specialised concerns about the specific care needs of vulnerable groups within an educational setting … (2013, 15)

Precisely this irony is evident in the Coalition Government's so-called 'new' approach to the care and education of young people designated as 'having SENs'. This approach is presented as a drive to retain a focus 'on achievement not labels', to tackling 'a culture of low expectations' and, above all else, of course, to 'empowering' parents to make choices about their children's education (DfES 2011, 3–4). Putting to one side the fact that the primary subjects of the government's commitment to empowerment are parents and not their (non-voting) children, there is the question of what type of 'empowerment' and care can be achieved by and within an education that is deprived of its authority. In other words, the question of empowerment cannot be untangled from the question of *telos*, of the end or ends for which people are being empowered. It is a question that is entirely negligible in relation to labouring, guided as it is by necessity, by the generation of commodities that can be predicted to stimulate and satisfy needs in persons reduced to life-processes. Equally, when teachers are required to give themselves over to the task of satisfying needs that, due to their very predictability and reducibility to quantities, must be located within the necessity of biological life, they are being asked to lose all sight of the *telos* of their education and care. For example, both Gillies and Robinson (2013), drawing on the findings of a study of young people at risk of being excluded from inner-city London schools, and Laurent (2013), reflecting on the experiences of disengaged young people in schools, point to the incongruity of a policy focus on personal development and emotional well-being that has given rise to a narrow and regulated approach to caring. Perhaps such ironies are the inevitable outcome of any attempt to 'empower' young persons that endeavours neither to prepare them for work (as opposed to labour) nor for action but merely for a life of labour and consumption in a mass society. It is an irony that Arendt expounds when she speaks of 'the real meaning of the emancipation of workers and women', to be included with others, 'not as persons, to be sure, but insofar as they fulfill a necessary function in the life-process of society' (Arendt 1993, 187–188). Following workers and women, we now witness the 'emancipation' or 'empowerment' of disabled people, again not in their individual distinctiveness but as the receivers of specialist forms of teaching and care that are conceived as mere labour.

However, care for the needs of disabled people might be conceived not only as specialist undertaking, a means to heal pain and ease impairment, but also as a way of preparing people to manifest their distinctly human capabilities of action and spectatorship, of beginning and giving witness to the beginnings of others. The potential depths of care have been illuminated by feminists, such as Nel Noddings. It is Noddings's (2010, 391) view that care can broaden the self by way of engaging the carer in a relation that 'is first of all attentive to the cared-for'. This attention or 'engrossment', which is 'an open, nonselective receptivity to the cared-for' (Noddings 2002, 15), takes educators out of themselves and reveals to them that they are related to others beyond the bounds of mutual labouring and consuming. Reflecting on the actions of a woman physician in her attentive care for an elderly woman in hospital, Gilligan (1993, 62) writes: 'The ideal of care is … an activity of relationship, of seeing and responding to need, taking care of the world by sustaining the web of connection so that no one is left behind'. Grounded in the experiences of women, this 'ethic of care' gives rise, not to a vision of justice, in which 'self and other will be treated as equal worth', but to 'the vision that everyone will be responded to and included, that no one will be left alone or hurt' (1993, 63). Immediately, this vision of care suggests that an education which is inclusive cannot be achieved by implementing the most effective kinds of strategies, techniques and methods to address and meet needs deemed 'special' or 'additional'. Instead, Arendt's (1998) 'web of relationships', Noddings's (2002) 'engrossment' and Gilligan's (1993) 'web of connection' together convey the primacy of interdependency, of the fact that before it is possible for us to include others we ourselves must have been included. Recognition of this fact renders indifference to another person impossible. For educators, such recognition might mean that attempts to include young people by way of labouring to meeting established biological needs take second place to works of care. Such works might, in turn, reassure all young people that they are not just one more segment in a social or medical category, but persons becoming towards a world in which they might realise the promise of distinctiveness that accompanied their birth. Thus, Laurent (2013, 40) observed 'caring moments' in schools engender relations that 'tend to have enduring effects on students'. Shelby (2003, 341) goes even further, suggesting: 'Care ethics … precisely because of the emphasis it places on the human capacity for response to connection and need, has the potential to strengthen in our schools the sense of humanity'. Harnessing this sense of interdependency in and beyond schooling might lead us to conclude that cuts to benefits and services, introduced in the name of austerity, have exclusionary conse-quences for us all as potential actors and spectators in a world that is always common.

Disability and inclusive education in a society of indifferent individuals

In the *Communist Manifesto*, Marx and Engels (1967, 223) famously spoke of the unending 'revolutionising of production, uninterrupted disturbance of all social conditions, everlasting uncertainty and agitation', which together mean that in 'the bourgeois epoch' all that was once 'solid melts into air'. This magnificent metaphor becomes, in Bauman's (2005a, 313) hands, piv-otal to comprehending what he names our 'liquid-modern condition'. Where Arendt saw that consumption depends upon labour, Bauman identifies, at the source of 'the glory and the blight of the consumer society' (2007a,

200), two crucial changes that make 'our form of modernity' both 'novel and different' (Bauman 2013, 29). The first of these changes, the loss of a common sense of an orderly society and a common faith in the institutions that might usher in this order, has given rise to the second, the individualisation of society, a process through which shared belief in the potency of 'society as a whole' has come to be supplanted by 'the self-assertion of the individual' (2013, 29). In this 'individualized society' (Bauman 2001a), where all established and prescriptive norms lose their hold, all traditional ties and customs fade and all solid institutions liquefy, women and men are, Bauman (2013) tells us (echoing Arendt's ironic use of the word), 'emancipated'. Alongside Bauman, Beck (2002, 131; original emphasis) offers an account of the *'inherent contradictions in the individualization process'*, which he summarises in the following way:

> The individual is indeed removed from the tradition commitments and support relationships, but exchanges them for the constraints of existence in the labor market and as a consumer, with the standardizations and controls they contain. (2002, 131)

As with Bauman, it is possible to detect Arendt's influence here. Liberation from the bonds of custom and tradition has left each individual prey to a new set of burdens within a society of labourers and consumers and, in particular, to the foremost demand of achieving individual independence.

Robert Nozick, in *Anarchy, State, and Utopia*, offers a defence of the individual and their independence that begins with an uncompromising rejection of the existence of a *'social entity'*, since in actuality, he contends, we are surrounded by 'individual people, different individual people, with their own individual lives' (Nozick 1974, 32–33; original emphasis). We should remember 'how different people are' and admit that any sensible conception of 'Utopia will consist of utopias, of many different and divergent communities in which people lead different kinds of lives under different institutions' (1974, 311–312; original emphasis). Nozick's words were, of course, to be famously echoed by Margaret Thatcher (1987), the former UK Prime Minister, when she proclaimed that there was 'no such thing' as society, only 'individual men and women' and 'families'.

In Bauman's work, two metaphors aptly illustrate the difference between the grand utopia, rejected by Nozick, and the individualised utopia, which he embraces. The first metaphor is of the *gardener*, who 'assumes that there would be no order at all in the part of the world in his charge were it not for his constant attention and effort', and who thereby embarks upon the task of 'encouraging the growth of the right type of plants and of uprooting and destroying all the others' (Bauman 2005a, 306). What the gardener wants, in other words, is to establish and to maintain a stable order. The second metaphor is of the *hunter*, who 'could not care less about the overall "balance of things", whether "natural" or contrived' (2005a, 306). For Bauman (2005a), the ascension of the hunters, for whom there are as many utopias as there are separate individuals or families, has accompanied the demise of the gardeners, who dream of forging a shared commitment to the production of (their version of) an orderly society. If Bauman is correct in his analysis, then we have witnessed a particular kind of validation of Nozick and Thatcher's rejection of society and of the ethic of care that stems from our interdependency.

The irony that permeates Arendt's (1993, 1998) discussion of 'emancipation' in a labouring and consuming society takes on a new harshness in Bauman's analysis of the emergence of the hunters; that is, of individuals 'freed' from all the demands of sustaining a solid identity. Bauman writes:

> One can argue … that having an unfixed identity that is eminently 'until further notice'; is not a state of liberty but an obligatory and interminable conscription into a war of liberation that is never ultimately victorious. (2005b, 32)

Bauman's account of the perpetual frustration of the individual in search of their freedom in a modern liquid society illuminates how care and responsibility can become privatised; that is, how the human capability to respond to and care for others can be subsumed by self-concern to such an extent that indifference becomes a way of life.

Living in an individualised society, and therefore no longer subjected to the visions and schemes of zealous and potentially demonic social planners or gardeners, what tests us is not the extent to which we successfully conform to pre-established patterns but the extent to which we are able to thrive without living towards such given ways of being. Indeed, it is precisely the gardener's imposition of order that stifles the progress of separate individuals in gaining and safeguarding their independence. Individualisation is thus a process that involves not order-building and order sustenance, but order disruption. In this society, the only prevailing norm is 'norm breaking (or rather the perpetual transcendence of norm, with a haste which denies habits the time they need to congeal into norms)' (Bauman 2001b, 131). Hence Bauman, employing a language he acknowledges amounts to 'a contradiction in terms', writes of 'liquid-modern culture' as 'a *culture of disengagement, discontinuity, and forgetting*' (2004, 71; original emphasis). This contradiction, conditioned by the process of individualisation itself, has significant implications for understandings of inclusion and exclusion. When all established metaphors for those persons who are deemed to be most included – the upstanding character, the pillar of the community and the honest citizen – give way to be replaced by images of separate individuals or hunters, successful in transcending any of the actual or imagined demands and pleasures of community life, then the most included of all is the indifferent individual *par excellence*. It is Slee's view that this process of individualisation has resulted in 'collective indifference', which:

> is not just a means of coping with the ongoing suffering of the developing world, it refers also to the ways in which we have come to routinely ignore suffering that stalks us in our neighbourhoods. (2011, 38)

In times of 'collective indifference', the hunters, dynamic and independent, able to submerge all aches of insecurity and all signs of weakness, are likely to be considered the most 'included' of persons. In these times, then, 'exclusion' does not so much designate a state of marginalisation within or ostracism from the social body or certain aspects of social organisation, but rather denotes separation from the class of persons who has achieved independence from society. On the basis of this account, and however paradoxical it might sound, 'exclusion' means dependency upon others and 'inclusion' independence from others. To be included, in this sense, is to secure one's own security, it is to sustain an 'identity in *not belonging*' (Bauman 2005b, 29; original emphasis).

Such is the pressure to be an independent hunter, Bauman insists, that a concerted effort is required by anyone seeking 'to spot a gardener who aims at predesigned harmony stretching beyond the fence of his private garden' (2005a, 307). However, perhaps Bauman is too hasty in announcing the demise of the gardener, since, while it might be hard to identify individuals who act and feel like gardeners, the function of the gardener might remain, broadly conceived as a mechanism for separating independent consumers from non-independent consumers. If in the past it was the gardener's function to cast persons aside in the name of an overarching vision of social harmony, now the gardener's purpose might be to segregate those pursuing their own, entirely private vision of the good life from those deemed unwilling or unable to secure a life that flourishes in its independence.

In relation to schooling, this new function of the gardener might be understood within the context of *mass education*. It is Arendt's contention that the rise of the social was accompanied by the creation of abundance, 'the ideal of the *animal laborans*', which has become so dominant that 'our whole economy has become a waste economy, in which things must be almost as quickly devoured and discarded as they have appeared in the world' (1998, 134). Bauman, who extends Arendt's insight to education, maintains that the art of learning has become so entwined with the art of forgetting that currently students are caught up in consuming 'knowledge' that 'is eminently *disposable*, good only until further notice and of only temporary usefulness' (Bauman 2012, 18; original emphasis). Education, thus dislodged from its place *between* the past and the future, has become *against* both the past, as it turns its back on tradition, and the future, as it seeks immediate and quantifiable ends. This change in education can be seen as yet another one of those many ambiguous emancipations that, together, constitute the character of 'liquid modernity' (Bauman 2005a). In this case, the emancipation takes the form of a 'gradual yet relentless' pressure to break away from 'the orthodox teacher–student relationship' and, instead, to embrace interactions organised along 'the supplier–client, or shopping-mall–shopper pattern' (2005a, 316).

The gardener's new function in this mass education might be detected in processes that see some young people classified as 'regular learners' and offered 'personalised' learning, while others are contained within the category 'children with special educational needs' and provided with 'individualised' learning within special or 'mainstream' schools (albeit, in specially designated centres, units and departments within these schools). Consider, for example, the following assertion from the Coalition government's Green Paper on SEN and disability:

> Parents of children with statements of SEN will be able to express a preference for any state-funded school – including special schools, Academies and Free Schools – and have their preference met unless it would not meet the needs of the child, *be incompatible with the efficient education of other children*, or be an inefficient use of resources. (DfE 2011, 17; emphasis added)

Granting parents and their children all the freedom of the consumer, the Coalition Government here identifies as 'special' those young people whose participation in education might disrupt the other, efficient consumers of education. In this way they offer us an insight into what the gardener's function in the liquid modern school might be, suggesting that the function is not to create classrooms of order but to sustain a culture of indifference by way of distinguishing independent learners from those unable to sustain the demands of consuming and disposing of mass education. It might then be that the function of the 'mainstream' or 'regular' school as gardener is no longer to separate those who can be educated from those young people once discarded as 'educational sub-normal', but is rather to segregate independent from non-independent learners. It might, in short, be the new role of the gardener in education to identify 'flawed consumers' (Bauman 2008, 149).

In their study of the experiences of sixteen parents of children with impairments in 'mainstream' schooling in South Africa, Swart et al. (2004, 99) learned that while the majority 'did not experience resistance from other parents', they did not 'however, … receive support', since 'in one parent's words, "you're part of the school community, but actually you're still on your own"'. In her small-scale study of the experiences of 17 mothers of children categorised as being 'learning disabled', Ryan (2005, 296) discovered that 'All of the mothers reported numerous instances in which they or their children were subjected to stares, looks and comments when they were out in public places'. In her reflections on the experiences of these mothers and their children, Ryan concludes: 'It is quite possibly the case that people are more generally concerned with protecting themselves and the social reality in which they live, than demonstrating negative responses towards learning disabled children or adults' (2005, 302). In other words, disabling attitudes can be informed, not by a hostility to that which diverges from given norms, but rather by a general stance of indifference that becomes antagonist only with the (imagined or actual) disruption of one's own, individual being in the world. Attitudes towards disability are, as Söder (1990) argues, complex and not stable, and this is especially so in a society where a dominant ideal is securing independence to accumulate and to consume. There are disabling attitudes that give rise to gazes that stretch out from one person to another with the intention to condemn or to classify, as with Foucault's (1977) infamous 'normalizing gaze'. But the absence of an attentive and caring attitude and gaze can, also, be disabling. We can be disabled, oppressed, excluded or marginalised from this perspective, not only by those attitudes that are pervasive in a society that responds with enmity to an impaired body (see here Bogdan 1988; Barnes 1992; Goffman 1990; Shakespeare 1994, 1999), but also when we are left alone to experience a numbing sense of invisibility within a society of indifferent individuals. We are all potentially disabled within a society without thoughtful and caring attention, but some people (i.e. those unwilling or unable to flourish alone) are more likely to be disabled than others. In this society, the physical reality that impairment may befall us all at any point is matched by the social reality of disability that awaits anyone incapable of uttering a proud boast of self-sufficiency. It is, perhaps, only in reference to this atmosphere of indifference that the Coalition Government's rejection of inclusive education and its active pursuit of the policy of austerity can be explained.

In their review of literature about the attitudes of parents' towards inclusive education, de Boer, Pijl, and Minnaert (2010, 178) observed that parents of non-disabled children 'are quite positive about inclusive education', before suggesting that a 'possible explanation' for this finding might be 'that the number of children with special needs who are full time in regular classes is still rather limited and that these pupils belong to the relatively easy-to-include subgroups of children with special needs'. They go on to suggest that due to limited experience of inclusive education, the parents of what they, too, insist on naming 'typically developing children' thus 'experience relatively few problems, resulting in a growing acceptance and a positive attitude' (2010, 178). Concluding their study of the attitudes of 338 Greek parents of primary school children without impairments towards inclusive education, Kalyva, Georgiadi, and Tsakiris (2007, 302) also note that their participants were 'positive about the expected outcomes of inclusion', and suggest that this might be due to the sense that 'benefits accrue to their own children as well as children with SEN', because their children 'are exposed to diverse learning opportunities'. In their research into the attitudes of 290 Greek parents of young children without impairments towards the inclusion of children with impairments into 'mainstream' kindergartens, Tafa and Manolitsis (2003, 169) discovered that 'Greek parents of typically developing children seem to recognize more benefits than drawbacks for their children's participation in inclusive programmes'. They go on to note that these parents 'seem to believe that their children, by virtue of being included in the inclusion classroom, will increase their respect, their awareness and their acceptance of other children's needs and will have fewer prejudices about people with special needs' (2003, 169). What both of these studies from Greece suggest is that the value parents place on inclusive education rests on the extent to which the child classified as being somehow 'other-than-normal' can be utilised as a means towards the advancement of the general education of their own children. Such attitudes hardly illuminate attentive care that involves respect for another person as they are, in and of themselves, beyond the confines of anyone's interest in or concern about them. The inference of all these studies might be that, in a culture of indifference, parents of children without impairments will accept all diversity and all the inclusion they can either benefit from or afford to be nonchalant about.

Thinking, caring attention and the possibilities of inclusive education

Rogers (2007, 65), in her study of 24 parents of children with impairments who attend 'mainstream' British schools, discovered that, despite the high hopes of the parents, a 'testing and examination culture' in these schools means that their 'children are excluded, ... at many different levels, although seemingly included'. Educationalists from countries as diverse as the United Kingdom, Malaysia, Brazil, Australia and South Korea are united in deeming the growing influence of market forces and competition between and within schools as subjugating the emergence of an inclusive education that might counter indifference and yield caring attention to all young people (Barton and Slee 1999; Booth, Ainscow, and Dyson 1997; Jelas and Ali 2012; Santos 2001; Slee 2001; Kim 2012). To create inclusive schools, what is required is a shift from a culture of mass indifference, fuelled by mass competition, to a culture of attentive care. In this culture, inclusion and exclusion, along with austerity, might be witnessed as having real consequences for individuals who are not simply like me but are persons to whom I am responsible with a responsibility that is the source of my becoming.

There is more that needs to be said about how indifference might be countered, and in order to say it we turn now to address Arendt's view of the spectator who, in absolute opposition to the indifferent individual, offers what she (1971a, 4) describes as their 'thinking attention' to the other person. Drawing on the insights of Socrates into the thinking process, Arendt (1971a) contends that to attend thoughtfully to another person I must first attend to myself, asking myself questions that I alone can provide answers for, answers that I alone can go on to question. This 'thinking dialogue between me and myself', this 'two-in-one' relation, is thus conditioned by the same plurality, the same 'difference and otherness', that is the life-breath of the common world (1971a, 187). As this world flourishes in spectatorship and action whenever 'people are *with* others and neither for nor against them – that is, in sheer human togetherness' (Arendt 1998, 180; original emphasis), so the life of the mind flourishes whenever I am *with* myself in the thinking process. Hence Arendt, who observes that 'thinking ... has split the one into a two-in-one', insists that 'for the thinking ego a "healing" of the split would be the worst thing that could happen; it would put an end to thinking altogether' (1971b, 70). But plurality and uncertainty, those inseparable characteristics of the vibrant mind and the flourishing common world, have been answered by the rise of the labouring and consuming society. In the same way that society endeavours to crush 'uncertainty and to save human affairs from their frailty' by way of seeking 'to eliminate action' (Arendt 1998, 230), so each of the 'prescribed rules' it propagates offers itself as a thread with which to seamlessly stitch up the split that separates the consciousness of the thinking ego (Arendt 1971a, 177). Social prejudices 'heal' the divided mind of its duality as behaviour 'cures' the plural realm of its distinctions and uncertainties.

By way of distinguishing thinking from contemplation and both from any mental activity that seeks to yield solutions and answers to practical quandaries, Arendt (1971a) considers the single word 'house'. This word, which contains and is a 'kind of shorthand' for the many differing meanings it has acquired for so many different groups of people, '*is something like a frozen thought that thinking must unfreeze* whenever it wants to find out the original meaning' (1971a, 171; original emphasis). Thinking thaws, but when, in the public realm, action becomes mere behaviour, so, within the life of the mind, words remain frozen, capable of forming nothing more than prejudgements, prejudice. So, while action necessitates forgiveness (Arendt 1998), the social, by attempting to eradicate all action and thinking, contains within itself the promise of an eternally, ice-clear conscience. Thus, we confront yet another of the contradictions that constitute times of mass indifference: in these times, as all established institutions melt, so thinking freezes.

Reflecting upon the 'aporetic character of Socratic thinking' (Arendt 1971a, 165), Arendt writes:

> What begins in wonder ends in perplexity and thence leads back to wonder: How marvellous that men can perform courageous or just deeds even though they do not know, can give no account of, what courage and justice are. (1971a, 166)

Equally, to receive the other in wonder is soon to be aware that at the edge of our awareness there is unknowing, and to accept this is to be returned once again to wonder. To further echo Arendt's words, it is marvellous that an educator can offer their caring and thoughtful attention to a young person and to include them into meaningful educational experiences, whilst being utterly unable to offer a definitive account of 'who' these young people are becoming. However, in the moment of categorisation, wonder and perplexity, those entwined characteristics of the spectator and of the caring and inclusive educator, freeze into the two negating forces of thoughtful attention, finality and monism. For example, when the search for a specialist pedagogy, for concrete, evidence-based and reliable techniques and strategies for the teaching of children categorised as 'having SENs', fills the specialist with 'the desire to find results that would make further thinking unnecessary' (Arendt 1971a, 176), young persons can find themselves frozen in the labels that have been attached to them. And when every thought about us is a frozen thought, we can find ourselves 'in invisibility, in that ... weird irreality that human relationships assume wherever they develop ... unrelated to a world common to all people' (Arendt 1995, 16). Only thoughtful and caring attention can thaw frozen thoughts about another person; only thinking can prepare us to attend to and to care for the other person, to begin to see and to hear, and thus to include them not for 'what' they seem to be but for 'who' they are perpetually becoming.

Conclusion

In a recent poll conducted in the United Kingdom about services offered by local councils, 65% of respondents reported that they had noticed no decline in the quality of these services since the introduction of cuts to their council's budget (Ipsos MORI 2013). The BBC's Economics' Editor, Stephanie Flanders (2013), described this as an 'austerity surprise'. Certainly, claims made for the 'empowerment' of local communities within the context of a 'Big Society' render the results of this survey surprising. But in its attempt to reach beyond such political rhetoric, this article has offered an account of the rise of a society that is characterised by just the type of extensive indifference to other people that explains the poll's finding.

It is within the context of a society of indifferent individuals that the social model of disability – for so long a tool utilised to illuminate those aspects of the built environments and institutions, along with those social attitudes and practices, that disable – might be called upon to prompt thoughtful and caring attention to those forms of community life that originate in a shared respect for the dignity and potential of all people. 'People with disabilities no longer want or need to be protected from community', Lord and Hutchison (2003, 85) contend, 'but require mechanisms for embedding their lives in community life'. It has been one of the central contentions of this article that in a society where individuals are increasing indifferent to one another, addressing disability means defending community and its possibilities for generating and sustaining caring, responsive and inclusive relationships. The society that is 'expert in branding and casting certain humans as "disabled" – in disabling such humans as would otherwise be able to live a human life, or in denying that they have such ability' – can, as Bauman (2007b, 58) insists, become a community 'that enables'.

Visions of community can be informed by what Ernst Bloch (1986, 146) names mere 'abstract utopian dreaminess', but they can equally be inspired by what he calls 'concrete utopia'. The abstract community represents the externalisation of the individual's inward self-concern, in which being at home with one's own self extends to being at home with others from whom one receives nothing but warm approval. This article has attempted to convey the possibility of generating visions of community life that begin not merely with such private wishes but in caring, thoughtful and responsible attention to other persons. The concreteness of the envisioned community is here distinguished from abstract fancy not by any of its imagined qualities but precisely by its incompleteness, for this community is no place to smugly proclaim one's own but is a place to create through caring relations.

A concrete and inclusive community, built up from the foundations of responsibility and care, begins in voyages from the borders of self-concern. This community is inclusive, not because it represents a safe haven wherein we might feel at home, but because it includes, and grows in accordance with, our capability to offer our caring attention to other persons, not as we or others define them but in their otherness, as they are in and to themselves. The central argument of this work has been that cuts to services and benefits, along with the rejection of inclusive education, have been encouraged not primarily by widespread negative thinking about disabled people, renewed and boosted by economic downturn and prevailing ideology, but first and foremost by the absence of such thoughtful and caring attention to the other person that has come to epitomise a society of labourers and consumers. In a society of indifferent individuals, the only cuts that hurt are the ones that strike directly, not at the community in which one lives but at the house in which one dwells. A sense of the disabling consequences of such indifference was announced on the streets of Madrid, where, in 2012, thousands of disabled people protesting against cuts chanted: 'Disabled people, abandoned' (Roders 2012). This article has suggested that such abandonment can be overcome only when persons turn from concern with what can be individually enjoyed and experienced to a commitment to what they can give.

References

Arendt, H. 1971a. *The Life of the Mind: Thinking*. London: Harcourt.

Arendt, H. 1971b. *The Life of the Mind: Willing*. London: Harcourt.

Arendt, H. 1993. The Crisis in Education. In *Between Past and Future: Eight Exercises in Political Thought*, 173–196. New York: The Viking Press.

Arendt, H. 1994. "What Remains? The Language Remains: A Conversation with Gunter Gaus." In *Essays in Understanding: 1930–1954*, edited by J. Kohn, 1–23. London: Harcourt Brace and Company.

Arendt, H. 1995. On Humanity in Dark Times: Thoughts about Lessing. Trans. C. and R. Winston. In *Men in Dark Times*, 3–31. San Diego: Harcourt Brace and Company.

Arendt, H. 1998. *The Human Condition*. Chicago: The University of Chicago Press.

Barnes, C. 1992. *Disabling Imagery and the Media: An Exploration of the Principles for Media Representations of Disabled People*. The British Council of Organisations of Disabled People and Halifax: Ryburn Publishing.

Barton, L., and R. Slee. 1999. "Competition, Selection and Inclusive Education: Some Observations." *International Journal of Inclusive Education* 3 (1): 3–12.

Bauman, Z. 2001a. *The Individualized Society*. Cambridge: Polity.

Bauman, Z. 2001b. *Community: Seeking Safety in an Insecure World*. Cambridge: Polity.

Bauman, Z. 2004. "Culture and Management." *Parallax* 10 (2): 63–72.

Bauman, Z. 2005a. "Education in Liquid Modernity." *Review of Education, Pedagogy, and Cultural Studies* 27 (4): 303–317.

Bauman, Z. 2005b. *Liquid Life*. Cambridge: Polity.

Bauman, Z. 2007a. *Society under Siege*. Cambridge: Polity.

Bauman, Z. 2007b. "Society Enables and Disables." *Scandinavian Journal of Disability Research* 9 (1): 58–60.

Bauman, Z. 2008. *Does Ethics Have a Chance in a World of Consumers?* Cambridge, Massachusetts: Harvard University Press.

Bauman, Z. 2011. *Living on Borrowed Time: Conversations with Citlali Rovirosa-Madrazo*. Cambridge: Polity.

Bauman, Z. 2012. *On Education: Conversations with Richard Mazzeo*. Cambridge: Polity.

Bauman, Z. 2013. *Liquid Modernity*. Cambridge: Polity.

Beck, U. 2002. *Risk Society: Towards a New Modernity*. Trans. M. Ritter. London: Sage.

Beck, U. 2013. *German Europe*. Trans. R. Livingstone. Cambridge: Polity.

Beresford, P. 2009. Whose Personalisation? *PIECES, Compass*, 47. http://clients.squareeye.net/uploads/compass/documents/CTP48Beresfordpersonalisation.pdf.

Beresford, P. 2013a. Are Social Care Personal Budgets Working? *The Guardian*. Tuesday February 12, 2013. http://www.theguardian.com/society/2013/feb/12/are-social-care-personal-budgets-working.

Beresford, P. 2013b. Social Care: From Personal Budgets to a Person-Centred Policy and Practice. *OpenDemocracy*. 30 April 2013. http://www.opendemocracy.net/ournhs/peter-beresford/social-care-from-personal-budgets-to-person-centred-policy-and-practice.

Bloch, E. 1986. *The Principle of Hope*. Translated by N. Plaice, S. Plaice and P. Knight. Oxford: Blackwell.

Blyth, M. 2013. *Austerity: The History of a Dangerous Idea* Oxford: Oxford University Press.

Bogdan, R. 1988. *Freak Show: Presenting Human Oddities for Amusement and Profit*. Chicago: The University of Chicago Press.

Booth, T., M. Ainscow, and A. Dyson. 1997. "Understanding Inclusion and Exclusion in the English Competitive Education System." *International Journal of Inclusive Education* 1 (4): 337–355.

Brown, G. 2012. Europe's Shortsighted Response to a Worsening Fiscal Reality, *Washington Post*. February 21 2012. http://www.washingtonpost.com/opinions/eu ropes-role-in-the-world-reshaped-by-economic-crises/2012/02/21/gIQAoNUiRR_ story.html.

Cabinet Office. 2010. *Building the Big Society.* http://www.cabinetoffice.gov.uk/ news/building-big-society.

Cameron, D. 2010. *The Big Society Speech.* https://www.gov.uk/government/ speeches/big-society-speech.

Catney, P., S. MacGregor, A. Dobson, S. M. Hall, S. Royston, Z. Robinson, M. Ormerod and S. Ross. 2013. Big Society, Little Justice? Community Renewable Energy and the Politics of Localism. *Local Environment: The International Journal of Justice and Sustainability* iFirst: 1–16.

de Boer, A., S. J. Pijl, and A. Minnaert. 2010. "Attitudes of Parents towards Inclusive Education: A Review of the Literature." *European Journal of Special Needs Education* 25 (2): 165–181.

DfCLG (Department for Communities and Local Government). 2010. *Decentralisation and the Localism Bill: An Essential Guide.* London: DfCLG.

DfE (Department for Education). 2011. *Support and Aspiration: A New Approach to Special Educational Needs and Disability.* London: DfE.

DfE (Department for Education). 2012. *Support and Aspiration: A New Approach to Special Educational Needs and Disability – Progress and Next Steps.* London: DfE.

DfEE (Department for Education and Employment). 1997. *Excellence for All Children: Meeting Special Educational Needs.* London: Stationery Office.

DfES (Department for Education and Skills). 2003. *Every Child Matters.* London: The Stationery Office.

DH (Department of Health). 2010. *A Vision for Adult Social Care: Capable Communities and Active Citizens.* London: DH.

Eagleton, T. 1991. *Ideology: An Introduction.* London: Verso.

Fergusson, E. 2012. "Review: Lessons for the Big Society: Planning, Regeneration and the Politics of Community Participation." *Urban Policy and Research* 30 (3): 349–351.

Flanders, S. 2013. A UK Austerity Surprise. *BBC News.* July 23, 2013. http:// www.bbc.co.uk/news/business-23424527.

Foucault, M. 1977. *Discipline and Punish: The Birth of the Prison.* Translated by A. Sheridan. Harmondsworth: Penguin.

Gillies, V., and Y. Robinson. 2013. "At Risk Pupils and the 'Caring' Curriculum." In *Critical Approaches to Care: Understanding Caring Relations, Identities and Cultures*, edited by C. Rogers and S. Weller, 42–53. London: Routledge.

Gilligan, C. 1993. *In a Different Voice: Psychological Theory and Women's Development.* Cambridge, MA: Harvard University Press.

Goffman, E. 1990. *Stigma: Notes on the Management of Spoiled Identity.* London: Penguin.

Ipsos, MORI. 2013. Ipsos MORI. *NLGN Poll. Topline Results.* Fieldwork: 12th– 14th January 2013. http://www.ipsos-mori.com/Assets/Docs/Polls/ipsos-mori-nlgn-top line-2013.pdf.

Jelas, Z. M. and M. M. Ali. 2012. Inclusive Education in Malaysia: Policy and Practice, *International Journal of Inclusive Education*, 1–13, iFirst Article.

Jones, K., A. Netten, J.-L. Fernández, M. Knapp, D. Challis, C. Glendinning, S. Jacobs, J. Manthorpe, N. Moran, M. Stevens, and M. Wilberforce. 2012. "The Impact of Individual Budgets on the Targeting of Support: Findings from a National Evaluation of Pilot Projects in England." *Public Money and Management* 32 (6): 417–424.

Kalyva, E., M. Georgiadi, and V. Tsakiris. 2007. "Attitudes of Greek Parents of Primary School Children without Special Educational Needs to Inclusion." *European Journal of Special Needs Education* 22 (3): 295–305.

Kim, Y.-W. 2012. Inclusive Education in South Korea. *International Journal of Inclusive Education*, 1–12, iFirst Article.

Labonté, R. 2012. "The Austerity Agenda: How Did We Get Here and Where Do We Go Next?" *Critical Public Health* 22 (3): 257–265.

Laurent, U. 2013. "Revisiting Care in Schools: Exploring the Caring Experiences of Disengaged Young People." In *Critical Approaches to Care: Understanding Caring Relations, Identities and Cultures*, edited by C. Rogers and S. Weller, 30–41. London: Routledge.

Lingard, B., and S. Sellar. 2012. "A Policy Sociology Reflection on School Reform in England: From the 'Third Way' to the 'Big Society'." *Journal of Educational Administration and History* 44 (1): 43–63.

Lister, R., and F. Bennett. 2010. "The New 'Champion of Progressive Ideals'? Cameron's Conservative Party: Poverty, Family Policy and Welfare Reform." *Renewal: A Journal of Social Democracy* 18 (1–2): 84–108.

Lord, J., and P. Hutchison. 2003. "Individualised Support and Funding: Building Blocks for Capacity Building and Inclusion." *Disability and Society* 18 (1): 71–86.

Luff, P., U. Laurent, V. Gillies, Y. Robinson, and M. Victoria. 2013. "Caring within Educational Institutions." In *Critical Approaches to Care: Understanding Caring Relations, Identities and Cultures*, edited by C. Rogers and S. Weller, 15–17. London: Routledge.

Marx, K., and F. Engels. 1967. *The Communist Manifesto*. London: Penguin.

Meacher, M. 2012. Austerity till 2018? Britain's Economy is Being Crucified on the Cross of Ideology. *The Guardian*. November 26, 2012. http://www.theguardian.com/commentisfree/2012/nov/26/austerity-2018-britain-economy-crucified.

Noddings, N. 2002. *The Challenge to Care in Schools: An Alternative Approach to Education*. New York: Teachers College Press.

Noddings, N. 2010. "Moral Education in an Age of Globalization." *Educational Philosophy and Theory* 42 (4): 390–396.

North, P. 2011. "Geographies and Utopias of Cameron's Big Society." *Social and Cultural Geography* 12 (8): 817–827.

Nozick, R. 1974. *Anarchy, State, and Utopia*. Oxford: Basil Blackwell.

Roders, P. 2012. Disabled Protest in Spain over Austerity Measures *Reuters*. Dec 2, 2012. http://www.reuters.com/article/2012/12/02/us-spain-disabled-idUSBRE8B108F20121202.

Rogers, C. 2007. "Experiencing an 'Inclusive' Education: Parents and Their Children with 'Special Educational Needs'." *British Journal of Sociology of Education* 28 (1): 55–68.

Ryan, S. 2005. "'People Don't Do Odd, Do They?' Mothers Making Sense of the Reactions of Others towards Their Learning Disabled Children in Public Places." *Children's Geographies* 3 (3): 291–305.

Santos, M. P.d. 2001. "Inclusion and/or Integration: The Debate is Still on in Brazil." *Disability & Society* 16 (6): 893–897.

Sen, A. 2012. Austerity is Undermining Europe's Grand Vision. *The Guardian*. Tuesday 3 July. http://www.theguardian.com/commentisfree/2012/jul/03/austerity-europe-grand-vision-unity.

Shakespeare, T. 1994. "Cultural Representation of Disabled People: Dustbins for Disavowal?" *Disability and Society* 9 (3): 283–299.

Shakespeare, T. 1999. "Art and Lies? Representations of Disability on Film." In *Disability Discourse*, edited by M. Corker and S. French, 164–172. Philadelphia: Open University Press.

Shelby, C. L. 2003. "Care Ethics in Education." *The Educational Forum* 67 (4): 337–342.

Slasberg, C., P. Beresford, and P. Schofield. 2012. "Can Personal Budgets Really Deliver Better Outcome for All at No Cost? Reviewing the Evidence, Costs and Quality." *Disability & Society* 27 (7): 1029–1034.

Slee, R. 2001. "Driven to the Margins: Disabled Students, Inclusive Schooling and the Politics of Possibility." *Cambridge Journal of Education* 31 (3): 385–397.

Slee, R. 2011. *The Irregular School: Exclusion, Schooling and Inclusive Education*. London: Routledge.

Söder, R. 1990. "Prejudice or Ambivalence? Attitudes Toward Persons With Disabilities." *Disability, Handicap & Society* 5 (3): 227–241.

Stuckler, D., and S. Basu. 2013. *The Body Economic: Why Austerity Kills*. London: Allan Lane.

Swart, E., P. Engelbrecht, I. Eloff, R. Pettipher, and M. Oswald. 2004. "Developing Inclusive School Communities: Voices of Parents of Children with Disabilities." *Education as Change* 8 (1): 80–108.

Tafa, E., and G. Manolitsis. 2003. "Attitudes of Greek Parents of Typically Developing Kindergarten Children towards Inclusive Education." *European Journal of Special Needs Education* 18 (2): 155–171.

Thatcher, M. (1987) *Interview for Women's Own*. http://www.margaretthatcher.org/document/106689.

Tomlinson, S. 2005. "Race, Ethnicity and Education under New Labour." *Oxford Review of Education* 31 (1): 153–171.

Tomlinson, S. 2012. "The Irresistible Rise of the SEN Industry." *Oxford Review of Education* 38 (3): 267–286.

United Nations. 2006. *UN Treaties 15. Convention on the Rights of Persons with Disabilities*. United Nations: UN Treaty Collection. https://treaties.un.org/doc/Publication/MTDSG/Volume%20I/Chapter%20IV/IV-15.en.pdf.

Wainwright, H. (2010) Cameron's 'Big Society' is a Toy Town, *The Guardian*. Wednesday 14, April. http://www.theguardian.com/commentisfree/2010/apr/14/david-cameron-big-society-conservatives.

Wolff, R. D. 2010. Austerity: Why and for Whom? *In These Times*. July 15, 2010. http://inthesetimes.com/article/6232/austerity_why_and_for_whom/.

Transforming marginalised adult learners' views of themselves: Access to Higher Education courses in England

Hugh Busher[a], Nalita James[b], Anna Piela[b] and Anna-Marie Palmer[b]

[a]School of Education, University of Leicester, Leicester, UK; [b]Vaughan Centre for Lifelong Learning, University of Leicester, Leicester, UK

Adult learners on Access to Higher Education courses struggled with institutional and social structures to attend their courses, but transformed their identities as learners through them. Although asymmetrical power relationships dominated the intentional learning communities of their courses, their work was facilitated by collaborative cultures and supportive tutors, and students gained the confidence to construct their own emergent communities of practice for learning. The students attended seven further education colleges in the East Midlands of England. Data were collected by mixed methods within a social constructivist framework from students and their tutors.

Introduction

People's identities are always shifting (Bauman 2000) but do so especially when they encounter new or challenging situations as liminal spaces (Bhabha 1994). The project of self-development is never ending (Giddens 1991). One group of people who experience particularly challenging circumstances are mature students on Access to Higher Education (HE) courses who return to formal education to enhance their cultural capital (Bourdieu 1990) and engage in a process of (re)construction and ongoing development (Brine and Waller 2004) of their identities as learners. Like other non-traditional learners, they are often initially tentative about this as their previous life experiences have frequently given them little confidence for engaging in formal learning (Crossan et al. 2003). They lack confidence that their habitus (Bourdieu 1990) will allow them to assert and develop their agency successfully in the field of formal learning in further education (FE) colleges, where Access to HE courses are conventionally located. They

156

fear their learning experiences will be riven with tensions between them as agents, others, and the social and institutional structures they encounter (O'Donnell and Tobbell 2007). FE colleges are the main educational institutions in England and Wales for 'providing opportunities for lifelong learning, and … promoting economic growth and social cohesion' (Jephcote, Salisbury, and Rees 2008, 164). They tend to offer a collaborative ethos or culture focused around values celebrating mature learners (Warmington 2002).

In England and Wales, Access to HE courses, originally established in the 1970s, are for those 'excluded, delayed or otherwise deterred by a need to qualify for (university) entry in more conventional ways' (Parry 1996, 11). Currently they recruit about 40,000 adults a year (Quality Assurance Agency [QAA] 2013) and are a major element in reducing educational disadvantage (Jones 2006, 485) and widening participation in HE. They are intended to provide adult learners (aged 19 years or older) with the subject knowledge and generic skills required for progression to and effective study at university. They lead to a diploma that is awarded by regional award-validating authorities (AVAs) which are regulated by the QAA on behalf of central government in England and Wales. The courses are usually offered through a variety of subject-focused pathways such as nursing and midwifery, social sciences, or business studies.

Government education policy in England and Wales, like that in the European Union, aims to widen participation in HE to satisfy the need of European economies for high-skilled labour (Field, Merrill, and Morgan-Klein 2010) in a global market. However, widening participation is a contested notion linked in part to social justice and equality of opportunity and in part to strengthening economic prosperity both for individuals and nationally (Burke 2007). Recently, in England and Wales it has been redefined as 'fair access' to HE through the development of particular admissions practices by HE institutions (Department for Business, Innovation and Skills [BIS] 2012, 4), rather than as free access for those people from marginalised social groups traditionally under-represented in HE. Further, since 2012, central government has encouraged Access to HE course providers to target younger people. Now only young adults aged 19–24 years undertaking their first full Level 2 (equivalent to GCSE, the school-leaving examination in England) or Level 3 qualification (equivalent to 'A'-level or Access to HE courses in England and Wales) will be fully funded (BIS 2010). Other older students will only be able to access government-backed loans to fund their Level 3 courses (BIS 2010). This new funding regime is likely to inhibit older people in financially straitened circumstances because of family commitments and/or lower paid employment from applying for Access to HE courses.

This paper considers how Access to HE students pursued the project of the self (Giddens 1991) in order to enhance their cultural capital (Bourdieu

1990), and how these projects are shaped by their struggles as citizens in the particular socio-economic policy contexts (Foucault 1977) since 2010, by their power-invested relationships (Handley et al. 2006) with their tutors and by their interactions with their colleagues on Access to HE courses that, possibly, generate communities of practice (Wenger 1998).

Transforming identities in the particular institutional contexts

People construct their work-related identities and values from their shared experiences with others in multiple communities (Wenger 1998; Holliday 1999), and from the dispositions of knowledge, skills, values and experiences they carry with them, their histories (Kearney 2003). People's identities develop throughout their lives (Bauman, 2000) through the interplay between individual agency and identity, institutional structures and social circumstances (Wyn and White 1998), including their families and friends through whom they develop social capital (Bourdieu 1990) and acquire a habitus (Bourdieu 1990). People's identities are the means by which they position themselves within a society or a community (Benjamin 2002) and shape their interactions with others, as well as being a persona or mask that allows them to play parts ascribed to them in a community (Hollis 1985).

For students on Access to HE courses their identities play out in various arenas, such as the local socio-economic and community contexts, the curriculum contexts of the Access to HE diploma and the institutional contexts of FE colleges that host these courses. The institutional context includes the classrooms where they encounter their tutors, college policies, teaching and learning practices, college cultures and course sub-cultures. It involves moral and political activity that constitutes the managing, monitoring and resolving of value conflicts, where values are defined as concepts of the desirable (Hodgkinson 1999). Resolving these conflicts ethically and transparently in keeping with previously established social and moral norms in an institution or community leads to greater social cohesion (MacBeath and MacDonald 2000) by constructing shared narratives or cultures. These define the core practices, values and boundaries in and of a community (Wenger 1998), such as a teaching group or institution, which occur in particular places/spaces at certain times.

Changing uses and demarcations of space through time reflect the changing relationships of people to each other and to the institution in which they are located (Paechter 2004). How people colonise the physical, online and organisational spaces they occupy, whether or not formally allocated to them by an institution, are part of the discourses about how they are constrained but try to assert their agency individually and collectively (Foucault 1976 in Gordon 1980) to construct the cultures of their work groups or communities within broader constellations of cultures (Wenger 1998; Holliday 1999) or institutions. In these spaces, organisational cultures, intertwined with power relationships, are negotiated by members of institutions to reflect and guide the values, relationships and practices that lie at the core of communities and institutions (Wenger 1998) in particular socio-political contexts.

A community's culture represent a nexus of particular values and beliefs that help members to have a collective work-related identity which encompasses subtle cultural dynamics such as members' perceived social functions and assumptions, rule-making, behavioural norms, and boundary and periphery definitions (Wenger 1998, 117), as well as articulated and unarticulated cues about members' status in a particular community. Cultures are constructed for a whole organisation like an FE college, as well as for communities or departments within it. While some authors (MacGilchrist, Myers, and Reed 2004; Senge 2006) perceive the cultures of communities within institutions (e.g. departments) as subcultures, emphasising the hierarchical institutional process of culture construction, Holliday (1999) describes them as small cultures to emphasise the agentic nature of culture construction that also draws on the socio-political contexts which community members inhabit. However, cultures are not fixed but shift (Holliday et al. 2010) as membership of communities shifts and as the social and policy contexts of those communities shift.

Whilst it is difficult to be prescriptive about what cultures in teaching and learning might be preferred, values and practices that sustain trust and collaboration between participants are likely to lead to a critical dialogue about the repertoire of teaching and learning practices (Smyth et al. 2000), which will enhance the conduct of participants' enterprise (Wenger 1998) by giving them a sense of ownership of it. Supportive learning cultures, which included informal support structures among the student body, help Access to HE students to cope successfully with the demands of the course and learn most effectively (Jones 2006). Group solidarity and mutual support were perceived by students in the study by Jones (2006) as significant factors in individual success.

Making particular choices in teaching, learning and institutional processes is a political act (Ball 1987) involving the use of power to assert some values or practices at a particular point in time in a particular situation to the exclusion of others. For example, decisions taken by Access to HE tutors about when work should be handed in excludes other times/dates, although students may try to negotiate these. Further, decisions taken by tutors and students are not taken in isolation but are also scrutinised by the gaze (Foucault 1977) of more senior members of their college's organisational hierarchy and of the AVA awarding the Diploma for the course. Teachers and students have to comply with the values and choices held by this gaze. Power and micro-political processes are used by institutional members to negotiate or enact particular policies and values within the contexts of institutional structures. The last are the reified outcomes of past power struggles.

Power flows in any organisation or community (Foucault 1986) and is accessible to all members of a community through the sources they can mobilise (Giddens 1984), the social networks of which they have membership (Busher 2006) and the negotiations they undertake. However, access to sources of power is unequally available in institutions because of the hierarchical distribution of authority (formally ascribed power) in a college (Hatcher 2005). For example, teachers are given authority to organise the processes of learning with their students (Bourdieu and Passeron 1977), allowing them to exercise control over their subordinates (Blase and Anderson 1995). Ignoring hierarchy risks making discussion of the negotiations of community members appear more egalitarian than they are and may not accurately reflect the lived experiences of the members of those communities (Busher, Hammersley-Fletcher, and Turner 2007).

There are many sources of power (Giddens 1984) linked to formal processes in organisations and to informal practices and personal knowledge (Busher 2006) that are available to people to try to achieve their agenda and assert their values (Ball 1987). Some influence the micro-political interactions of students (Benjamin 2002). Others influence negotiations between students and tutors or between Access to HE tutors and college systems. For example, teaching and learning can only take place through students assenting to the processes chosen by their tutors, even if only tacitly. Through such processes and their interactions with other people in various social and institutional structures, students on Access to HE courses struggle to assert their agency and modify their identity and habitus as learners.

Conceptualising communities of learners

The term 'community' has a wide range of meanings but is unavoidable in trying to conceptualise how people coalesce together for particular purposes, such as learning on Access to HE courses. In this paper we draw a distinction between learning communities that are intentionally set up by institutions (Andrews and Lewis 2007; Mangham 2012) and communities of practice (Lave and Wenger 1991; Wenger 1998) that are emergent or naturally occurring (Mittendorf et al. 2005) amongst people coalescing to work together. The former emerges out of the literature on learning organisations (Senge 2006; MacGilchrist, Myers, and Reed 2004) and assumes the communities are carefully constructed by the activities of their leaders (Mitchell and Sackney 2006) with the help of other members to construct particular cultures that engage members in purposeful work. This overlooks the importance of power as a constituent factor in the construction of communities (Hatcher 2005; Handley et al. 2006).

There are important similarities and differences between intentional learning communities and emergent communities of practice. Both models of community share several similar features, such as emphasising the importance of collaborative cultures, differentiating between core and peripheral members, recognising the importance of boundaries both to demarcate communities and to act as semi-permeable membranes through which members of different communities interact, and recognising that communities often have overlapping membership. However, while individual communities of practice are said rather vaguely to relate to wider constellations of similar communities (Wenger 1998; Holliday 1999), learning communities are firmly placed within the boundaries of the institution to which they belong (MacGilchrist, Myers, and Reed 2004; Senge 2006). Emergent communities of practice are said to develop their own small cultures (Holliday 1999) while intentional learning communities (Mangham 2012) are said to construct subcultures of their host institutions, as has already been discussed. In intentional learning communities, hierarchically appointed leaders are viewed as essential in constructing cultures and practices of working and acting as gatekeepers. They exert control over new members (Lave and Wenger 1991) by expecting them to conform to codes of practice and language, or to learn these, before they are permitted full membership of a group. In emergent communities of practice the role of formal leaders is vague, although informal leadership is said to be exercised by existing core members of communities, the old lags (Lave and Wenger 1991), who teach new entrants the ropes.

Methodology

The study took a social constructivist perspective (Lave and Wenger 1991), using a linked case-study design (Miles and Huberman 1994) across seven FE colleges in the East Midlands of England in 2012/13. It used mixed methods to triangulate the perspectives of students on Access to HE courses within and across colleges to enhance the trustworthiness of the study. It investigated the perspectives of marginalised adult learners, who were students on Access to HE courses, on their past and present learning experiences, on the transformation of their views of themselves as learners during the Access to HE courses, and on the impact on their learning of their socio-economic contexts and their relationships with their families, friends, Access to HE tutors and fellow students.

Subject to their ethical consent, all Access to HE course students in each college were invited to complete two questionnaires about their views of themselves as learners, one at the start of their course and one at the end. This instrument was intended to give a broad view of Access to HE students' perspectives and to complement the in-depth views gained from the student focus groups and concept maps, the last mainly being used as a trigger to stimulate students' positioning of themselves in relation to the Access to HE courses and the social contexts in which they lived and worked before the focus groups began. In each college, seven Access to HE students were invited to participate in focus group interviews on three occasions during the academic year, although the number of participants in each focus group tended to diminish during the year, raising questions about the representativeness of the views we were hearing at later stages in the study. The choice of students in each college for the focus groups was guided by our criteria for as wide a spread of students by social status and subject pathway within the Access to HE courses as possible but was, nonetheless, to some extent influenced by tutors. Access to HE tutors were also invited to take part in individual semi-structured or group interviews on two occasions during the year to provide an institutional perspective on the courses.

Data were analysed on a college by college basis as well as across colleges. We had 365 questionnaire responses (out of more than 700 possible replies) from the seven colleges/institutions in autumn 2012. Overall, 70% of respondents were female, but in College 4 no men answered the questionnaire while 50% of the answers in College 6 came from men. The quantitative data were analysed with simple descriptive statistics while the open-ended answers were scrutinised to generate numeric codes that would help to illustrate trends and patterns within the cohort of the study. The qualitative data from the interviews were audio-recorded, transcribed and analysed using a grounded approach (Corbin and Strauss 2008) powered by NVivo to construct themes that reflected participants' own constructs of themselves and their contexts. The visual data from the concept maps, through which students could express their views of their transitions and transformations (Wall and Higgins 2009), were analysed hermeneutically, an approach that took account of the views of Prosser (2006) and Pink (2001).

Findings

The distribution of the population for this study is consistent with QAA (2013) figures for the national population of Access to HE students. Fifty-two per cent of the students were aged between 19 and 24 years, with 3.6% being aged 45 years or over. However, the study sample was less ethnically diverse than QAA (2013) figures (76% white compared with 69%). Only 10% of the sample of this study had not previously worked, while 60% were currently employed, albeit mainly in low-paid jobs. Nearly 12% of the respondents to the questionnaire did not have Level 1 qualifications while 18% did not have Level 2 qualifications (GCSE). Seventy per cent of the respondents did not have Level 3 qualifications (equivalent to 'A'-level). The most popular Access to HE pathways in our study was nursing and midwifery (54%), followed by social science (22%), health education (19%) and science (17%).

The perspectives of students from the focus groups held during the autumn term 2012 fall into four main themes: discourses, significant others and the developing self; courses as arenas for student self-development; constituting a sense of community; and facilitating learning through community. The different colleges in the study are referred to by number (e.g. College 5) to keep them and their participants anonymous.

Discourses, significant others and the developing self

Students on the Access to HE courses had to negotiate a range of social and policy processes or discourses (Gee 1999), in part because Access to HE courses are defined as full-time, to assert their agency, despite their relative powerlessness in many of the situations. Many of these students were married, had children, and worked as well, even if only part-time, 'because I can't afford to pay for [the course] without contributing. My husband works, but on his wage, we can't live' (College 1).

Some employers were sympathetic to the pressures on the students and converted full-time jobs into part-time jobs or reduced the hours the students were working. One student was allowed by her employer to 'drop down [from two days] to one day, [but] he's still paying me for two days and I'm paying him those days back in my spare time' (College 3). However, other firms were not so sympathetic: 'I asked [for] my job to go part-time but they didn't allow it. So I had to leave and this made me ineligible for Job Seekers Allowance' (College 5).

The impact of performativity and neo-liberal market economics (Jeffrey and Troman 2012) on students was very visible. Agencies of the state seemed particularly unhelpful. In one case a student was refused benefit 'because I still live at home, they've judged my parent's income, whereas obviously I'm an adult and I support myself [and] I am desperately trying to seek a job' (College 5). Although another student gained funding because 'I got made redundant from my job' (College 3), 'the Job Centre … said that if a full-time job became available I'd have to quit the course and start the job' (College 3). Colleges, too, constrained as they were by the guidelines of central government (BIS 2010, 2012) and the college inspectorate about how colleges should be organised, were sometimes less than helpful. In one case a student was at first told 'that I would be funded, but when I came for the enrolment [College] said, "No". So now I am struggling to pay the rest of the tuition fee … it's really frustrating' (College 2).

The financial constraints students faced were a burden to many of them although their desire for self-improvement also raised the skills of the British labour force, as central government policy encouraged (BIS 2010) to generate economic growth: 'People like us, will probably be going on to get better jobs … to make the economy better (College 4). It was also enhancing their own cultural capital (Bourdieu 1990) by improving their, 'careers so that we can be better people' (College 4). However, students acknowledged that, 'without the degree and the things that come after, it's just ruled out' (College 5). Their personal and socio-political contexts forced students into regimes of work that were hectic: 'I work full-time and I come here to school full-time and it's tiring and it can be hectic, and if you analyse it, it's almost impossible' (College 6).

For students under these pressures, their families were a major source of practical support in students' struggles for education:

> I get a lot of help from my mum with childcare because me and my husband both work and I'm here. So he's taking up the slack of other cooking and cleaning duties and the childcare. (College 3)

Families, as well as students' previous life experiences, were also an important source of inspiration for students, illustrating the importance of social capital (Bourdieu 1990) to people: 'Now I've had my little boy, I want to show him that it's important to learn and what you can do when you apply yourself' (College 7). 'If we don't do it [get to university], we're just wasting our life like again … we've all like learnt from our past experiences' (College 4).

Students thought the lack of free Access to HE courses, implemented since 2010 (BIS 2010), was most unfair to people who were trying to study and work and not rely on state benefits:

> You've got to be on … not just low income, but you've [also] got to be getting council tax benefit … Basically you are penalised for being outgoing and doing what you are supposed to do in society. (College 2)

In particular, several women students thought it essential to have free or grant-aided Access to HE courses:

> If I had to pay for [the course], I would have had to save this year to do it next year and I would have had to work as well because there was no way that would [cover] my nursery fees as well. (College 4)

Courses as hierarchical but collaborative arenas for student self-development

On the Access to HE courses the formal hierarchies of the college were less visible, in part perhaps because students thought 'most [tutors] treat us like adults I think. I've had a few problems with some' (College 4). '[Tutors] understand that we're not school children who have no commitments outside college' (College 1). This fits with the view of college cultures as collaborative, acknowledging the needs of adult students in them (Warmington 2002; Jones 2006). That students always referred to their tutors by the tutors' given names, without title, was, perhaps, an indicator of the relationships between them being collaborative but respectful.

Tutors tried to act as friendly facilitators and supporters of students. As one student commented about her course and her tutor:

> I was quite worried that I would be lost and wouldn't have a clue, but after the support and having some feedback, I feel a lot more confident going forward. (College 5)

In part, tutors' support arose from their expertise in their subject areas, 'making you sort of appreciate a subject and teaching it in a way that is both interesting and accessible' (College 5), and the provision of a range of learning resources to students. In one college a student spoke of endless telephone calls with her tutor at home when developing her UCAS form (College 4). In another, tutors seemed to provide an endless stream of tutorials if students 'didn't understand anything in the lesson or [didn't] understand the assignment' (College 7). Another resource was extensive use of formative assessment: 'Even now the teachers are still telling us how we should set out our assignments and helping us with things like referencing and it's been very helpful' (College 5).

These supportive relationships served a critical function in helping students to be successful by seeing students' 'strengths and weaknesses and help[ing them] to develop from those' (College 5). Further, tutors also cared for the whole person and not just the academic aspects of student development:

> When you're talking about families and past experiences of loss of loved ones and things like that ... [tutors] won't just like brush it away. They will have time for you to sit and discuss. (College 3)

However, the relationships between students and tutors were laden with power (Handley et al. 2006). The formal authority of the tutors (Bourdieu and Passeron 1977) subtly indicated the unavoidably hierarchical nature of the relationships between tutors and students. It was tutors whom students notified when they could not attend the course for some reason. Tutors kept registers of student attendance as part of their functions as staff of a college. Tutors marked assignments and gave feedback to students on how to improve their work. These practices projected power over students (Blase and Anderson 1995). Consequently, students always seemed to be aware of the hierarchical relationship between them and the tutors, although tutors placed 'emphasis on independent learning and [gave students] enough support so that [they didn't] feel like [they]'re completely lost and like got nobody to turn to' (College 5).

Nonetheless, the Access to HE courses offered spaces (Paechter 2004) for students to share with other like-minded people their aspirations for the future and the practicalities of developing their confidence, skills and knowledge to achieve those. It was an important space for developing confidence because students met 'different people from different backgrounds and different behaviours' (College 2). It helped them to learn who they were and what they were supposed to do (College 2), developing their senses of identity through their interactions with others in particular situations (Giddens 1991). In doing so, students seem to have shifted their habitus (Bourdieu 1990) and sense of agency (Wyn and White 1998) through their interactions with others. As one student explained: '[it] helped me to find out who I am [so] I can be what I want because it's the choice that ... will take me to my destination' (College 2). The students' development of their identities helped them to re-position themselves within their society (Benjamin 2002) and alter their interactions with others.

Constituting a sense of community

The Access to HE courses provided important sites for student transitions because their physical spaces helped students to develop social networks that facilitated their learning: 'We all talk to each other because we're all sat in a room together and sort of forced together' (College 4). This sense of being part of a community had a dramatic effect on some students: 'It's absolutely changed my life and I've got complete focus now. I thought I'd just come here and be quite solitary' (College 3). The nature of the community depended on the quality of relationships developed by the students among each other: 'We've got a really good mix and everybody's really focused and we're all wanting everybody to succeed and we're all supportive of each other' (College 3). These collaborative cultures were purposeful and work focused, constructing a community of practice (Wenger 1998): 'I think in the classroom time everybody will work with everybody and then at lunch and break people like group with who they feel they gel with better' (College 4). This illustrates that learning is a form of intellectual, physical, emotional and social work (Hodkinson 2004) in which people use their resources and those of others, such as their teachers and colleagues, to construct new (social) artefacts of knowledge and skills and networks of relationships.

The development of a sense of community was facilitated by students' having common purposes for joining an Access to HE course: 'We all know why we're here. They [sic] want to get to university' (College 6) and 'It helps to all be in the same boat ... everybody here has either experienced education or has come to it fairly late' (College 5). These purposeful communities generated collaborative cultures creating a mutual engagement in learning (Wenger 1998).

In these emergent communities (Mittendorf et al. 2005), Access to HE students were supportive of each other's endeavours: 'Everyone respects each other's opinions, respects why they're here … [are] people that want to help me and I want to help them' (College 6). This made it possible for people to make mistakes but learn from them without feeling threatened: 'Even though I was embarrassed, I wasn't like, "Oh my god. That was horrible". No one … bullies or anything' (College 7). This tolerance and trust of others is an important feature of collaborative cultures in learning communities (Andrews and Lewis 2007). Students in one college feared that breaching these norms would threaten the sense of community in their classes:

> When your peers in your own class are like laughing at you [or] they're making sarcastic comments. I think we need to work on that. (College 4)

Facilitating learning through a sense of community

Students thought that sharing a sense of a community depended on positive interpersonal relationships. In one college a student noted 'a very positive learning environment' (College 1). In another college a student noted that 'it helps having the same people around you obviously if you get on with them. We all kind of feel like we can depend on each other and support each other' (College 5). It helped them to work successfully together: 'We do help each other with assignments' (College 1), 'community spirit here definitely' (College 5), and diminished people's individual sense of stress and worry: 'If you can ask other people about problems with an assignment or just the workload, then it takes a massive stress off' (College 1).

The values that students held were made visible through the ways in which they worked: 'We don't often let people lag behind. If there's a problem, then we will help' (College 1). In one college this led to 'study groups in the library … and get stuff done there, which is a good help' (College 6). In another college, some students set up a group on Facebook: 'so we could post if we were at home saying, "Can anyone help me with this or does anyone know how I can get around doing this sort of work?"' (College 3)

These views highlight a sense of responsibility as individuals and as a community, with people working to benefit other members of the community, not just themselves, through shared practices, artefacts, patterns of action and language. This reflects how Wenger (1998) and Holliday (1999) think people build small communities with their own distinctive cultures, yet linked to those of their host institution. In the liminal spaces (Bhabha 1994) of the Access to HE courses, students who were initially strangers to each other and to the tutor built successful communities of learning practice.

Discussion

Access to HE students discussed how their struggles with their socio-economic contexts helped them to recognise what they wanted to achieve in life. Their discussions showed the interplay between individual agency and identity, institutional structures and social circumstances (Wyn and White 1998), including their families and friends, and how this led to their personal development. The development of the self was manifestly an ongoing project (Giddens 1991; Bauman 2000; Brine and Waller 2004). It was these struggles that gave Access to HE students the motivations to return to formal education, even though it was an arena in which many of them had previously had little success. The asymmetrical nature of power was visible in many of these struggles where students felt they had limited power but, nonetheless, negotiated the best deals they could to meet their values and interests.

Students thought their Access to HE courses helped them to alter their identities as learners and develop their sense of agency as people, as did participants in the study of O'Donnell and Tobbell (2007). The cultures of their courses gave students a sense of community although these were imbued with asymmetrical power relationships (Hatcher 2005). The collaborative cultures of the intentional learning communities (Mangham 2012) that the tutors tried to construct on the courses were mediated by flows of power (Foucault 1986), shaping how formally powerful people, such as course tutors, acted as leaders or hosts (Derrida 2000) and interacted with students, and *vice versa*. Students perceived their tutors as having formal power derived from their authority of office (Bourdieu and Passeron 1977). They welcomed tutors organising the courses carefully and supporting them personally in their work of learning (Hodkinson 2004). Tutors also played important boundary or peripheral roles for their courses, as models of communities of practice (Wenger 1998) predict, negotiating with college leaders and AVAs on how to meet the demands of the curriculum and the regulatory contexts of college, course and wider policy frameworks, such as university deadlines for applications. It left them socially slightly apart from the students, but allowed them to project power to steer the community in directions to make learning as successful as possible.

The flows of power were not pathological constraints on the efficient working of the courses but part of the normal (political/ negotiative) processes of the course communities (Ball 1987) about means and ways of learning and the construction of acceptable knowledge outcomes. For example, students negotiated work schedules with tutors to meet the constraints on their time and the requirements of the courses. Tutors projected power over students (Blase and Anderson 1995) through their access to resources of knowledge that could help students pass the Access to HE course, as well as regulatory or disciplinary power and powers of surveillance

(Foucault 1977) on behalf of their colleges and the AVAs giving Access to HE diplomas.

Students also asserted power in the relationships in the course communities; for example, by asking tutors for extensive help with developing aspects of their knowledge, drawing on the values made manifest in these communities to legitimate their requests. Flows of power also shaped how students began to construct emergent or naturally occurring (Mittendorf et al. 2005) communities of practice, sites and processes of informal learning to complement the formal learning spaces of their courses. In these emergent communities of practice, students negotiated with each other for help with learning and the logistics of attending their courses, using various forms of media to communicate, such as face-to-face contacts such as library study groups, emails, telephones, and online (Facebook) discussions. Most of the electronic communications excluded tutors suggesting Access to HE students held their own sources of power and influence over the ways in which these sites developed, including their practices and values.

The spaces of the Access to HE courses (Paechter 2004) were the arenas that developed intentional learning communities, organised by the colleges and managed by the Access to HE course tutors, and emergent communities of practice, constructed by students. Both were focused on the enterprise of learning (Hodkinson 2004). In the intentional learning communities, participants constructed collaborative cultures under the guidance of the tutors as formal leaders or hosts (Derrida 2000). At the core of these cultures were values of respect for other people and collaboration in achieving the purposes of the courses. Collaborative cultures are said to be at the core of learning communities and communities of practice (Lave and Wenger 1991; Wenger 1998; Andrews and Lewis 2007). The course cultures were sub-cultures of adult-learner-oriented college cultures (Warmington 2002) constructed collaboratively between tutors and students, albeit with asymmetrical power relationships of hierarchy (Hatcher 2005) imbuing them. They helped students to become independent learners and meet the demands of their course validators and course providers.

Alongside and intermeshed with these intentional learning communities developed emergent communities of practice constructed by the students to help each other develop as learners. The small cultures (Holliday 1999) of these communities that emerged in the liminal spaces (Bhabha 1994) of courses again appeared to be collaborative, perhaps reflecting those of the intentional learning communities with which they shared overlapping membership. In these communities, tutors were servants to the students, providing resources for learning in a multiplicity of ways but marginal or peripheral to the social and linked work processes of the groups. Further study needs to be undertaken to find out how power flows in these emergent communities of practice that seem similar to those investigated by Lave and Wenger (1991). As a result of their growing confidence and competence as learners, their enhancement of their social and cultural capital (Bourdieu 1990), students began to shift the habitus (Bourdieu 1990) with which they had entered the field of the Access to HE courses to become accomplished independent learners who could organise their own work.

Conclusions

While Access to HE has provided a valuable entry route into higher education for many mature students, there is a lack of up-to-date empirical research in England and Wales on the processes of transition and transformation that they experience. This study, based on Access to HE students in seven colleges, albeit in only one region of England, is the largest of its kind in England and Wales since the year 2000 and addresses this dearth. It also takes account of how policy contexts have shifted since the studies of the earlier twenty-first century.

This study offers important insights into how Access to HE students pursued the project of the self (Giddens 1991) shaping teaching and learning by negotiating with their teachers, although the teachers had greater access to sources of formal power, located in the institutional structures of teachers' and students' work than did the students. Students enhanced their social and cultural capital (Bourdieu 1990) through being active participants in constituting their learning, working with teachers to build communities of practice (Wenger 1998). These had purposeful, collaborative cultures based on trust and mutual respect, albeit with asymmetrical power relationships between participants (Hatcher 2005). Despite students' power-invested relationships (Handley et al. 2006) with their tutors, the negotiations amongst students and teachers were viewed as legitimate and normal, not pathological aspects of teaching and learning that helped students to develop their sense of agency as citizens that went beyond the requirements of the tightly framed academic curriculum of their Access to HE courses that formed part of the performative cultures of their colleges. The works of Watkins (2005) and Sebba and Robinson (2011) show similar cultures can also be applied in schools for students under the age of 16 years and will improve the success and quality of learning amongst those students.

The flows of power in the Access to HE course revealed two types of communities of practice, intentional learning communities (Mangham 2012) established by the tutors, and emergent communities (Mittendorf et al. 2005) constructed by the students as their confidence grew in their abilities as learners and their sense of agency developed during their courses. The membership of these two types of community were heavily overlapped but in the latter the tutors were marginalised as providers of learning resources, whilst in the former they were leaders of learning.

Access to HE students' ongoing struggles with their socio-political and economic contexts (Foucault 1977) seemed only to have strengthened their resolutions to do something with their lives that contributed to the social well-being of their society. In doing so, they also met government strictures about the need to improve the skills of the labour force. However, central government appeared to do little to help them financially in their endeavours.

References

Andrews, D., and M. Lewis. 2007. "Transforming Practice from within: The Power of the Professional Learning Community." In *Professional Learning Communities: Divergence, Depth and Dilemmas*, edited by L. Stoll and K. Louis, 132–148. Maidenhead: Open University Press.

Ball, S. J. 1987. *The Micro-Politics of the School*. London: Methuen.

Bauman, Z. 2000. *Liquid Modernity*. Cambridge: Polity Press.

Benjamin, S. 2002. *The Micro-Politics of Inclusive Education*. Buckingham: Open University Press.

Bhabha, H. 1994. *The Location of Culture*. London: Routledge.

Blase, J., and G. L. Anderson. 1995. *The Micro-Politics of Educational Leadership: From Control to Empowerment*. London: Cassell.

Bourdieu, P. 1990. *The Logic of Practice*. Translated by R. Nice. Cambridge: Polity Press.

Bourdieu, P., and J.-C. Passeron. 1977. *Reproduction in Education: Society and Culture*. London: Sage.

Brine, J., and R. Waller. 2004. "Working Class Women on an Access Course: Risk, Opportunity and (Re)Constructing Identities." *Gender and Education* 16 (1): 97–113.

Burke, P. J. 2007. "Men Accessing Education: Masculinities, Identifications and Widening Participation." *British Journal of Sociology of Education* 28 (4): 411–424.

Busher, H. 2006. *Understanding Educational Leadership: People, Power and Culture*. Buckingham: Open University Press.

Busher, H., L. Hammersley-Fletcher, and C. Turner. 2007. "Making Sense of Middle Leadership: Community, Power and Practice." *School Leadership and Management* 27 (5): 405–422.

Corbin, J., and A. Strauss 2008. *Basics of Qualitative Research: Techniques and Procedures for Developing Grounded Theory*. 3rd ed. Los Angeles: Sage,

Crossan, B., J. Field, J. Gallacher, and B. Merrill. 2003. "Understanding Participation in Learning for Non-Traditonal Adult Learners: Learning Careers and the Construction of Learning Identities." *British Journal of Sociology of Education* 24 (1): 55–67.

Department for Business, Innovation and Skills (BIS). 2012. "Government Response to 'Students at the Heart of the System' and 'A New Regulatory Framework for the HE Sector'." http://www.bis.gov.uk/assets/biscore/higher-education/docs/g/12-890-government-response-students-and-regulatory-framework-higher-education.

Department for Business, Innovation and Skills (BIS). 2010. "Further Education – New Horizon: Investing in Sustainable Growth." http://www.bis.gov.uk/assets/biscore/further-education-skills/docs/s/10-1272-strategy-investing-in-skills-for-sustainable-growth.pdf.

Derrida, J. 2000. *Of Hospitality*. Stanford, CA: Stanford University Press.

Field, J., B. Merrill, and N. Morgan-Klein. 2010. "Researching Higher Education Access, Retention and Drop-out through a European Biographical Approach: Exploring Similarities and Differences within a Research Team." European Society for Research on the Education of Adults, Sixth European Research Conference, University of Linköping, September 23–26.

Foucault, M. 1976. "Truth and Power." In *(1980) Power Knowledge: Selected Interviews and Other Writings by Michel Foucault*, edited by C. Gordon, 1972–1977. New York: Pantheon Books.

Foucault, M. 1977. *Discipline and Punish: The Birth of the Prison*. Translated by A. Sheridan, London: Allen Lane.

Foucault, M. 1986 "Disciplinary Power and Subjection." In *Power*, edited by S. Lukes, 5–16. Oxford: Blackwell.

Gee, J. P. 1999. *An Introduction to Discourse Analysis: Theory and Method*. London: Routledge.

Giddens, A. 1984. *The Constitution of Society*. Cambridge: Polity Press.

Giddens, A. 1991. *Modernity and Self-Identity: Self and Society in the Late Modern Age*. Cambridge: Polity Press.

Handley, K., A. Sturdy, R. Fincham, and T. Clark. 2006. "Within and beyond Communities of Practice: Making Sense of Learning through Participation." *Identity and Practice, Journal of Management Studies* 43: 641–653.

Hatcher, R. 2005. "The Distribution of Leadership and Power in Schools." *British Journal of Sociology of Education* 26 (2): 253–267.

Hodgkinson, C. 1999. "The Triumph of the Will: An Exploration of Certain Fundamental Problematics in Administrative Philosophy." In *The Values of Educational Administration*, edited by P. T. Begley and P. E. Leonard, 7–22. London: Falmer Press.

Hodkinson, P. 2004. "Research as a Form of Work: Expertise, Community and Methodological Objectivity." *British Educational Research Journal* 30 (1): 9–26.

Holliday, A. 1999. "Small Cultures." *Applied Linguistics* 20: 237–264.

Holliday, A. 2010. "Introduction." In *Intercultural Communication, an Advanced Handbook*. 2nd ed, edited by A. Holliday, M. Hyde, and J. Kullman, 1–6. London: Routledge.

Hollis, M 1985. "Of Masks and Men." In *The Category of the Person: Anthropology, Philosophy History*, edited by M. Carrithers, S. Collins, and S. Lukes, 217–233. Cambridge: Cambridge University Press.

Jeffrey, B., and G. Troman. 2012. "Introduction." In *Performativity across UK Education: Ethnographic Cases of Its Effects, Agency and Reconstructions*, edited by B. Jeffrey and G. Troman, 1–5. Painswick: E&E Publishing.

Jephcote, M., J. Salisbury, and G. Rees. 2008. "Being a Teacher in Further Education in Changing times." *Research in Post Compulsory Education* 13 (2): 163–172.

Jones, K. 2006. "Valuing Diversity and Widening Participation: The Experiences of Access to Social Work Students in Further and Higher Education." *Social Work Education* 25 (5): 485–500.

Kearney, C. 2003. *The Monkey's Mask: Identity, Memory, Narrative and Voice*. Stoke-on-Trent: Trentham Books.

Lave, J. and E. Wenger. 1991. *Situated Learning: Legitimate Peripheral Participation*. Cambridge: Cambridge University Press.

MacBeath, J., and A. MacDonald. 2000. "Four Dilemmas, Three Heresies and a Matrix." In *Leadership for Change and School Reform*, edited by K. A. Riley and K. S. Louis, 13–29. London: Routledge Falmer.

MacGilchrist, B. K. Myers, and J. Reed. 2004. *The Intelligent School*, 2nd ed. London: Sage.

Mangham, C. W. 2012. *A Combined Framework for Investigating Communities of Practice and the Function of the Learning Organization: A Case Study of an Industrial Training Unit in the United Arab Emirates*. Leicester: University of Leicester.

Miles, M. B, and M. Huberman. 1994. *Qualitative Data Analysis: An Expanded Sourcebook*, Thousand Oaks, CA: Sage.

Mitchell, C., and L. Sackney. 2006. "Building Schools, Building People: The School Principal's Role in Leading a Learning Community." *Journal of School Leadership* 16: 627–640.

Mittendorf, K., F. Geijsel, A. Hoeve, M. D. Laat, and L. Niewenhuis. 2005. "Communities of Practice as Stimulating Forces for Collective Learning." *Journal of Workplace Learning* 18: 298–312.

O'Donnell, V. L., and J. Tobbell. 2007. "The Transition of Adult Students to Higher Education: Legitimate Peripheral Participation in a Community of Practice?" *Adult Education Quarterly* 57 (4): 312–328.

Paechter, C. 2004. "Space, Identity and Education." *Pedagogy, Culture and Society* 12 (3): 307.

Parry, G. 1996. "Access Education in England and Wales 1973–1994: From Second Chance to Third Wave." *Journal of Access Studies* 11: 10–33.

Pink, S. 2001. *Doing Visual Ethnography*. London: Sage.

Prosser, J. (2006). *Image-Based Research: A Sourcebook for Qualitative Researchers*. London: Routledge Falmer.

Quality Assurance Agency. 2013. *Access to Higher Education: Key Statistics*. http://www.accesstohe.ac.uk/AboutUs/Publications/Documents/Key-statistics-2013.pdf

Sebba, J., and C. Robinson. 2011. *Evaluation of UNICEF UK'S Rights Respecting Schools Award Paper Presented to British Educational Research Association Annual Conference*, 7–9. University of London, London, UK: Institute of Education.

Senge, P. M. 2006. *The Fifth Discipline*. New York: Currency Doubleday.

Smyth, J., A. Dow, R. Hattam, A. Reid, and G. Shacklock. 2000. *Teachers' Work in a Globalising Economy*. London: Falmer Press.

Wall, K., and S. Higgins. 2009. *Pupils' Views of Templates: A Visual Method for Investigating Children's Thinking*. ESRC Seminar: Leicester University.

Warmington, P. 2002. "Studenthood as Surrogate Occupation: Access to HE Students' Discursive Production of Commitment, Maturity and Peer Support." *Journal of Vocational Education and Training* 54 (4): 583–600.

Watkins, C. 2005. "Classrooms as Learning Communities: A Review of Research." *London Review of Education* 3 (1): 47–64.

Wenger, E. 1998. *Communities of Practice: Learning, Meaning, and Identity* New York: Cambridge University Press.

Wyn, J., and R. White. 1998. "Young People, Social Problems and Australian Youth Studies." *Journal of Youth Studies* 1 (1): 23–38.

Home education, school, Travellers and educational inclusion

Kate D'Arcy

Department of Applied Social Studies, University of Bedfordshire, Luton, UK

The difficulties Traveller pupils experience in school are well documented. Yet those in home educating go unreported. Monk suggests this is because some groups are overlooked; that gypsies and Travellers are often not perceived as home educators. This article highlights how the move to home education is seldom a free choice for Traveller families. Although existing literature suggests this is a consequence of Traveller culture and mobility patterns, this article argues that problems in school drive uptake. Issues of race and ethnicity continue to drive educational inequality and there is an urgent need to redress this is in educational policy and practice.

Introduction

Travellers are a distinctive, yet often disregarded group of home educators in England (Monk 2009). The term Traveller is commonly accepted as one which covers a range of identifiable ethnic groups, the largest being Romany Gypsies and Irish Travellers. The term Traveller is also sometimes extended to include Occupational Travellers, the most significant being the Fairground or Showman community,[1] and more recently New Age Travellers. Defining a Gypsy, Traveller or Showman is a matter of self-ascription and does not exclude members of these communities who live in houses because ethnic and cultural identity is not lost, it simply adapts to new circumstances. This article reports on research involving Showmen and Romany Gypsy families; the term Traveller is applied when discussing all groupings.

Having worked in a Traveller Education Service (TES) for many years I am passionate about improving access and attainment in education for Traveller children and their families. A main focus of work concerned Traveller pupils' move to secondary school as they continue to experience difficulties there; hence there was a high drop-out and uptake of home education. TES

174

are not generally funded to support home education and little is known about the home-educating practices of Traveller families. Existing reports on home education justify Travellers' uptake of home education as a consequence of the communities' culture and mobility patterns. My experience suggested otherwise. I therefore undertook empirical research into home education as I wanted to challenge the discourse which suggests that the Travellers' move to home educate is a cultural choice. I argue that it is driven by inequality in school and that the current freedom to choose children's sites of education (i.e. home rather than school) is not an inclusive practice for already marginalised groups.

The specific contribution of this article is thus that it reports on an under-researched area; little is known about the reasons for choosing home education and consequential outcomes. A literature review discovered only two other studies on the topic of home education and Travellers in the United Kingdom. Most research on home education is based on professionals' views; however, this research asserts the voices of Traveller families in order to illuminate continuing educational inequality and draws on Critical Race Theory (CRT) to do so. Although CRT is not often applied to Travellers, I propose that it is a valuable and practical theory to highlight ongoing inequalities in education for Traveller children.

The article begins with an overview of Elective Home Education (EHE) and the difficulties Travellers experience within mainstream school. The research project and its design are then elaborated upon. The findings of the reported research include two short stories or vignettes that depict different Traveller families' experiences of EHE. The article concludes by summarising the challenges the current EHE system presents and several recommendations in working towards educational inclusion.

Elective home education and Travellers

In England education is compulsory for children of statutory school age; however, schooling is not. The official UK government wording to describe home education is 'Elective Home Education' (DCSF 2007) and this term is used throughout this article. There is little research on EHE in England and no information about the exact number of children who are home educated. Current EHE guidance does not require parents or carers who are home educating their children to make themselves known to their Local Authorities (LA), and Rothermel (2002) suggests up to two-thirds of home educators may be unknown. LAs can estimate numbers from school data regarding withdrawn pupils, which suggest that home education is on the rise. In 1997 estimated national figures were around 50,000 (Meighan 1997), in 2009 the total number was estimated to be 80,000 (Badman 2009). Still, regional figures are variable and Ofsted (2010) reported that the number of home-educated children ranged from 32 to 620 across the 15 LAs they visited.

Over the years the subject of home-educating Traveller families has been noted sporadically (Kiddle 1999; Ofsted 2001, 2003; Derrington and Kendal 2004). As early as 2003 Ofsted documented the growing trend among secondary-aged Traveller pupils to be home educated and stated concerns about its suitability because 'the adequacy, suitability and quality of such provision is uneven' (2003, 5).

The number of home-educating Traveller families is also growing and varies across England. The TES have reported a marked annual increase and research across 23 LAs, and Ivatts (2006) observed that approximately one-third of all home-educated children were Travellers. Traveller children therefore make up a significant proportion of home-educated children.

At this point it is also important to acknowledge the diverse reality of educational provision. EHE is only one of the various educational options open to and used by families in England. Not all children who are out of school will be home educated. This article concerns two legal educational options – school and EHE – but there are additional educational alternatives such as Pupil Referral Units and private education, which are not covered. It is also important to stress that there are significant numbers of children who are not registered in any educational provision. Once again exact data is hard to find, but Ofsted (2003) estimated that 12,000 Traveller pupils of secondary age were not registered in any educational provision.

Elective home education

In England, Section 7 of The Education Act guides current workings of EHE policy and practice:

> The parent of every child of compulsory school age shall cause him to receive efficient full-time education suitable (a) to his age, ability and apti-tude, and (b) to any special educational needs he may have, either by regular attendance at school or otherwise. (The Education Act 1996)

While there is a duty for parents to educate their children, they are not obliged to send them to school (Gabb 2004) as 'suitable' educational alter-natives are legal. EHE guidance states that LAs must 'make arrangements to enable them to establish the identities, so far as it is possible to do so, of children in their area who are not receiving a suitable education' (DCSF 2007, 5). This is particularly challenging for EHE children (Hopwood et al. 2007) as there is no legal definition of what a suitable education looks like or comprises.

Moreover, LAs do not currently have any statutory duties to monitor EHE on a routine basis. They cannot legally insist on entering the homes or seeing children for the purpose of monitoring EHE provision (DCSF 2007). Many LAs therefore have to ask parents to inform them of their decision to home educate and to agree to a visit by an EHE advisor. Consequently, the

LA's abilities to fulfil their EHE duties are reliant on positive relationships with home-educating parents.

The vagueness of current EHE legislation has resulted in EHE becoming a very indistinct area of education. Practices and expectations across LAs regarding EHE are diverse and applied inconsistently. Ofsted (2010) found little uniformity across the 15 LAs they studied on how monitoring visits were managed and what they were to include. In a time when mainstream education and the achievement of children within school is regularly scrutinised and monitored, it seems surprising that the area of EHE has not until recently attracted the same attention (Monk 2004).

The Labour government's Every Child Matters agenda[2] encouraged a scrutiny of any policies or practices that did not protect children and ensure the development of their potential. This scrutiny, coupled with the growing numbers of home-educated children and increasing disquiet from LA children's services[3] regarding the current effectiveness of EHE systems, came to a head with the death of a seven-year-old girl who was home educated (Webb 2010). Consequently, in January 2009 the government commissioned Graham Badman to assess whether the current system of supporting and monitoring home education enabled all home-educated children to receive a good education and stay safe and well (DCSF 2010).

Badman (2009) reviewed and reported on EHE and suggested that regulatory and legislative changes to the EHE system were necessary. Twenty-eight recommendations were proposed, which included: setting up a national registration system for EHE children and allowing EHE officials the right to access home-educating children's homes to monitor provision and establish their safety and well-being. Although the government initially accepted Badman's recommendations, the public rejection by home-educating organisations and the political pressures of an upcoming general election meant that, in actual fact, none were upheld. Many professionals and practitioners were disappointed with this outcome. Indeed, Ofsted suggested that the failure to:

> register all children with the LA, irrespective of where they were educated – in LA or in independent schools, at home or in other educational provision – contributed to making it possible for young people to disappear. (2010, 24)

EHE remains a complex, yet vague area of education. The purpose of this article is not to advocate for or against home education but to investigate the effect of current EHE systems on already marginalised groups of children. It reports on the reasons a small sample of Traveller families took up EHE and documents their home education practices to evidence that the move to EHE is not necessarily an inclusive practice. To substantiate this argument it is essential to provide a brief overview of the difficulties Traveller pupils experience in school, as this article will highlight how in some cases neither school nor EHE provides Traveller children with a suitable education.

Traveller pupils' experiences of mainstream schooling

The issues concerning Traveller pupils' low attendance in school are well documented. Traveller children's achievement was noted in the 1960s (Department of Education and Science 1967), yet in 2010 Traveller children were still among the lowest achieving groups. Indeed, Romany Gypsy and Traveller of Irish Heritage pupils were the only ethnic groups in the United Kingdom whose performance had deteriorated (Equality and Human Rights Commission 2010).

Research has highlighted the barriers to Traveller pupils' achievement and attainment: high levels of racist bullying and harassment from pupils and staff (Lloyd and McClusky 2008; Lloyd and Stead 2001), a lack of understanding and respect for Traveller cultures in school (Tyler 2005; Wilkin et al. 2010), low expectations of Traveller students and a high drop-out rate during the secondary school phase. Racism and discrimination underpin all these barriers.

Racism and discrimination

Issues of race equality are a significant factor in Travellers' educational success. Ulreche and Franks reported that Roma, Gypsy and Traveller children experienced 'prejudice, bigotry and institutional racism as part of their daily lives' (2007, 9). Among the 201 children they consulted, 63% were bullied or attacked physically and 86% had received racist comments. Within wider society, Travellers are all depicted as Others and stereotyped according to a set of negative descriptions that justify their exclusion from full participation in society (Devine, Kenny, and Macneta et al. 2008). As a consequence, teachers may either deny Traveller pupils' cultural differences or construct this as deviant (Lloyd and Norris 1998).

The literature on Travellers' experiences in school highlights many problems within an educational system in which stereotypes and misunderstandings of Traveller communities and cultures are commonplace (Wilkin, Derrington, and Foster 2009). Lloyd and McClusky (2008) suggest that central to the negative educational experiences of so many Travellers lies a denial of difference and the complexity of cultural identity. Accounts of Travellers' failure in education commonly emphasise Travellers' reluctance to participate in education and this is presented as a feature of Traveller culture (Piper and Garrett 2005; Wilkin et al. 2010).

Consequently, there is a discourse that Traveller parents are not interested in or committed to their children's education, this being more pertinent at secondary level than primary (Wilkin, Derrington, and Foster 2009). Such discourses are concerning as they inform educational practices; practitioners may use them to predict and explain away the poor outcomes for Traveller pupils. Such judgements are also used to justify why high numbers of Traveller families home educate, and as a consequence ongoing issues of educational inequality are ignored.

Research method and design

The research drew upon an interpretive paradigm that recognises research participants' views are diverse and numerous and seeks to document their understandings of the situation being studied. Data were collected through two sets of semi-structured interviews with 11 Traveller families (nine Romany Gypsy families and two Showmen families) over six months. The research sample concentrated on family units. This was for ethical and practical reasons. Families could themselves select who was part of the interview; children could be part of the interview if the family wished and parents were present at all times. Many family units included more than one child who was home educated. Across the 11 families there were 42 children, 32 of whom were being home educated or had been in the past. The other 10 children were in education, of pre-school age or old enough to work.

The main selection criteria specified that families needed to be registered as providing EHE. As a professional who worked in the field, it was my expectation that there were many more home-educating families than those registered, as there is no current legal requirement for families to inform the LA of their intent to home educate. Nevertheless, I only approached those on the registered list because I might otherwise be inviting children who were not registered in any educational provision and were deemed 'Missing from Education'.[4] This could have difficult ethical implications regarding the responsibility to report such families to the LA.

Further subgroup criteria related to different geographical locations, different travelling patterns, a range of socio-economic status and different Traveller groups in order to represent broadly the characteristics of the LA Traveller population and build up an unbiased and trustworthy sample. The main groups of Travellers residing in the LA under study were English Romany Gypsies, Travellers of Irish Heritage and Showmen. Romany Gypsy families are reasonably settled whereas Travellers of Irish Heritage and Showmen are highly mobile. There were no Irish Travellers registered as EHE and they were therefore not included.[5]

EHE practices are varied and it is important to note that this research sample is quite particular in its social characteristics. Thus, as previously suggested, the incidence of EHE take-up by Travellers in this LA may not be typical when considered on a national scale. Consequently, findings must be acknowledged with caution and no generalisations regarding all Travellers and EHE must be made. No names are referenced; those provided in the text are pseudonyms to protect all respondents' identities.

I recognised that I was potentially in a more privileged position than other researchers as I was working with Traveller families. However, my TES was not funded to support EHE and I relied on gatekeepers to initialise contact with EHE families. My methodological approach included a deliberate choice to focus on Travellers' voices and I used storytelling to highlight

Travellers views, and not those of other educators as they have been documented before and form part of the discourse that so often portrays Travellers in a negative light.

Storytelling is one of several CRT tenets. CRT provides ways to problematise Travellers' inclusion and exclusion within education – stories can document the lived experiences of racism and oppression. Who tells whose stories is a fundamental concern in CRT, and in reporting on my research I made a conscious choice to document the stories of Travellers in their own words, rather than mine. My book documents Travellers' voices verbatim (D'Arcy 2014), and this article offers a smaller selection due to word limitations. I member-checked my findings and the sections of interview I planned to report on with all families to ensure they agreed with the way I was presenting their views. I recognise that I am asserting these stories on Traveller families' behalf, but do so to raise awareness of how education systems continue to deal with difference and how this results in ongoing inequalities in education.

CRT recognises the complicated and deeply embedded nature of racism (Gillborn 2005). CRT has emerged as a focus point for work on race and is frequently applied to education in the United Kingdom. CRT is academic and practical. It challenges hidden operations of power that disadvantage minority ethnic groups by asking critical questions about inequality (Gillborn 2008). Travellers' stories can challenge what the dominant discourse suggests; for example, the dominant discourse implies that Travellers take up EHE for mobility reasons, yet research (Ivatts 2006; Bhopal and Myers 2009; D'Arcy 2014) suggests that the Travellers' decision to home educate is associated with discrimination in school. Consequently, the voices of the marginalised provide counter-stories which oppose stereotypical assumptions that blame Traveller communities themselves for their educational exclusion and a lack of appropriate educational response to their needs. In a CRT fashion, I document my findings by telling the stories of two different Traveller families.

Traveller families' experiences and practices of EHE

Research tells us that home-educating practices are diverse (Rothermel 2003) and this was reflected within the Traveller families interviewed. Nevertheless, there was one broad distinction that could be made. Seven out of the 11 families paid for private tuition, and the rest of the families delivered educational provision themselves. The stories that follow capture the experience of one of a family who employed a tutor and another who provided home education themselves.

The Smith family

Mrs Smith had four boys, ranging from seven to 13 years old. They had only lived in the county for six months. They had been settled in another city where the boys all attended school regularly. Mrs Smith spoke of their excellent progress there and referred to the head teacher and staff who supported the boys and made them feel included:

> It was like they cared. They were in cricket team, they were doing ever so well, it upset me to move. The rules in secondary were good; there was no bullying, no swearing.

Due to unforeseen and unplanned events the family moved suddenly, but mum was not happy with the local school and therefore decided to home educate all her boys herself:

> Well, there was a couple of reasons [for home education] really … for one main reason I did not like the things what was said in the playground, it wasn't things I like my kids to be involved in. The things my kids were having said to them were disgusting … Alfie told me about it. Home education is the way to go with Alfie anyway, because he's … well he is at home and he was uncomfortable at school.

Mum did not feel that her children were safe in the new school environment, she also felt that Alfie's needs would not be met there. Alfie had been diagnosed with autism and at least three other children in the families I interviewed had a statement of special educational needs (SEN) and this played a part in families' decision to home educate. Educational support for families is an important consideration, and in the EHE literature the issue of support for vulnerable groups of children in schools is a recurring factor. It is interesting to note that children with additional needs (including Travellers, those referred to as Gifted & Talented and having SEN and children who are bullied) often resort to EHE because the school system does not support them. Indeed, Arora's (2006, 62) research on the experiences of children with SEN found that the need for home education would not have been contemplated if flexible school support had been available at the time.

Practice

Mrs Smith had purchased several books covering a wide age range. The boys work from handwriting, counting, tables, multiplication, basic mathematics, spelling, science and other text books and reading schemes. Routine was important:

> The boys sit down round the table, I bought books and they sit and do their lessons. We try to do everything in the lessons and they sit and write an essay about what they did or where they have been or whatever. You know, so they have practiced their writing. Then they have sit and read it back so I can see their spelling mistakes.

Mrs Smith felt that the good things about EHE were:

> You can stick to the way of life they are used to ... our way of life.

> EHE is different – they enjoy it – it's in a different environment, its more easy going. The lessons are different. The main thing is routine ... leaving school they were out of routine ... but we set up our own. The boys do their chores [look after dogs, chickens and tidy up]. It makes them independent for when they grow up. It teaches them respect and clean living. Books provide the basics then they explore wider stuff through their interests like history. You can channel them, instead of sitting in with kids doing things they don't like you can channel them so that they do get interested in what they like and do reading. Once they have read about it, got excited about it then they can also write about it – it just goes round and round ... I get by, I can read a bit but I want my kids to be better than that. My friend does up mobile homes – when they get older he will take the boys with him. So if they have that and reading, writing and calculations they are all the main things they should be concentrating on.

The type of education Mrs Smith describes is one that is self-generated and driven by the children's interests; it was also felt to be a more relevant education than school. But EHE was also challenging:

> Getting the boys to do what I tell them to do was difficult. I had a new role – as teacher ... has taken a while for boys to get used to. If they don't do it – they will be going back to school ... I enjoy it because it gives me time with the kids, it's nice. I enjoy it and I think they enjoy it with me as well.

> I felt a bit lost at the start, I did not know if I was teaching them the right things. I though logically about it. Well ... what are the main things they will need? I picked out the things I thought they needed.

EHE is very much left to parents' resources, and Mrs Smith was waiting on the EHE adviser to visit for guidance and reassurance; in this LA such visits took place just once a year:

> I see EHE as 'You have made the choice you do it'. I would not be happy if I did not speak to anyone because I would feel a bit lost. I don't want to do wrong by my kids education. I did not have much education, only went to school until I was seven. I said I was going to home educate and the children wouldn't be left without an education. I need the adviser[6] to point me in the right direction ... I'll be ok ... I will be pleased when he has been.

> I think EHE is ok. You make decision you do it, but I think there a lot of chances that kids can slip through. It's the ideal option for people who don't really want to take their kids to school – EHE but not for the right reasons. They use it as an excuse and because there is not a lot of back up I think there were a lot of kids will fail and that a shame because I do think kids need their education.

Mrs Smith is committed to her children's education and is doing the best she can with available resources. Her comments do reveal concerns with the current, liberal EHE system that, in her opinion, does allow children to fall through the education net as it is solely reliant on parents' input, which can limit their educational experiences and long-term opportunities.

The Young family

Mrs Young has three children – Gary the eldest, Rosanne and Bob.

> Gary went to secondary school and he had a terrible experience, yes … because he's a Traveller. He got picked on; even by the teachers … I don't know … I was not prepared for Rosanne to go through that. We had the same when I went to school, my brothers and sisters so … I think she would have liked secondary education but it doesn't just come like that does it … I think she would have enjoyed it all but … you got all the bad points … like with being a Traveller haven't you? Like being picked on. I tried with Gary because I thought it might be different … but no.

Rosanne went to primary school: 'It was a lovely school, it was a good school'. Mum was reluctant to send her to secondary because Gary was bullied there, but she also did not feel confident about taking up EHE so she asked the primary school if Rosanne could repeat her final year. Her request was refused. Rosanne told me that:

> She [mum] did not know what she had to do to home educate, she thought if she could keep me in [school] another year, it would just be easier all round.

The fact that Gary's bullying issues in school were not addressed, led to his withdrawal but also mum's reluctance to send her daughter to this school. Mrs Young's concern about doing home education properly also highlights lack of confidence in taking on sole responsibility for educational provision, yet this was preferable to her daughter being bullied and the family chose the safer option – EHE.

Practice

> We have not heard of EHE, we call it home tutoring. Rosanne was home tutored since 11, for five years. She never did go to big school at all. Well, I knew other people that had their children home educated so at first we had different tutors coming out … In the first beginning we had a tutor come out, but she was not a lot of good. The work that she was setting was not good. Then we went to the learning centre for a long while … I took her every fortnight. She had a tutor there – a really good lady. She was setting her work out for two weeks and then going back and then going there for two hour lesson.

Rosanne has stopped now because she is 16. She had her inspector come out, he gone through all the work she's done and give her a really good report. If I'd of thought I could of showed you. He was really pleased. He loved all the social stuff she did. He said that is their biggest worry ... that they are not socialising with other people.

For Rosanne EHE was overall a positive experience and they had learnt by trial and error. She had spent more time with her family and had flexibility around her learning; these were the good things about EHE:

I have been able to be with me sister more, she's only little, so I have been able to be with her a lot more. I can do what I want, when I want and how I want, that sort of thing ... that was good.

Mrs Young felt that EHE had worked out well for Rosanne; however, Bob was now coming up to the end of primary school and they were planning on trying to send him to secondary school:

Yes, we are trying again now because he is leaving school in September and he'll be going ... we will let him have a go. Gary had a go and did not like it, Rosanne did not get a chance because I wouldn't let her and now with him we are deciding again to try again. See how he gets on, if he doesn't we'll pull him out and home educate him.

Bob really, really wants to go and all, he wants to go to other school. He's got lots of his friends going up as well. They all know where he comes from, he goes round lot of their houses and they all know where he comes from ... what all helps ...

That's how it should be [Nan].

Yes, but it ain't always like that, when he gets up there ... we'll see when he gets up there, but there are a lot of different children in a year, it is bigger than the little school. So ... I don't know – we just got to try it.

Mrs Young's story reveals the effect of racism on educational progression; it prevented her completing her school education and that of her two oldest children. The youngest was going to transfer – his situation was different because he had friends who knew he was a Traveller and accepted him; highlighting that identity, acceptance and inclusion is key in educational progression. Her story also reveals the concerns about secondary school, it is bigger than primary and she is concerned about other children who might bully her own. Although the family are willing to try secondary school they are also ready to withdraw him at the first sign of difficulties. This is a common approach and one seldom appreciated by schools.

Quick intervention can prevent EHE in cases of racism, bullying, and discrimination in school, which were mentioned by every family I spoke to. Seven out of the 11 families talked about direct bullying experiences because they were Travellers. Some children were also bullied because they could not read or write by the time they got to secondary school. Lots of families talked about the way their child was treated differently because they were a Traveller. Most parents felt worried about their children's safety and well-being in school. Families who did not feel supported opted for home education as a way to avoid racism and discrimination. Traveller families were attracted to EHE because it represented a safer place to educate their children legally.

Both stories counter the idea that Travellers are not interested in their children's education and confirm that discrimination underpins school access and inclusion; they also dispel the discourse that EHE is a free choice. These findings correlate with previous research in this field, which suggested that Travellers' reasons for EHE and their withdrawal from school had 'less to do with not wanting their children to receive an education and far more to do with concerns about the school institution itself' (Bhopal and Myers 2009, 4).The illustrative examples from Mrs Smith and Young were confirmed by the wider sample of voices. Traveller parents wanted their children to go to secondary school, but the fact that children experienced racism and bullying and did not get the right support for their educational needs meant that they did not feel able to continue sending them there.

Elective home education and exclusion

Reviewing the literature on EHE confirms that this is not just an issue for Travellers; there are other groups of children whose parents feel compelled to home educate. Thus, it might be argued that if systems in school were better prepared in meeting the needs of those children considered to be 'different', then there might be less need for these children's parents to resort to home education in the first place. I also propose that in seeking to escape mainstream school, Travellers' pupil's exclusion is further reinforced by home education as they may have limited access to educational resources. The lack of support for EHE parents also creates uncertainty about their competence at home schooling.

Levels of financial and social resources did vary among families and this was reflected in the provision they were able to offer their children. Those children living in families with fewer financial and social resources had more restricted activities and opportunities. Affluent families took children on trips, social activities, purchased laptops to work on and books to study; others could simply not afford this. Several low-income families spoke about the challenges of home education due to the cost of tutors and books and not always knowing whether what they were doing was right, especially if their child had SEN.

The current EHE system does not ensure that all children receive an equitable education and the most vulnerable children may therefore not receive the education they need because of their financial circumstances or SEN. Within school such inequalities are addressed in part through free school meals and additional support, yet those who are home educated receive no support at all. In this way the move to EHE is likely to limit some children's ability to become autonomous in later life. These children can as a result of inequality in school and EHE not access their right to an education.

Educational inequality

> One way of looking at the patterns of inequality in education is to look at the 'outputs' of the system … who stays on, who does what and who goes where. (Ball 2013, 181)

Reay, Crozier, and Clayton (2010) researched the benefits and challenges of the unfamiliar surroundings of higher education institutions for working-class students. Many of the working-class parents interviewed as part of this study wanted their child(ren) to go to university but had underlying fears that this move could result in 'abandoning the family and its norms and values' (Thomas and Quinn 2007, 63). Thus there is a price to pay in trying to fit in. The same could be said for the sample of Traveller families interviewed.

Some were fearful about revealing their child's Traveller identity in a secondary school environment where they were in the minority and did not feel safe. Research has shown that many Traveller children do not feel confident in revealing their Traveller identity publicly because of fears of racism and discrimination and 'play White'. Derrington describes this as 'passing identity by concealing or denying one's heritage' (2007, 357). The extent to which Traveller children feel safe and accepted is therefore an essential criterion in school attendance and achievement.

Others struggled with 'cultural dissonance' – the different expectations in school and home meant it was hard to fit into either world. Safety and survival is always in question and where there is no history of secondary transfer in the family there might be additional lack of confidence in this educational process. In some cases children tried to return to mainstream education at the post-16 stage, but this also posed challenges: Kyle had dropped out of school in Year Seven (first year in secondary school); he was home educated until he was 16 but enrolled on a construction access course to specialise in plumbing. Kyle completed his access course but as he had dyslexia and limited literacy and numeracy skills the college suggested he was not able to carry on. His mother related this decision to being a Traveller:

I see it as a lot of excuses. It was a bit of a smack in the mouth. I thought those days were over. There are a lot of things, unless you live this lifestyle you think things have changed but they are basically the same.

Kyle did not see the relevance of secondary education but this did not mean that he was totally disengaged from education or learning. Still, the fact he had SEN, was a Traveller and did not attend secondary school limited his opportunities at college. Such setbacks can confirm families' suspicions about mainstream education establishments.

This tale confirms the vulnerability of those with intersecting inequalities. Although many home-educated children will undertake GSCE examinations, Traveller families often find the education systems complex and may struggle finding information about GCSEs. The route to EHE can thus prevent social mobility as no qualifications are achieved and consequently securing a job is challenging, especially one in education, law or other professions where by community role-models can begin to establish themselves. The reality that a significant number of Traveller children are not attending school has a direct impact on the communities' social inclusion and families' opportunities for social mobility. This is why education in the broadest sense of the word is a fundamental human right. As Save the Children (2001) confirm, the denial of education can affect the enjoyment of other rights such as employment, health and economic well-being.

Critically observing EHE highlights interesting parallels between those who are labelled or managed differently in mainstream systems. The literature shows that the difficulties Traveller children experience in school are not theirs alone, Gifted and Talented children and those with SEN also struggle to have their needs met. These studies confirm that inequality in schools is ongoing and this is driving uptake of EHE. It is therefore important to note the relationship between school experience and uptake of EHE. An emerging equality issue is the perceived differences of learners who are problematised according to a non-specified but dominant view of what is considered 'normal' (Armstrong, Armstrong, and Spandagou 2010, 37).

Studying EHE provides important information about inequality for Travellers as well as different groups of children. Many home-educated children end up outside mainstream education through no fault or desire of their own, but simply because they are different to teach or culturally diverse. It cannot be denied that meeting the needs of all children via one educational system is challenging. However, schools are places that hold real potential in creating inclusive and democratic societies. Yet EHE facilitates the exclusion of particularly vulnerable groups of children and is therefore not an inclusive practice. The concluding section of this article will now briefly summarise the challenges raised and propose some recommendations in working towards educational inclusion.

Working towards educational inclusion

Attention has been drawn to the effects of a very liberal EHE system, whereby Traveller children drop-out of school with ease, cannot necessarily access further education and may experience limited educational provision. This challenges the dominant discourse that suggests home education is a free choice which derives from Travellers' mobility. Families referred frequently to racism and discrimination, particularly in secondary school systems, which compelled them to home educate their children. Yet these families were all committed to their child's education. Educational systems are therefore still not enabling all children to feel included and achieve.

Analysing EHE draws attention to the relationship between school and EHE, the complexities of inclusion and exclusion and the consequences for those children labelled as 'different'. Travellers' explained their strategies to ensure that their children continue learning in a safe environment. Home education can be safer and remains a legal educational alternative but it is also unequal. The EHE system as it stands is problematic because it cannot ensure all children can access the resources and support they need to become autonomous. Support and resources for EHE are limited, especially if the child has SEN. The freedom to legally choose home education over school is thus not necessarily, from these data, an inclusive practice. Depending on the capital and social resources available, some children will have a positive experience whereas others will be much more limited.

Enabling school inclusion is a complex task. Sociological thinking about educational inclusion has certainly drawn attention to the social construction and perpetuation of inequality because of perceived differences of learners. The liberal EHE system in many ways continues segregation as home-educated children are removed from the mainstream. There is a need for further sociological debate to consider how children defined as 'different' can be supported without stigmatising them on that basis (Minow 1985). The issue for contemplation is not how to educate those who are 'different' but how to educate all children.

Gewirtz and Cribb (2009) suggest that sociologists should take seriously the practical judgements and dilemmas of the people we are researching. This research has shown that Traveller parents' motivations for EHE are comparable with other parents with children who have SEN. These parents may be seen to be expressing as choice to home educate but closer investigation indicates that this is driven by discrimination. This research has begun to document the educational experiences of those who experience EHE first hand, and further research is needed to establish a better understanding of the number of children who are home educated and their needs. A useful next step would be to ask LAs to record to reasons why parents are withdrawing their children from school and analyse this information, as such data would be hard to ignore.

Opportunities for debate within sociological and educational communities are important to ensure that such issues do not continue to be disregarded. The aim of this article has been to raise awareness of ongoing inequality in education, both school and EHE. The hope is that it will act as a reminder to researchers, educators and policy-makers alike; there is much to be done to ensure educational inclusion for all.

Notes

1. This community will be referred to as 'Showmen' in this article.
2. The aim was for every child, whatever their background or their circumstances, to have the support they need to 'be healthy, stay safe, enjoy and achieve, make a positive contribution and achieve economic well-being' (DCSF 2003, 6).
3. Practitioners working for and with children and young people.
4. Children and young people who are not receiving education and whose whereabouts are unknown.
5. Undertaking research into those not registered formally as providing EHE would be a further research study of interest because there remain many Traveller children who are not registered in any educational provision.
6. The adviser is an EHE staff team member. In the LA under study there are three EHE staff in total: a manager, an administrator and an adviser, the latter visits families when they register and monitors provision on an annual basis. Please note that such arrangements vary and this example will not reflect practice in all LAs in England.

References

Armstrong, Armstrong, and Spandagou. 2010. *Inclusive Education, International Policy and Practice*. London: Sage Publications.

Arora, T. 2006. "Elective Home Education and Special Educational Needs." *Journal of Research in Special Educational Needs* 6 (1): 55–66.

Badman, G. 2009. *Review of Elective Home Education in England, a Report to the Secretary of State*. London: The Stationery Office.

Ball, S. J. 2013. *The Education Debate*. 2nd ed. Bristol: Polity Press.

Bhopal, K., and M. Myers. 2009. *A Pilot Study to Investigate Reasons for Elective Home Education for Gypsy and Traveller Children in Hampshire*. Report for Hampshire County Council. Ethnic Minority and Traveller Achievement Service.

D'Arcy, K. 2014. *Traveller and Home Education: Safe Spaces and Inequality*. London: Institute of Education Press.

Department for Children, Schools and Families. 2007. *Elective Home Education, Guidelines for Local Authorities*. London: DCSF.

Department for Children, Schools and Families. 2010. *Independent Review of Elective Home Education*. Accessed September 2010. http://webarchive.nationalarchives. gov.uk/20101213224929/http://dcsf.gov.uk/everychildmatters/ete/independent reviewofhomeeducation/irhomeeducation/.

Department of Education and Science. 1967. *Children and Their Primary Schools, the Plowden Report*. Central Advisory Council for Education (England) London: HMSO.

Derrington, C. 2007. "Fight, Flight and Playing White: An Examination of Coping Strategies Adopted by Gypsy Traveller Adolescents in English Secondary Schools." *International Journal of Educational Research* 46 (6): 357–367.

Derrington, C., and S. Kendall. 2004. *Gypsy Traveller Students in Secondary Schools*. Stoke-on-Trent: Trentham Books.

Devine, D., M. Kenny, and Macneta. 2008. "Naming the 'Other': Children's Construction and Experiences of Racism in Irish Primary Schools." *Race, Ethnicity and Education* 11 (4): 369–385.

The Education Act. 1996. Accessed June 2013. http://www.legislation.gov.uk/ukpga/1996/.

Equality and Human Rights Commission. 2010. *How Fair is Britain? Equality, Human Rights and Good Relations in 2010*. The First Triennial Review. Equality and Human Rights Commission.

Gabb, S. 2004. *Home-Schooling: A British Perspective*. University of Buckingham. Accessed July 2012. http://www.seangabb.co.uk/academic/homeschooling.htm

Gewirtz, S., and A. Cribb. 2009. *Understanding Education, A Sociological Perspective*. Cambridge: Polity Press.

Gillborn, D. 2005. "Education Policy as an Act of White Supremacy: Whiteness, Critical Race Theory and Education Reform." *Journal of Education Policy* 20 (4): 485–505.

Gillborn, D. 2008. *Race and Education Racism and Education: Coincidence or Conspiracy?* Abingdon: Routledge.

Hopwood, V., L. O'Neill, G. Castro, and B. Hodgson. 2007. *The Prevalence of Home Education in England: A Feasibility Study*. York Consulting LTD, Nottingham, Department for Education and Skills. Accessed February 2013 http://www.parliament.uk/deposits/depositedpapers/2008/DEP2008-1324.pdf.

Ivatts, A. 2006. *Elective Home Education, the Situation regarding the Current Policy, Provision and Practice in Elective Home Education for Gypsy, Roma and Traveller Children*. London: Department for Education and Skills.

Kiddle, C. 1999. *A Voice for Themselves*. London: Jessica Kingsley Publishers.

Lloyd, G., and G. McClusky. 2008. "Education and Gypsy Travellers: Contradictions and Significant Silences." *International Journal of Inclusive Education* 12 (4): 331–345.

Lloyd, G., and C. Norris. 1998. "From Difference to Deviance, the Exclusion of Gypsy Roma and Traveller Pupils from School." *International Journal of Inclusive Education* 2 (4): 359–369.

Lloyd, G., and J. Stead. 2001. "The Boys and Girls Not Calling Me Names and the Teachers Believing Me: Name Calling and the Experiences of Travellers in School." *Children & Society* 15 (5): 361–374.

Meighan, R. 1997. *The Next Learning System and Why Homeschoolers are Trailblazers*. Nottingham: Educational Heretics Press.

Minow, M. 1985. "Learning to Live with the Dilemma of Difference. Bilingual and Special Education." *Law and Contemporary Problems* 48 (2): 157–211.

Monk, D. 2004. "Problematising Home Education: Challenging 'Parental Rights' and 'Socialism'." *Legal Studies* 24 (4): 568–598.

Monk, D. 2009. "Regulating Home Education: Negotiating Standards, Anomalies and Rights. University of London." *Child and Family Law Quarterly* 21 (2): 155–185.

Ofsted. 2001. *Managing Support for the Attainment of Pupils from Minority Ethnic Groups*, HMI. Crown Copyright, 2001.

Ofsted. 2003. *Provision and Support for Traveller Pupils*, REF: HMI 455, November 2003. Crown Copyright, 2003.

Ofsted. 2010. *Local Authorities and Home Education*, June 2010, HMI. Crown Copyright, 2010.

Piper, H., and D. Garratt. 2005. Inclusive Education? Where Are the Gypsies and Travellers? *British Educational Research Association Presentation*. Glamorgan, September 14–17.

Reay, D., G. Crozier, and J. Clayton. 2010. "'Fitting in' or 'Standing out': Working-Class Students in UK Higher Education." *British Educational Research Journal* 32 (1): 1–19.

Rothermel, P. 2002. "Home Education: Aims, Practices and Outcomes." Paper presented at BERA Educational Research Conference." Accessed November 2012. www.educationotherwise.org/publications%20Files/leaflets/research.pdf.

Rothermel, P. 2003. "Can We Classify Motives for Home Education?" *Evaluation and Research in Education* 17 (2): 74–89.

Save the Children. 2001. *Denied a Future: The Right to Education of Roma, Gypsies and Traveller Children in Europe*. London: Save the Children.

Thomas, L., and J. Quinn. 2007. *First Generation Entry into Higher Education*. Maidenhead: Open University Press.

Tyler, C. 2005. *Traveller Education, Accounts of Good Practice*. Stoke-on-Trent: Trentham Books.

Ulreche, H., and M. Franks. 2007. *This is Who We Are: A Study of the Views and Identities of Roma, Gypsy and Traveller Young People in England*. London: The Children's Society.

Webb, S. 2010. *Elective Home Education in the UK*. Stoke-on-Trent: Trentham Books.

Wilkin, A., C. Derrington, and B. Foster. 2009. *Improving the Outcomes for Gypsy, Roma and Traveller Pupils, Literature Review*. DCSF, Research Report DCSF-RRO77.

Wilkin, A., C. Derrington, R. White, K. Martin, B. Foster, K. Kinder, and S. Rutt. 2010. *Improving the Outcomes for Gypsy, Roma and Traveller Pupils: Final Report*. Department for Education. Research Report DFE-RR043.

Index

Note: 'N' after a page number indicates a note; 'f' indicates a figure; 't' indicates a table.